DRY-LAND GARDENING

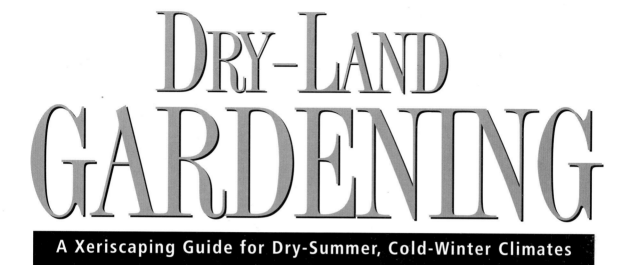

A Xeriscaping Guide for Dry-Summer, Cold-Winter Climates

Jennifer Bennett

DRY-LAND GARDENING

A Xeriscaping Guide for Dry-Summer, Cold-Winter Climates

FIREFLY BOOKS

BOOKMAKERS PRESS

A FIREFLY BOOK

Cataloguing-in-Publication Data

Bennett, Jennifer
    Dry-land gardening

ISBN 1-55209-221-6

1. Xeriscaping.   I. Title.

SB439.8.B46 1998   635.9'525   C98-930015-3

Published by
Firefly Books Ltd.
3680 Victoria Park Avenue
Willowdale, Ontario
Canada M2H 3K1

Published in the U.S. by
Firefly Books (U.S.) Inc.
P.O. Box 1338, Ellicott Station
Buffalo, New York 14205

Produced by
Bookmakers Press Inc.
12 Pine Street
Kingston, Ontario
K7K 1W1

Design by
Andrew McLachlan, Kroma Design

Color separations by
Friesens
Altona, Manitoba

Printed and bound in Canada by
Friesens
Altona, Manitoba

Printed on acid-free paper

Front cover photograph © Turid Forsyth
Back cover photograph © John Ruskay

Acknowledgments

This book represents the commitment and cooperation of several individuals. They include: Andrew McLachlan of Kroma Design; editorial associates Catherine DeLury and Mary Patton; principal photographers John Ruskay and Turid Forsyth; and Susan Dickinson and Tracy Read of Bookmakers Press.

I would also like to express my thanks to Cedar Valley Gardens, Port Hope, Ontario; Mason Hogue Gardens, Uxbridge, Ontario; VanDusen Botanical Garden, Vancouver, British Columbia; and Devonian Botanic Garden, Devon, Alberta, for the opportunity to take photographs in their beautiful gardens.

To John, for working on this project with me

Contents

Introduction
Dry Summers, Cold Winters

◆

"THERE ARE NO UNIVERSALLY ACCEPTED DEFINITIONS OF DROUGHT.
ANY EXTENDED DRY WEATHER THAT IS WORSE THAN EXPECTED
AND THAT LEADS TO MEASURABLE LOSSES CAN CORRECTLY
BE CALLED A DROUGHT."

—David Phillips, *The Climates of Canada,* 1990

It is early August, and we have had no rain to speak of for a month. Measurable losses? A few delicate plants that I should never have subjected to a dusty bed on the other side of the driveway and even a seedling caragana that would have been tough as nails in a few weeks had I not neglected to water it in its infancy. I guess, by Phillips' definition, this is a drought. Certainly, the local farmers are unhappy. One night, a shower wet the surface of the ground just enough to keep it damp till 8:00 the next morning.

In the meantime, the temperature has been high, around 70 to 85 degrees F (21-29°C), and it has often been windy. I watch storm clouds brew to the south and west and slowly move north and east, a repetitive weather pattern that is frustrating but also results in the kind of beautiful weather which brings tourists here with their canoes and bicycles. I listen for the weather forecasts, trying to guess the difference between "isolated showers" and "scattered showers," "occasional thunderstorms" and "thunderstorm warnings."

My drought is real, but it is a challenge, not a tragedy. This is not the Sahara, nor is it the Dust

Rudbeckia hirta is able to survive the difficult combination of dry summers and frosty winters.

Bowl. This drought will be over in a couple of weeks, so except for a few unwisely situated plants, it is survivable. As the quotation at the beginning of this chapter makes clear, drought is relative. But

An eastern Ontario garden contains a variety of cold-hardy, drought-tolerant plants on a gravel-mulched, stone-edged slope.

for a gardener, those "measurable losses" can be disastrous. If I had a conventional English-style perennial border, for instance, many of my plants, given the amount of watering I do, would be dead by now and the rest would look pathetic.

Of course, some of them wouldn't even have survived the winter. I live in eastern Ontario, in a place where January and February temperatures sometimes dip to minus 33 degrees F (–36°C). Worse, the winters are variable: snowy one week,

rainy the next, glazed with ice the next. In spring, the soil stays soggy and cold for weeks. It's hard on people, but harder still on plants.

This limestone hilltop is a beautiful spot, but when I moved here almost a decade ago from a garden only a 15-minute drive away, I was in for a setback. That garden and this garden are in the same climatic zone, but they have little else in common. That one was lush and shady, with a stream out back. This one is exposed and windy.

Plants that flourished for me there looked tired and refused to grow here. Several of my perennials didn't survive their first winter. In summer, the soil quickly dried after a rain, and rains came seldom. Daily watering, a tiring chore, became part of my routine, yet plants still withered. That wasn't my idea of an enjoyable gardening experience. I didn't want to be tied to my plants by an umbilical water hose all summer, nor did I want to be one of those tiresome gardeners who is forever wishing for rain when everyone else is enjoying the sunshine of our brief summer.

There is one more limitation where I live. Our water comes from a well. The water is wonderful to drink—cold and full of minerals—but it is hard on plants, especially in summer. Plants do best with what they are meant to be watered with: soft water that is the same temperature as the air. Rainwater. Every gardener notices the difference in the garden's response to a rainfall compared with a sprinkler. Sprinkling, especially with cold water, does little more than keep plants alive. There they sit, huddled and soaked, waiting to warm again in the sun. Rainfall revives them and gets them growing again, sometimes so fast that you can almost see them getting bigger.

I decided to water with saved rainwater as much as possible. When there is no rain to fill the barrels, I do the next best thing, allowing well water to warm in the barrels, then using a watering can. My plants don't get much watering—the lawn gets none—but everything does as well as I can hope for. Quality watering wins over quantity watering. The garden gets no watering at all during the weeks when I'm away on vacation, but I don't want to return home to a landscape of brown stems and crackling foliage. Almost anyone with a garden at the summer cottage can sympathize. If you can't be there all the time during dry weather, plants that need coddling are out of the question.

But still, many gardeners see lush borders and difficult plants as the gardening ideal. When I speak to horticultural societies, even in climates harsher than my own, I am often asked how to grow French hydrangeas, saucer magnolias, wisteria, hybrid tea roses or tropical hibiscus. Maybe the

A watering can regularly dipped in a rain barrel takes care of thirsty container-grown plants.

questioners, usually beginners, have been inspired by pictures in Southern or British gardening magazines and encouraged by dealers responding to market demands. The fact is that all these plants are tricky, if not impossible, to grow in zone 4, where I live, let alone in a place with dry summers and little or no water to spare. Let them be fussed over by those who truly love them. For the rest of us, there are many lesser-known plants that are even more beautiful, I think, and undoubtedly much easier to grow. Increasingly, these plants and their seeds are becoming available from retailers.

The plants I'm talking about are winter-hardy and drought-tolerant. They are just one aspect of a gardening system known as xeriscaping, a term created in the Arizona desert—a very different climate from mine—to describe landscaping with xeric, or drought-tolerant, plants. Xeriscaping, which means choosing the best plants as well as growing them the best way, is virtually a lifestyle. It is an approach to gardening that favors not only water conserva-

Rather than depending on tender, fussy plants, the harsh-climate gardener grows such stalwarts as yarrow.

tion but also the conservation of time, energy and other resources. Xeriscaped gardens look quite different from English perennial borders or French *potagers*. Dry gardens are distinctive: brighter, more open, with the waxy foliage of succulents and much more gray foliage. These gardens depend more on groundcovers and mulches than on stately flowering perennials. There are apt to be more tall grasses and fewer vines.

If the dry garden is different in space, it is also different in time. I concentrate my gardening activities in spring and fall and leave the garden alone as much as I can during its two stressful seasons, summer and winter. Spring and fall are times for planting, moving, dividing, pruning, fertilizing and mulching in preparation for the difficult seasons to come. In summer, virtually all I do is deadhead flowers, harvest edibles and spot-water, making the rounds when necessary with my watering can after supper.

Whether or not they call what they do

xeriscaping, dry-garden enthusiasts are everywhere, from the American deserts to the Canadian prairies and the midwestern states, even England. One of the best dry gardens I have visited is in England, not a country usually associated with drought, although Beth Chatto writes in her classic *The Dry Garden* that "many years, little measurable rain fell from May to September."

Chatto runs a commercial enterprise and writes only about the plants in her own garden. Like me, she lives in a place where sunny summers delight tourists but challenge gardeners: "…every year brings weeks and often months of concern for our plants, the 'good' weather for the sportsman and camper becoming the despair of the gardener."

This book is not just about my own garden. My garden is modest, one I have built and maintained myself, with a body more prone to aches and weariness than I would like. It is not a botanical garden, nor is it a display garden. It's simply my own pleasure, though I now have hundreds of species and cultivars mostly chosen for drought tolerance as well as perennials, shrubs and trees chosen for winter hardiness. To make this book as useful as possible, I have included expert advice and the results of university, government and public-garden reports from across the continent, mainly in zone 4 or 5.

I am not in the business of selling plants, so I am not out to convince you to buy anything. You can grow the newest hybrids purchased at upscale garden stores or the most tried-and-true of the heirlooms obtained as divisions from your neighbors. You can have a beautiful garden made up of just one or two types of plants as easily as you can have one full of an array of things, as I do. So long as your climate is similar to mine, a garden suited to dry summers and cold winters will be the most self-reliant garden you can grow.

As freshwater supplies become scarcer, the dry garden is also well suited to the new millennium. This is a garden that gives more to the environment than it takes away. A few skills and the right plants add up to a garden with a different sort of beauty, one that leaves your time and your conscience free and easy.

CLIMATE ZONE MAP

This simplified version of the U.S. Department of Agriculture's climatic-zone map indicates general temperature trends throughout most of Canada and the United States. The temperature ranges indicate average minimum winter temperatures. Colder zones have lower numbers. Nursery catalogs usually indicate the coldest zone in which a plant will thrive. Plants that are successful in your zone and in zones with numbers lower than yours should survive winters in your garden. Plants that prefer zones with higher numbers than yours may not be winter-hardy for you. But conditions vary locally, so experimentation is often worthwhile.

Zone 1
Below −50°F
Below −45°C

Zone 2
−50°F to −40°F
−45°C to −40°C

Zone 3
−40°F to −30°F
−40°C to −34°C

Zone 4
−30°F to −20°F
−34°C to −29°C

Zone 5
−20°F to −10°F
−29°C to −23°C

Zone 6
−10°F to 0°F
−23°C to −18°C

Zone 7
0°F to 10°F
−18°C to −12°C

Zone 8
10°F to 20°F
−12°C to −6°C

Zone 9
20°F to 30°F
−6°C to −1°C

Zone 10
30°F to 40°F
−1°C to 4.5°C

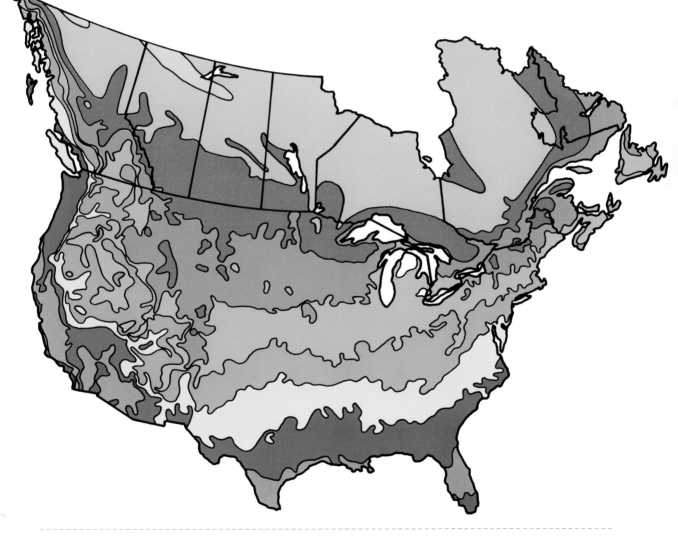

Water Ways

◆ *1*

"IF A WELL BE LACKING IN THE GARDEN, THEN DIG A DEEP PIT
IN SOME CONVENIENT PLACE OF THE GARDEN, TO DRAW WATER OUT
OF THE SAME. FOR A GARDEN GROUND NEEDETH OFTEN TO BE
WATERED, THROUGH WHICH ALL SEEDS COMMITTED TO THE EARTH,
AS PLINY REPORTETH, BOTH SOONER BREAK FORTH,
AND SPEEDIER SPREAD ABOUT."

—Thomas Hill, *The Gardener's Labyrinth*, 1577

Seeds and plants need water, as Thomas Hill pointed out more than four centuries ago. Water is the lifeblood of the garden, even the dry garden. The lack of fresh water is the most important limitation to agriculture worldwide. Since water is so critical to the survival of not only plants but all other living things, it is important that it be managed carefully and consciously in the garden. How you water, when you water, if you water—these are important questions in the dry-summer, cold-winter garden, questions that will determine what plants you can grow, where you can grow them and how. The less water you have, the more careful about it you must be and the better able to conserve it when possible and use it where necessary.

Plants need an almost constant supply of water, and virtually all of that is taken in through the roots. The soil may look dry to you, but a heavy dew can refresh roots near the surface, while those deeper underground search for enough moisture to keep their cells plump even in the midsummer heat. A fresh leaf is about 80 percent water, as are we, but plants, unlike humans, must constantly take in water from the bottom to replace what is lost out the top through pores that are always at least partially open. Weight for weight, plants need about 17 times as much water as humans do. Stop the intake of water for long, and most plants soon wilt, then die. Fortunately, the deeper-rooted the plant, the more self-reliant it is. Once trees are established, gardeners pretty much forget about them, and there are many shrubs and even perennials that likewise seldom require watering.

Watering needs depend upon many things, as outlined in the next chapter. Plant choice, soil quality, exposure to sun or shade and even the garden's location all play a part. *Rudbeckia hirta* (black-eyed Susan, gloriosa daisy) will grow without watering in Atlanta, Georgia, and in my own garden in eastern Ontario, but it needs regular watering in Albuquerque, New Mexico.

My own equivalent of Thomas Hill's "deep pit," described at the beginning of this chapter, are four rain barrels along with an aboveground pond, all of which collect rainwater from downspouts connected to the eavestroughs. For most of the summer, these reservoirs supply all the water I

Plants in containers are high priorities at watering time. If foliage covers the pot, rainfall may not even touch the soil.

need. Only after about two weeks of drought do I have to fill the barrels with water from the hose. This is better than watering the garden directly from the hose, because my home's water supply comes from a well and is very cold, even in mid-summer. Cold water on warm roots is not much better than no water at all. In the barrel, the water is allowed to warm to air temperature, then is applied with a watering can just where needed.

Using Rainwater

Making the most of the supply of rainwater is an important survival strategy of the dry-summer gardener. Rainwater has several advantages over tap water:

• It is free.

• It is soft. Hard tap water not only leaves a whitish residue of calcium or magnesium carbonate on leaves, soil and plant pots but also can interfere with the uptake of nutrients in the soil.

• It is the ambient temperature. Water that is colder than the air temperature slows seed ger-mination and plant growth. In hot weather, cold irrigation can actually cause wilting.

• It is not treated with chlorine, fluorine or other tap-water additives. Fluoridated tap water normally contains about 1 part per million (ppm) fluorine, but as little as $\frac{1}{4}$ ppm can damage many plant species, in the garden or in a vase. Symptoms range from burning of leaf tips to leaf death. Chlorine, too, is toxic to plants in sufficiently large amounts, although it is very volatile and will dissi-pate into the air if the water is allowed to sit for a few hours.

• Rainwater is naturally acidic due to carbon dioxide and other acid-producing substances in the atmosphere, which means that rainwater has a pH of less than 7, generally 5.6 to 5.7. On a scale of 1 to 14, pH 7 is neutral. Numbers higher than 7 indicate increasing alkalinity; numbers lower than 7, increasing acidity. In industrialized places, such as the northeastern United States, the pH of rain-water can be as low as 4.1, because sulfur and nitrogen oxides from the burning of fossil fuels react with raindrops to form sulfuric and nitric acids. This intensifies the acidity of acidic soils, where limestone must be added for certain crops, but most garden plants do best in soil that is neutral or slightly acidic. Where I live, the bedrock is limestone, so the soil and well water are alkaline. Using rainwater helps neutralize my garden soil.

• Using rainwater in the garden means that precious, expensive treated tap water can be used for the purpose for which it is intended: drinking. One of the reasons the Denver, Colorado, water department began an extensive xeriscaping plan was that 40 percent of its treated water was going to residential landscape use. In Victoria, British Columbia, a relatively humid place, 36 percent of the residential water supply goes to lawns and gardens in summer. Only 2 percent is used for drinking and cooking.

Watering in the rain might sound like nothing more than a strange way to get wet, but it makes sense to people with dry gardens. A downpour usually means wasted water; suddenly, water overflows my rain barrels and runs down the driveway. Meanwhile, the garden soil is so dusty that it sheds water, and by the time the rain ends, only the surface is wet. So if I'm lucky enough to be home during a summer rainstorm, I'll be outside scooping water out of the barrels and dumping it here and there on the neediest places. A watering like that results in a deep soaking that can set the garden up for a week of drought.

Measuring Water

Most watering is done in summer, of course, when water supplies are generally lowest and all needs are highest. In Georgia, where summers are relatively humid and gardening goes on year-round, household water use in summer is about double that in winter. In Kamloops, British Columbia, a semi-desert city where only about 10 inches (25 cm) of rain falls each year and where cold weather prohibits winter gardening, the figure for midsummer water use is about five times that for midwinter. There is a program in that city to reduce summer water use by 25 percent. The most effective way to do this is to decrease landscape use, which accounts for at least half of the residential water supply.

It isn't usually necessary to know how much rain falls on your garden. It's enough to know that sometimes your garden is dry. But you may want to keep track—to give a lawn its allotted 1 inch (2.5 cm) per week, for instance—so that you can make up the difference from a sprinkler. Some hardware stores and garden-supply sources sell rain gauges, or you can make one from a large can set just deep enough into the garden soil that it stays securely upright. After each rainfall, simply measure the water level with a ruler, then empty the can before replacing it. For an ongoing record of water accumulation, mark a plastic drinking straw from the bottom in inches or centimeters. After a rain or after sprinkling, insert the straw to the bottom of the can, put a finger on top, pull the straw out and read the level.

How can you tell when to water? Mostly by the appearance of the soil and by wilted plants. The most needy plants will wilt and may even die before more drought-tolerant ones show any signs of stress at all. Wilting in the evening can be caused by a day of hot, windy weather and can even occur when there is moisture in the soil, but wilted leaves in the morning are a sign of dry soil and imminent damage to plants. Water immediately.

Another way to gauge dryness is with one of the soil-moisture meters on the market. When the meter is inserted into the soil, a bimetallic tip generates electricity in the presence of moisture, causing the pointer to move. In experiments in California, even inexpensive meters were somewhat effective, although salts in the soil made the meters indicate more moisture than was present. The California researchers concluded that gardeners should get to know their own soil-moisture levels and plant responses before relying on meters.

Watering is best done when the air is calm and relatively cool—that means morning or evening. Evening is best, because most plant growth occurs at night, the seeds of many desert species germinate in darkness and plant cells can take time to plump up and prepare for the heat of the following day. The only caution about evening watering is that you should water the ground, not the foliage.

Foliage that stays wet all night is easy prey for fungal diseases. If you use a sprinkler, choose the morning instead.

Never overwater—watering so heavily that it leaves puddles on the ground. Too much watering weakens plants, making them more vulnerable to diseases, to future drought and to winterkill.

Saving Water in the Garden

Don't have a set schedule for watering, because the garden's needs will vary from place to place and time to time. Prioritize your plants according to their water requirements. They are as follows, starting with the greatest need:

Young plants. Watering priority goes to any plant in its first year in your garden, even drought-tolerant perennials, shrubs and trees. Shrubs and trees under stress may look perfectly fine until they reach the point of death, when the leaves wilt. By then, it is likely too late. As these plants represent your greatest garden investment in terms of time, space and probably money, they must be considered top priority at planting time and then once a week during dry weather. Water deeply. Thorough watering helps roots go deeper, making the plant more self-reliant. A tree needs soaking to a depth of about 14 inches (35 cm). If the ground is really dry and you don't want to haul buckets of rainwater, the easiest way to accomplish this is to place a hose near the trunk and let the water trickle gently for several hours. If there is runoff, the water is flowing too fast or the ground is saturated. In experiments in California, privet plants given the most frequent watering developed 18-inch (45 cm) roots, compared with 12-inch (30 cm) roots on plants watered half as often. By their second year, drought-tolerant trees, shrubs and perennials should be able to get by with watering no more frequently than every two weeks in dry weather.

Annuals. Like all plants in their first year of growth, vegetables and annual flowers also demand high priority. Most vegetables do best with about 1 inch (2.5 cm) of water per week, although drought-tolerant annuals require watering only during the first few weeks after seeding or transplanting. Self-sown annuals need even less. Annuals that are not drought-tolerant should be grown only in areas with shade, deep soil and easy access.

Plants in containers. Because their root systems are restricted, container plants can't draw water from as large an area as plants in the ground. Also, once container-plant foliage becomes dense, any rain that falls may be shed outside the container, making the plant totally dependent upon the gardener. Only very drought-tolerant plants, such as cacti and succulents, can be left untended in pots. Adding wetting agents—hydrogels—to potting soil may help. These water-absorbing polymers take in large amounts of water and, in theory, gradually release it to plant roots. Research on their effectiveness has been controversial, but trials at the University of Georgia indicated that hydrogels enhanced the growth of summer annuals in nonirrigated soil.

Plants that are not drought-tolerant. You may decide to grow a group of thirsty plants, even though you know they'll require more attention during dry weather.

Lawn. Some people like to have a lush, green lawn all summer and are willing to make it a watering priority. Sprinkler systems are the only practical way to water a lawn, and such watering is best done first thing in the morning. Even the thirstiest types of lawn grasses need only 1 inch (2.5 cm) of water per week. If it rains that much, no more water is needed. See the directions on page 17 for making a simple water-measuring device. See Chapter 3 for suggestions about cutting down on watering by planting drought-tolerant grasses and alternative groundcovers.

Watering Systems

How you water your garden will depend on many considerations: How big is it and how dry? How often are you away? How much time and money do you want to spend?

Watering can. A watering can may be old-fashioned, but it is the cheapest water-conserving device available. Needless to say, it doesn't suit every situation. Lugging water around by hand takes time and energy, and somebody has to be around to do it. If your watering needs are modest,

With the trickle system, gardeners can ensure that water is not wasted on the foliage but reaches the soil directly.

however, this might be your most valuable piece of gardening equipment, especially when combined with rain barrels. Using a watering can has the double benefit of giving you a good excuse to wander through your garden.

Rain barrel. When 1 inch of rain falls on 1 square foot of roof, that equals a little over ½ gallon (U.S.) of water. If ¼ inch of rain falls, then, 1,000 square feet of roof collects about 150 gallons of water. (In metric terms, 1 centimeter of rain on 10 square meters of roof provides 1,000 liters.) So it doesn't take much of a rainfall to fill a barrel placed at each downspout from the eavestroughs. Recycled metal oil barrels or plastic pails used to ship foods such as olives can be called into service, or there are special plastic barrels made just for this purpose. Some have lids, some have a tap near the base, and some can be connected together for added capacity. If these barrels dry out in summer, fill them from the hose and let the water warm to air temperature before using it in the garden. In late fall, before freeze-up, empty the

barrels and lid them or turn them upside down to prevent their being cracked or swollen by ice.

Cistern. At one time, my old farmhouse, which was built soon after the turn of the century, had a cistern in the basement, filled by runoff from the roof. Water could be pumped out whenever it was needed. A cistern may be above ground or buried and may be made of plastic, wood, metal or concrete.

Subirrigation. A long word for a simple procedure, subirrigation means that the soil under the surface is watered. The usual method is to insert topless cans or other open containers in the soil near plants, with just the rims above the soil surface. Punch a few small nail holes in the cans before you bury them, then fill with water. The water will gradually soak into the soil at root level, where it is most useful. You can also buy subirrigating watering fixtures that can be attached to plastic soda bottles.

Furrows. An ancient system still used wherever farm fields are irrigated from rivers, furrows are ditches that direct water between rows of culti-

In June, the soil around an ornamental-grass transplant is mulched with straw to slow drying.

vated plants. Not particularly attractive, furrows are most practical in the vegetable garden. You must follow the contours of the garden, and the water supply must be plentiful enough to reach the end of the furrows. The advantages of furrows are that they are inexpensive, they water the soil only, not the foliage, and they allow you to leave a hose in one place and get on with other things while gravity does the work.

Soaker, drip or trickle irrigation. In a way, these are simply more expensive, more attractive forms of furrowing. Again, water goes onto the soil, not the foliage, and the system is relatively or totally automated, so you don't have to stay in the garden while watering is going on. Rather than flowing down an open furrow, however, water flows down a perforated hose or tube. Most hoses can be hidden with mulch, so these systems are appropriate for ornamental as well as vegetable gardens.

Soaker Hose: Made from recycled tires, the soaker hose is the most economical choice. It has tiny pores that allow water to seep from it slowly and evenly. About half a gallon (2 L) of water per minute seeps from every 100 feet (30 m) of hose. Water soaks in directly under or close to the hose. The chief disadvantage of the soaker hose is that because of the small size of its pores, it can easily clog from hard or alkaline water or from solids in the water, even if you install a filter. Treated tap water or fresh rainwater from a lidded barrel are among the best sources of water for a soaker hose. If you are in doubt about the clarity of your water, try a short length of hose for a season to see how it works for you. These systems operate at lower water pressure than normal household water pressure, so you must have the tap only partially turned on or install a pressure regulator next to the filter on the line leading to the hose.

Drip or Trickle System: The choice of many professional growers, this system has smaller feeder tubes fitted with emitters plugged into the larger tube where needed. Some systems can handle normal household water pressure.

There are several disadvantages to this system:
• The initial setup can be labor-intensive.
• It is not frostproof.
• Rodents, insects or foot traffic can cause damage.
• The water from such a system is likely to be cold, and overwatering is as possible as it is with more conventional systems.

If you are interested in a soaker, drip or trickle system, ask several manufacturers for descriptions of their products (see Sources). Also, most hardware and garden stores sell basic systems in spring. If you buy from more than one manufacturer, make sure that all the components are compatible.

Sprinklers. These are not very efficient watering devices. About half of the water applied by sprinklers can be lost to evaporation, especially if you use a fine spray on a windy day. However, sprinkling is the most practical method for shallow-rooted plants like grasses and for large areas like lawns, especially if water is not scarce. To conserve water when you do sprinkle, settle for a coarse spray rather than a fine one. Spray during calm weather, preferably first thing in the morning. Because spraying wets foliage, it should not be done in the evening, which can encourage fungal diseases.

An underground sprinkler system can be professionally installed. Make sure the application rate suits the absorbing ability of your soil; otherwise, runoff will occur. Keep track of the amount of water your sprinkler uses by placing three or four rain gauges in the irrigated area for a certain length of time, usually an hour. See the directions for making a rain gauge on page 17. Average the water level among the gauges.

Household and gray water. Water used for cooking and washing is called gray water, as opposed to "white" drinking water and "black" sewage water. Gray water cannot legally be used in all places, especially in cities, so check with local officials before you redirect your wastewater.

Where it can be used, gray water is especially good for lawns and flowerbeds. It should not be used on vegetables and fruits or new plantings because of possible contamination. As it is likely to be alkaline, do not use it on acid-loving plants. Dilute it with fresh water whenever possible, and don't always use it on the same area. A certain amount of soap does not harm most plants, including grasses, and can even act as a fertilizer and pesticide. Too much soap, however, can burn the foliage of sensitive plants.

If you intend to use your gray water, use simple soaps rather than detergents containing softeners and whiteners. Dish-washing or cooking water should be allowed to cool, then poured into the soil around plants near the kitchen. Water from a dehumidifier is pure and safe to use. Water from the rinse cycle of the washing machine is better for the garden than water from the wash cycle, which may contain chlorine bleach, borax or other substances that can harm plants. Boron (borax) is especially dangerous—it is sometimes deliberately used as a herbicide. In any case, gray water should be applied directly to the soil, not the foliage. Regularly test soil watered with gray water to measure salt or boron accumulation.

Do not use gray water:
• if it is contaminated with black water. For

A terraced slope facilitates water retention while also allowing soil to drain as efficiently as possible.

instance, do not use water in which diapers have been washed.

• if it has been softened, because softened water contains too much sodium.

• if it comes from a swimming pool, because it will contain too much chlorine and/or bromine.

• if it comes from a sink where a garburetor has been used.

• if you intend to direct it into a drip-irrigation system, unless you install both a filter to remove suspended particles and a grease trap for kitchen-sink water.

• if it has been sitting any length of time, because bacteria in it may multiply. Handle carefully.

• if soil drainage is poor, because salts may accumulate in the soil.

Garden-Water Conservation

Anything that will hold rain near roots, rather than letting it flow away, will maximize the efficiency of watering. On flat or slightly sloped

The advantages of rainwater in the dry garden are many: it is free, it is soft, it is acidic, and it is the ambient temperature.

ground, make a ring dike a few inches high around each plant. Slopes are best terraced if you can manage it. This gives plants the ideal conditions of good drainage, water retention and relatively deep soil. Support the terrace banks with rocks, boards or logs, and build the flat surfaces up with compost or topsoil.

Soil drainage is critically important for many plants that can survive drought, especially in a garden like mine, which may be soggy for weeks in spring. Gardening on a slope helps plants survive, especially xeric plants. In places where water collects, I have to grow some of my toughest plants—or nothing at all.

In the next chapter, there are more suggestions about how to conserve soil moisture.

Household-Water Conservation

Water-conservation practices are seldom limited to the garden alone but are connected with saving water in other areas of life.

If children want to play in the water, give them a wading pool rather than letting them play with a sprinkler or hose.

Use a bucket of water to wash the car rather than using a sprinkler or going to a commercial car wash, an extravagant water waster.

Swim in a natural body of water rather than a swimming pool, especially your own swimming pool. Residential swimming pools lose enormous amounts of fresh water through evaporation and backwash. And swimming-pool water cannot be recycled, as it is contaminated with chlorine. If you do have a swimming pool, fill it to 6 to 8 inches (15-20 cm) from the top to reduce the water loss from splashing. Also, a swimming-pool cover will cut down on evaporation while it holds in heat and keeps out dirt.

Install a water-saving device in your toilet tank. Old models can use as much as 7 gallons (26 L) of water per flush, while most modern toilets use less than half that amount. Old toilets can be retrofitted with toilet-tank banks that lessen the tank capacity.

Make sure your plumbing is not leaking. A dripping toilet, for example, can waste as much as 17 gallons (64 L) of water a day.

An automatic dishwasher uses about 12 gallons (45 L) per run. Make sure it's fully loaded before turning it on.

Store a jug of ice water in the refrigerator rather than letting the water run until it's cold every time you want a drink.

Take short showers rather than baths, and if you do have a bath, don't fill the tub to the top. Install a water-saving showerhead.

Many washing machines use 40 gallons (150 L) or more per load. Wash a full load rather than a few items, or set the water level lower.

How Much Do You Use?

If you have a water meter, it will record the amount of water your household uses in cubic meters, gallons or cubic feet. If it measures in cubic feet, multiply the number by 7.5 to translate into gallons. One cubic meter equals 220 gallons. Turn on your sprinkler or other watering device for a minute, and record how far the meter turns. Multiply the number of gallons times the number of minutes you usually leave the sprinkler running. You can use the same method to calculate the number of gallons used in the shower, the dishwasher or the washing machine. If all appliances are turned off and the meter continues to turn, there is a leak somewhere in the system.

You can also measure the flow rate by collecting and measuring the water that flows from, say, your shower in 10 seconds. Multiply by 6 to arrive at the total number of gallons per minute, then figure out how many minutes you generally spend in the shower to arrive at the total.

DRIEST OF THE DRY

The plants in the following chapters vary in their water needs. Almost all require a certain amount of watering, especially in their first year or two. There are a few, however, that once established—which may take only a few weeks—are virtually self-sustaining, no matter how dry the weather. If you want a garden that almost never needs watering, consider the following genera, as well as the hardy bulbs and rhizomes listed in Chapter 4:

Achillea
Artemisia
Caragana
Centaurea
Hemerocallis
Juniperus
Paeonia
Sedum
Sempervivum
Yucca

In a hanging basket of xeric plants, hardy sedum surrounds a tender agave and echeverias in an arrangement that demands little or no watering.

Garden Survival Techniques

◆2◆

"THESE THINGS HAVE GROWN HERE FOR THOUSANDS OF YEARS.
THEY CAN TAKE CARE OF THEMSELVES. THEY DON'T NEED WATERING."

—John P. Morgan, Prairie Habitats Nursery

When John Morgan, owner of the plant nursery Prairie Habitats, in Argyle, Manitoba, describes the native plants of central Canada and the midwestern United States, he sums up the meaning of the word adaptation. Native plants are able to survive without our help and have done so for a very long time. Not only do they not need us, but when we interfere with them, we often do more harm than good. We water too much, drowning the roots. We fertilize too much, encouraging fast, weak, disease-susceptible growth. One of the best ways to grow a garden which needs little care, then, is to stick with plants that are native to or naturalized in your area or in other drought-prone places and let them take care of themselves.

Some of these wildlings are little known in gardens; others, like black-eyed Susans and Shasta daisies, are common. Some domestic flowers are virtually the same as their wild forebears, but in other cases, the garden cousins have been substantially changed, usually to produce larger, longer-lasting flowers, perhaps in a wider color range,

even with differently shaped petals or many more petals per flower. Sometimes, invasiveness is reduced in the domesticated version. The drier the garden, however, the less important long-lasting flowers and polite root systems become. The more a plant's innate survival abilities are bred out of it, the less suitable it is for tough growing conditions.

Plant Choice

The plants suitable for unwatered gardens are natives of dry places, not necessarily in North America, although you may choose to grow plants that are native to your area—a worthwhile conservation effort. Some lovely prairie grasses and wildflowers can be purchased as plants or grown from seed (see Sources). I don't care where my plants' ancestors grew, although my garden does include many North American natives.

Here are five things to consider when choosing plants for the dry garden:

• Plants that other people consider weedy might be just right for you. Goutweed (*Aegopodium podagraria*), for instance, is considered too weedy for a manicured border, but it is beautiful and re-

Choosing plants for the dry garden may mean passing up plants that demand attention in favor of self-sufficient plants.

liable when the chips are down, even in the dry shade under trees or under the eavestroughs against a house wall. So are certain grasses, bellflowers, yarrows and plants that drop their seeds after blooming. In my garden, a wild buttercup (*Ranunculus acris*) arrived on its own in an area of stone mulch. With its deeply divided leaves and waxy yellow flowers on tall stems, it was beautiful from early spring until late fall. It was finally done in by a front-end loader. All garden books say this plant is too aggressive for a garden, yet surrounded as it was by a stone mulch, it showed no inclination to spread, and I cut back its finished flowers to discourage self-sowing.

• The deeper and longer-lived the root system, the more self-sufficient the plant is likely to be. Taking simply that fact into consideration, plants are drought-resistant in roughly this descending order: trees, shrubs, perennials and annuals, including vegetables.

• Almost anything that has survived two winters in your garden, whether it comes back in spring by self-sown seeds or from a perennial root, will be better able to take care of itself than anything freshly planted.

• Lawn grasses can be difficult, expensive and environmentally harmful to keep pristine, but they are among the easiest plants if you choose the right grasses and accept summer brownness or occasional weediness.

• Many plants that will survive drought are intolerant of extended wetness. Just because a plant can live in dry ground doesn't mean it can put up with anything.

Choosing plants that will grow in your climate and in your garden is a first step to success in a drought-prone place with cold winters. Plants not sufficiently hardy for your climatic zone (see page 13) may survive a year or two until they are polished off by a so-called test winter, one with record low temperatures or seesaw variations. In the meantime, you will probably have to contend with winter-killed shoots each spring. If you have acidic soil, it is best to grow plants that prefer acidity—the same with alkaline soil. You can fight nature, of course, but be prepared to work hard and to put up with discouragement. Eventually, nature always wins.

How can you tell whether a plant will survive without water? Much of this book consists of lists of suitable plants. All of them will tolerate a considerable stretch of dryness. Most nurseries and seed catalogs give some indication of relative needs for moist or dry ground, and that ubiquitous term "well-drained soil" applies to virtually all the probable drought survivors. Some companies specialize in dry-land plants. Plants developed on the prairies are usually good bets. There have been especially successful breeding programs in Alberta, Manitoba and North Dakota. And, of course, experimentation is worthwhile and often rewarding, but you must be prepared to accept a few losses.

Remember, however, that while many plants can survive with little or no watering after they have been established in your garden for a year or two, all must be watered regularly when newly sown or planted. And if a plant looks wilted first thing in the morning, it needs watering right away.

Once plants are established, some surprising choices will survive a dry summer. Astilbe and lady's mantle, reputed to be lovers of damp ground, grow in my garden in a small patch of shade provided by a large rock on an otherwise exposed slope. Hosta grows happily in the shade of a stump. I have Siberian irises in many places. None of these plants grow as big as they would in wetter places, but they survive and flower every year.

Sowing Seeds

The easiest way to obtain some unusual plants is to grow them yourself from seed. I always include a few perennials amongst my tomatoes and peppers, which are started indoors in late winter under lights or by the window. In this way, I have obtained some lovely species of allium, dianthus, euphorbia and verbascum, to name just a few. Some perennials and shrubs can be a bit tricky from seed, but those four are examples of many that are as easy to grow as peppers, especially if you have a simple fluorescent light fixture which can be raised or lowered so that it is always just slightly

above the plant tops. Seed catalogs and packets give instructions about seed depth and any special needs the seeds have. Many prairie species, for instance, require light to germinate, so the seeds should be sprinkled on top of the soil, not buried.

For seeding, use a special seedling mixture, such as the type made from peat and vermiculite, which is available in garden stores. Any pots or containers that will hold soil securely and drain from the bottom can be used, but stay away from terra cotta, which dries out too quickly. The soil mixture must be kept thoroughly moist until the seeds sprout, then misted whenever the surface dries. Hardy species can begin to spend part of the day outdoors in their pots in partial or full shade as soon as the temperature rises above freezing. Gradually increase their outdoor exposure until planting time.

Some seeds can be sown directly in the garden. These are divided into two groups: seeds sown before the last spring frost date and seeds that wait until later. Many annuals are most easily grown this way, and most of the hardy ones can be sown anytime in spring. They germinate as soon as the soil is warm enough and sprout in the moisture left from winter. Seeds of frost-tender species—those which have to wait until after the last spring frost—are best sown directly in the garden in early summer soon after a rain, but if this is not possible, wet the ground before seeding. To catch water, the seeded area should be slightly lower than the surrounding soil. If you are seeding in rows, sow the seeds in shallow ditches.

Within the perennial flowerbed, I sow curving rows of the seeds of annuals, such as cornflower, snow on the mountain and Shirley poppy, and mark their position with twigs inserted at both ends of the row. If you are seeding in drifts or patches, you may want to mark the perimeter with white flour or string; seedlings can take a week or more to emerge, and identification can be tricky when they do. Check the seeded area every day, and water with a fine spray if it dries out. Once the seedlings emerge, they quickly develop a deep root system if watering is limited to no more than once a day. Self-sown seeds of hardy annuals take care of themselves, sprouting when conditions are best.

Adventurous gardeners can grow almost all their plants, such as these annual flowers, from seed.

Cuttings

Many of the plants in the dry garden can be multiplied from softwood cuttings. Artemisia, perovskia, lavender, rosemary and penstemon are a few. In early summer, when the new growth is still soft, take a stem tip about as long as your finger, strip off all but the top couple of leaves, dip the base in rooting hormone and plant the cutting to about half its length in a pot of damp sand or seedling mixture, several cuttings per pot (you will probably have some failures).

Place the pots in a shady spot outdoors, water them, and cover with something transparent. Single cuttings can be covered with drinking glasses; flats can be covered with the plastic domes that protect baked goods. Weight the top down so that it will not blow off.

When new growth starts, remove the lid, but replace it if the cuttings wilt. As soon as they can survive without the lid, transplant each cutting into its own pot. Let it grow for another couple of weeks before planting out. Then follow the rules as for any potted transplant, whether purchased or homegrown.

Transplanting

Make sure the soil in the plant pot is wet, then tip the plant out. If the plant is root-bound—roots circle round and round inside the pot—tease the roots away from the soil ball before planting. Pour water into the planting hole, and set the plant at the same depth it grew in its pot. Press the soil down around the roots, and water again.

The general rule with transplants, including annuals, perennials, shrubs and trees, is to water them regularly until new growth begins—the sign that roots have grown into the surrounding soil. This may not mean daily watering (in fact, watering too frequently encourages shallow root growth, and you want the roots to grow deep), but it may be as often as twice a week for shrubs and trees, every second day for annuals and perennials. At Prairie Habitats Nursery in Manitoba, owner John Morgan marks with red flags anything newly planted to remind himself that these plants need close watching and may need watering. Fall-planted trees, shrubs and perennials need deep soaking, just as they would if planted in spring. Do not fertilize them. It is no longer recommended that top growth be pruned back after planting, but dead or damaged branches should be trimmed off. Perennial plants need as much foliage as possible for root development. More information about watering is given in the previous chapter.

Shading transplants in sunny places for the first few days will help them adjust to the stress of planting. Temporary shade can be provided by cut fern fronds, evergreen branches or a portable lath roof.

The only trees and shrubs that require staking are any which are top-heavy or are growing in windy places. In most cases, the stake should be removed after one growing season. The trunk will strengthen if the tree is allowed to move in the wind.

Planting Time

In the dry garden, all planting and transplanting are best done in spring or fall. In spring, the soil is still moist from winter. The northern plant-nursery business hits its stride in spring, and most mail-order shipping is done then. But hot, dry summer weather may soon follow planting time, making it difficult for new plants to become established. Fall planting often works better, from August through October, or at least six weeks before freeze-up in your area. Soil temperatures are still high enough for root growth, fall rains may arrive, and the new roots will have all next spring to grow. Also, plant prices are usually marked down in fall.

Fall planting is not wise for any species considered only marginally hardy in your area. These plants need the advantage of an entire growing season before they must endure their first winter. Herbaceous perennials that are best planted in spring include aconitum and platycodon. Shrubs and trees that are best planted in spring include betula, carpinus, cercis, ginkgo, populus and quercus.

Antidesiccants

Evergreens should be watered in late fall the year they are planted and, thereafter, following a very dry summer. Otherwise, they should be able to survive the winter on their own, although they may suffer some browning and needle loss. To help prevent this, some growers use antidesiccants, waxy products that coat the leaves of evergreens in winter to minimize moisture loss. Though antidesiccants are sometimes used on needle evergreens, they are most valuable on broad-leaved evergreens —few of which are adapted to dry-summer, cold-winter gardens. The antidesiccants themselves are difficult to use where winters are cold. They must be reapplied at least once during the winter and can be applied only when the temperature stays above 40 degrees F (4.5°C) long enough for the substance to dry without freezing, a winter intermission that may not occur in your garden.

INVASIVE PLANTS

Some of the most reliable plants for dry places are invasive in certain climatic areas and certain types of soil. These plants, especially imported species, termed aliens, are receiving increased attention and may become more difficult to obtain. The following species, recommended in this book as species for dry-summer, cold-winter gardens, are considered invasive somewhere in Canada or the northern United States, according to two sources. One is a survey by 35 botanists reported in *Invasive Plants of Natural Habitats in Canada* (Canadian Wildlife Service, Environment Canada, Ottawa, 1993). The other is Brooklyn Botanical Gardens publication number 149, *Invasive Plants* (100 Washington Avenue, Brooklyn, NY 11225-1099). While invasiveness is too large and complex a subject to treat fully in this book, suffice it to say that it is controversial. And although the following species are sometimes invasive, cultivars

Dependable in the dry garden, Vinca minor *can be invasive in kinder climates.*

of the same species may be fine. Check with local government agencies and plant nurseries.

Aegopodium podagraria; Artemisia absinthium; Berberis thunbergii; Caragana arborescens; Centaurea cyanus; Coronilla varia; Cytisus scoparius; Euonymus alatus; Euonymus fortunei; Gypsophila paniculata; Hesperis matronalis; Lonicera maackii; Lonicera tatarica; Miscanthus sinensis; Phalaris arundinacea; Poa compressa; Poa pratensis; Polygonum cuspidatum; Sedum acre; Spiraea japonica; Syringa vulgaris; Verbascum thapsus; Vinca minor.

Windbreaks

Any object, however small, on the windward side of a plant will provide that plant with a certain amount of drought protection. Most windbreaks are hedges or rows of wind-tolerant plants situated on the side of the garden that faces the prevailing winds. As wind blows against the windbreak, the air pressure builds up on the windward side and air moves up and over or around. There is some protection close to the windbreak, even on the windward side, and the higher the windbreak, the farther the protected area extends on the leeward side (away from the wind)—up to 30 times the height of the windbreak. Windbreaks that allow about half the wind to pass through are more effective at preventing turbulence on the leeward side. Windbreaks also help keep snow around the garden. High-density windbreaks, including buildings, create a narrow band of deep snow, while lower-density windbreaks spread the snow out and away.

Windbreaks have a couple of side benefits. Trees and shrubs screen roadside dust and absorb sound, providing a pleasant rustle of their own. They protect wildlife, affording nesting sites for birds as well as food for birds and other animals. And they cut down the wind around any buildings in their wake, lessening the need for heat in winter and shading the buildings in summer. According to the USDA Forest Service, homes protected by shade trees or windbreaks may use 15 to 30 percent less heating energy in winter and 10 to 20 percent less cooling energy in summer.

This effect can be especially dramatic in a city. The average temperature of city cores is rising 1 Fahrenheit degree (0.5 C°) per decade relative to the surrounding countryside. Near a reflective surface or paving, temperatures may soar. Preliminary data indicate that an increase of 5 percent in a landscape's tree canopy in city or country can lower July temperatures by 2 to 4 Fahrenheit degrees (1-2 C°), while reducing wind speeds by about 10 percent.

In cold-winter places, it makes sense to plant deciduous trees on the southerly side of the yard. These will lightly screen the house and garden during the summer but will allow solar heat and sunlight to pass through in winter, when the trees are leafless. For a rural or prairie property that needs extensive windbreaks, ask for current species and spacing recommendations from the nearest Extension Service in the United States or from the provincial Department of Agriculture in Canada.

The genera most commonly used for low windbreaks in dry-summer, cold-winter areas are caragana, cotoneaster, euonymus, lonicera, physocarpus, pinus, potentilla, prinsepia, prunus, ribes, spiraea, syringa, taxus, thuja and viburnum. Any of these plants can be used for an informal hedge, one that requires minimal pruning. For a formal hedge, one with a geometric shape, avoid fast-growing plants and plan to prune at least once a year or as often as every two weeks during the growing season. Do not prune coniferous evergreens beyond the current year's growth, as they will not recover. Only evergreens offer good windbreak value year-round.

Sun and Shade

Windbreaks also provide shade to the garden. Most drought-tolerant plants are described as needing full sun, but full sun in a place with blue sky from horizon to horizon every day is quite different from full sun in a place that is often overcast. All plants need a certain amount of sunlight, even if it is reflected from a nearby surface, but almost all appreciate a bit of shade too, and some shade can allow you to grow plants that would otherwise be impossible. While daylong shade makes any garden difficult, the dappled shade provided by trees, shrubs and tall perennials—or, for that matter, the intermittent shade afforded by a fence, porch railing or slatted roof—provides the best environment for healthy plant growth, especially in a sunny, windy place.

Obviously, some balancing has to be done. Trees are water hogs themselves, and those with a lot of feeder roots near the surface will take water you might want for other plants. In a small garden, grow only shrubs or trees that mature at a reasonable height, and provide additional shade with fences, gazebos and other landscape features.

A stone mulch reflects heat around xeric plants such as Anemone pulsatilla, *but it needs occasional touching up.*

Using Rocks

Rocks suit dry gardens aesthetically and practically. Consider rocks not only as accents, borders and mulches but also on their own—in the establishment of gravel paths or stone patios, for example (see page 43). Many drought-tolerant plants are native to rocky or scree areas. The soil under and shaded by rocks stays cooler and wetter than the surrounding ground, and large rocks act as windbreaks, enabling high-alpine plants, for instance, to survive the full-sun exposure and constant wind. Lowland plants can benefit in the same way. On arid sites in California, simply placing a few large rocks around each transplant has been shown to increase rooting success. If your soil is rocky, the initial planting can be difficult, but plants directly seeded or set in place when small will make their own way through the rocks and may ultimately be tougher than those in deep soil.

Rocks can be gardens on their own. I include lichen-covered rocks here and there and consider myself lucky if I find a rock covered with moss.

Moss will not survive on the fully exposed south-facing side, but it will survive on the shady side. It turns brown and looks lifeless during dry weather but becomes green and soft almost instantly in the rain, a metamorphosis (and an indication of sometimes unseen rainfall) that I find enchanting. Small birds collect moss from my rocks for nest building.

Lichens are more weather-resistant than mosses. Some can endure the extremely dry, cold conditions of the Arctic and high mountains. Again, if you find rocks already decorated with lichens, consider yourself fortunate. John Morgan of Prairie Habitats Nursery in Manitoba brought some beautiful lichen-covered rocks home from the Arctic. Some of the lichens survived indoors, he says, even spreading to neighboring rocks—a lovely idea for a no-care "houseplant." Bright orange lichen colonizing a bone he found on the prairies survived when the bone was indoors but quickly died when the bone was moved to a sunny outdoor spot. "I guess I should have hardened it off," he muses.

Improve clay and other soils with organic matter, which makes them more droughtproof and helps prevent cracking.

There are a few things to keep in mind when working with rocks. Remember that it is difficult to mow or keep weeds down directly around rocks. Leave an area of bare ground or low groundcover between rocks and mowed lawn. Either plant something between the rocks, or be prepared to pull out weeds or use a string trimmer whenever they show up. Rocks exposed to the sun should not be used as mulches near the south side of a home in places where summers are hot. They can act as a heat sink, heating during the day and releasing heat at night, contributing to the warmth of the house. Gravel or larger stones make an attractive mulch for the dry garden, but fallen leaves and other organic matter will eventually create soil pockets between the stones, and where there is soil, weeds will follow. Rake or clean your stone mulch at least once a season.

Soil, Fertilizer and Compost

Soil in the dry garden should be improved before you begin planting. Good drainage is especially important. If you are working with an existing weedy garden or a garden that does not thrive, consider salvaging whatever plants you can by digging them up with big rootballs and temporarily putting them in big pots in the shade or heeling them into a cleared area. Then remove all the weeds in the bed, and start again by working plenty of organic matter into at least the top 12 inches (30 cm) of soil.

One inch (2.5 cm) of water will penetrate clay soil 4 inches (10 cm), loam 6 to 8 inches (15-20 cm) and sandy soil 12 to 14 inches (30-35 cm). Sandy soil encourages deeper rooting and drains well but needs watering more frequently than loamy soil. Clay soil holds water longer, but drainage is poor, and once dry, clay is difficult to rework. Compost or another type of organic matter will improve all soil types and their ability to retain water without interfering with drainage. In the *Journal of Soil and Water Conservation*, Berman Hudson states that soils high in organic matter have a significantly higher available water capacity (the amount of water available to roots). The available water capacity of a silt loam containing 15 percent organic matter by volume is more than twice that of a silt loam containing 5 percent organic matter. "Other factors being equal," says Hudson, "soils containing more organic matter can retain more water from each rainfall and make more of it available to plants."

It's tempting to apply fertilizer, but plants that tolerate drought don't need much, if any, and fertilizer, especially nitrogen, can easily do more harm than good. The vegetable garden often benefits from spring fertilization, but otherwise, err on the side of moderation. Phosphates and potash may help, but plants grow lush, green and leggy when fed a high-nitrogen diet. Then, when dry weather comes, they quickly wilt. Organic matter is what a dry garden needs—the more, the better. And for most gardeners, organic matter means compost.

If you have a dry garden, you need a compost pile. Compost, a decomposed mixture of vegetable scraps and garden clippings wetted and layered with soil, is free and will help the soil absorb and retain water. It is also a gentle fertilizer. Compost can be piled in the open or within an enclosure. I have a three-sided homemade bin about 3 feet (1 m) high and wide. There are also all kinds of compost bins on the market. Small amounts of compost can even be made in plastic garbage bags tied, left in the summer sun and turned once a week. Alternatively, to make a simple rodentproof bin, cut off the bottom of a plastic garbage pail, drill holes around the bottom half, bury the pail so that all the holes are underground and use this receptacle for compostable food scraps, replacing the lid between additions. Add earthworms, if you like, to speed the process. Start a second pail so that there is always one to fill and one ready to use.

If you don't have much compost or livestock manure, green manuring is a method of adding the same quality of nutrients and humus. A crop such as ryegrass or buckwheat is grown just a few inches high, then turned into the soil. In a vegetable garden, the rotation of crops can include one bed being devoted to a green-manure crop each season. In a flower garden, green manuring must be done the season before the bed is planted.

Mulch

Mulches are blankets, usually of organic materials, laid between plants. Suitable mulch materials include grass clippings, bark chips, salt hay (stiff grass that grows in some coastal marshes), evergreen needles, seaweed and leaf mold (partially composted leaves from the previous fall). The leaves themselves can also be used directly: Run a lawnmower through piles of leaves to shred them, or put the leaves in a garbage can, then chop them with a string trimmer. Leaves make a better soil additive, however, if left to compost for a year. To compost them, add them in small amounts to a compost pile or pile them on their own within an enclosure made of wire or snow fencing. A sprinkling of high-nitrogen fertilizer or a layer of manure will speed composting. Grass clippings are most easily handled if they dry before use. Evergreen needles make an ideal mulch in dry areas with alkaline soil, but where soils are naturally acidic, they should be confined to acid-loving plants. A power chipper/shredder will turn all weeds, vines, leaves and branches into a good mulch.

There are two types of mulch: summer and winter. Both should be at least 2 inches (5 cm) deep. Each has different advantages.

Summer Mulch: Summer mulches of organic materials hold in moisture, limit weed growth and moderate temperatures. Recent research in North Carolina has shown that mulches reduce the maximum daily temperature at the soil surface by 4 to 6 Fahrenheit degrees (2-3 C°) and increase the minimum daily temperature by around 2 to 4 Fahrenheit degrees (1-2 C°). The temperature is not affected by the type of organic mulch; the North Carolina test used pine bark, hardwood bark, cedar chips and pine needles. There are additional advantages of a summer mulch. While bare soil can lose three-quarters of the rain that falls on it to runoff and evaporation, almost all that rainfall can be saved by summer mulches. In the vegetable garden, mulching greatly reduces the incidence of fungal-disease infection, especially on tomatoes and potatoes. Soil splashing onto foliage during rain or watering causes most fungal infections.

To apply the mulch, wait until around mid-

A year-round water-saving mulch can be maintained with occasional additions of dry organic matter.

snow can maintain a soil temperature of 32 degrees (0°C), whereas without snow, the soil would freeze to a depth of 4 feet (1.2 m). Anything you can do to concentrate snowdrifts on planted areas will help protect roots from low winter temperatures and provide more soil moisture in spring. Leave perennial stems in place in fall to help hold snow.

Year-Round Mulches: In some gardens, mulches remain more or less permanently around trees and shrubs and are simply augmented to whenever necessary. For instance, there are permeable landscape polypropylene fabrics that are meant to be used around perennials, shrubs and trees. The mulches are covered with gravel, wood chips or another covering that looks more attractive and prevents ultraviolet degradation of the mulch. The fabric, in turn, increases the durability of the organic mulch above it. But these mulches are not for everyone. They are expensive, and some growers have had problems with mice tunneling underneath. Not only that, but in some studies, these mulches have been found ineffective against perennial weeds. An organic mulch at least 4 inches (10 cm) deep has been shown by the Denver Water Department to be just as effective.

Mulch steadily composts into the soil, so if you want a permanent mulch, you must add to it in spring and fall. Because mulch keeps the soil cool in spring, early growth will be delayed.

Truly xeric plants such as cacti, succulents, artemisias and perennial salvias are better left without a mulch, which can keep too much moisture around the roots.

Additional Winter Protection

Dry winters can be hazardous to plants—especially evergreens, anything newly planted and anything only marginally hardy—which is one reason to apply a winter mulch. Evergreens that turn brown in winter may be losing moisture more quickly than their roots can take it up. Desiccation progresses from buds and needle tissues inward from the edges and tips. Pine and spruce needles turn yellow, then brown. Branch tips of junipers and cedars may die. Sometimes, severe or even complete defoliation follows and may lead to the death

June, or whenever the soil has warmed and the plants are tall enough to stand above the mulch. Organic mulch applied too early keeps the soil cool. The exception to this timing is a clear plastic mulch, which is meant to be placed on the vegetable garden early to help the soil warm up. If you have an unexpectedly wet summer, remove any mulch. It can hold too much moisture against plant roots and will attract slugs and snails.

Winter Mulch: Winter mulches also hold moisture in the soil, but their main function is to help protect roots during cold winters. They are most valuable on new plantings or on plants that are only marginally hardy for your area. They are best applied after the ground freezes. If you are mulching trees, make sure the mulch does not come into contact with the bark, or it can cause rotting of the bark and will attract pests and rodents. Remember that snow has been called the poor man's mulch. When the air temperature is minus 22 degrees F (–30°C), 6 feet (1.8 m) of

When young, these windbreak trees may suffer in winter, but as they mature, they begin to protect neighboring plants.

of the plant the following spring or summer.

As soon as the ground thaws in spring, damaged evergreens should be given a good watering. Deciduous trees and shrubs may lose branch tips, which appear brown and dried out and may not blossom or leaf out properly in spring. Do not prune away branches until you are sure they are dead. Then prune carefully to restore a balanced shape to the plant.

Young smooth-barked trees and shrubs, such as apple, elm, horse chestnut, linden, maple, poplar and willow, are susceptible to frost cracking—lengthwise splits on the south or west sides of trunks or branches. These form scars that can provide fungi an entrance. To prevent frost cracking, wrap the trunks of young trees and shrubs with plastic fruit-tree spirals, burlap or foil. Alternatively, trunks can be painted with white latex paint. Any type of tree wrap should be applied in late fall and removed in early spring to prevent its becoming a shelter for pests and fungi.

As well as mulching after the soil freezes, there are other ways to prevent cold and drought injury:

• Grow plants suited to your climatic zone.

• Make sure the soil is reasonably well drained.

• Avoid poor planting locations. Trees and shrubs near white or aluminum-sided buildings may be damaged by reflected heat. Only the toughest plants should go in places that are very windy or have poor soil drainage.

• Water trees and shrubs before the ground freezes, especially if the summer or fall has been dry. Plants near the house will probably be especially dry.

• In late summer or fall, do not fertilize, especially with nitrogen, and do not prune plants. Both practices encourage growth that is less winter-hardy. Wait until spring.

Containers

Containers can be attractive and useful in any garden, including a dry one. Roots confined within a small area, such as a container, are more dependent than ever upon the gardener for their water supply,

Keep container plants that need frequent watering, such as these marigolds and peppers, near a water source.

but containers afford the possibility of gardening in places like patios and porches and can be the best way to show off demanding plants that you'd have to coddle no matter where they grew, such as small azaleas or miniature roses.

Place containers, especially dark-colored ones, in partly shaded places. The black plastic pots that nursery trees and shrubs are sold in can heat to over 120 degrees F (48°C) in the summer sun, hot enough to bake the roots. Unless the plants in the pots are drought-tolerant, be prepared to water at least once a day. Containers set into the ground, to their rims, will stay cooler, cutting down on watering needs. They may even root through the drainage holes into the soil. If you have to leave the containers untended for more than a day, place them in a shallow basin of water in an area that is shady all day.

Any sort of container that is porous, from a basket to a wood-fiber or terra-cotta plant pot, should be lined with plastic to retain soil moisture, unless the container is partially buried. Drainage holes are usually not needed, except in deep shade.

Containers can also display drought-tolerant plants. Certainly stone or hypertufa troughs, which are made from a mixture of peat, vermiculite and Portland cement, are perfect for cacti and succulents, but any type of container will do. Drought-tolerant plants that are content with relatively little soil are good choices for containers such as pottery bowls, terra-cotta pots and even old leather boots, all of which are too shallow for more demanding plants. A few examples, which require very little watering but are decorative all season, include:

- any of the trailing types of sedum
- upright sedums such as 'Autumn Joy'
- any of the sempervivums, echeverias or jovibarbas
- artemisias such as 'Valerie Finnis'
- variegated Solomon's seal
- tall succulents such as yucca and agave
- cacti, whether houseplants or hardy types
- ribbon grass

Even if plants are hardy perennials, they may not survive the winter in a container. Take the plants out of the pots in fall, and plant them in the ground to ensure winter survival.

Heatproofing the Gardener

Heatstroke is a potentially deadly condition that can arise from working for hours in the hot sun, causing the body's core temperature to rise. There are many warning signals that cooling is needed. Early symptoms of heat stress are mild dizziness, fatigue, irritability, decreased concentration and impaired judgment. Heat rash, heat cramps and heat exhaustion can be followed, finally, by heatstroke. Heat cramps are caused by loss of body salt in sweat. If they occur, rest in a cool place and drink a lightly salted beverage. There are a few ways to avoid heat stress:

- Do your midsummer gardening in the morning or evening, especially on days that are hot and humid.
- If you do garden during the heat of the day, wear a hat and loose, woven clothing that admits air.
- Drink enough water to replace body fluid lost by sweating.
- Take periodic breaks in a shaded or air-conditioned place.

If you notice any of the above symptoms in somebody else, take that person immediately to a cool place. One symptom of heat stress is a resistance to treatment. Make the person rest for at least half an hour. If heatstroke occurs, take the person to a shaded place, wrap him or her in a wet sheet and arrange transportation in an air-conditioned vehicle to a hospital as quickly as possible.

TREES UNDER STRESS

Trees have different growth patterns and so show drought damage in different ways. Some, including spruce, hemlock, beech and certain ashes, maples and pines, are described as having predetermined growth. Their buds expand the year after they were produced. Therefore, if there was drought when the buds were forming, it will show up in stunted growth of new leaves the following year.

Species described as heterophyllous have winter buds that grow during the current season. These species, including birch, poplar, elm, apple, silver maple and some ashes, leaf out sparsely and show the effects of drought during the season when it occurs.

Others, including junipers, produce several flushes of growth each year and can stop or start growing as the weather changes, so they may look normal.

All evergreens can develop brown needles, which can simply be pruned back.

In many species, mild water stress stimulates flower production.

Browning of the needles of evergreen trees and shrubs during hot summer weather need not be serious, unless it carries on for two or three seasons. All evergreens show some browning by fall. Lost needles do not grow back, but the plant continues to grow from growing tips. To minimize losses, soak the ground around the stem in fall before the soil freezes.

Lawns, Grasses and Groundcovers

3

"AND WHEN THE WIND IS BLOWING, YOU GET THESE BEAUTIFUL
WAVE PATTERNS IN THE GRASS: THE SEA OF WIND."

—Robert Wrigley, from *In a Sea of Wind: Images of the Prairies*, 1991

North Americans love lawns. It is said that if all the lawns in the United States were joined together, somebody would have to water and mow an area the size of Indiana. All this lawn should make for acres of drought resistance; grasses are, after all, the plants that dominated the dry, windy prairies for eons. But lawns are very different things. We've selected and pampered some of them until they can no longer survive without special care. Bluegrasses and ryegrasses kept unnaturally juicy and bright green no matter how hot and dry the weather are among the greatest water wasters on the continent. At 18 gallons per square foot (7 L/0.01 m²) per year, a bluegrass lawn may use more water than a swimming pool. Lawn grasses need regular fertilizing too, and they're susceptible to myriad insects and diseases.

On the other hand, lawns can be self-sustaining without extra water—or at least with much less than the weekly 1 inch (2.5 cm) usually recommended. My own lawn, which has evolved over decades, is never watered (or fertilized, for that matter), and it easily survives weeks of hot, windy summer weather without rain. Many gardeners wouldn't be content with a lawn that blooms with dandelions in spring and hawkweed and daisies in summer, then turns brownish in late July, but it is easy to maintain and suits my family just fine. When it is green and newly mowed in spring, early summer and fall, it looks much like any other. If I were fussier, I'd dig out the broad-leaved weeds by hand.

Existing Lawns

If you already have a lawn but want to do less watering, the Turf Resource Center in Rolling Meadows, Illinois, offers the following tips:

• Reduce or stop fertilizing at least one month before you expect hot weather. Lush, recently fertilized grass is less able to withstand high summer temperatures.

• Gradually raise the height of your mower blade as the temperature increases. Longer grass shades the soil and encourages deeper roots.

• Mow often enough that you are never removing more than the top third of the grass at a time. Make sure your mower blade is sharp.

• If you do water, do it late at night or early

in the morning so that the water can soak deeply into the soil. Infrequent deep watering encourages deeper roots.

• Confine watering to areas that are seen the most or receive the most traffic.

• In fall, aerate, dethatch, if necessary, and apply a balanced fertilizer. If your soil is deficient in potassium, add this nutrient, as it improves rooting and therefore heat tolerance.

If you have fallen heir to a labor-intensive lawn, the most sensible course of action is to replace what you don't need with a different groundcover, either something not living, such as a patio, or any of the plants listed on pages 49 to 65. Simply lift the unwanted sod in chunks, and turn them upside down in a pile to compost into topsoil, which they will do in about a year. Difficult lawn can also be replaced with easier lawn. Seeds of white Dutch clover or fescue can be sprinkled on an existing lawn about a month before the first mowing in spring.

New Lawns

A lawn of mixed plant species is more able to put up with varying weather conditions. If you don't use herbicides, a mixed plant population will develop naturally, but if you want to get off on the right foot, there are also self-reliant mixtures on the market, especially if you are starting a lawn from seed rather than sod. One recommended mixture for prairie lawns that are not watered contains 35 percent 'Park' Kentucky bluegrass, 35 percent creeping red fescue and 30 percent 'Streambank' wheatgrass. There are also ecological mixtures on the market, such as Fleur de Lawn and Fragrant Herbal Lawn, both developed by Tom Cook of Oregon State University. Cook's lawns may include English daisies (*Bellis perennis*), yarrow (*Achillea millefolium*) and strawberry clover (*Trifolium fragiferum*). Dwarf perennial ryegrass keeps the lawn green through winter.

Many other ecological lawn mixtures contain a portion of clover (*Trifolium* species), not a grass at all but deep-rooted, drought-tolerant and green all summer. Because clover is a legume, it contributes nitrogen to the soil; it also tolerates medium-to-low mowing and some shade. In cold-winter areas, it will winter-kill if there is insufficient snow cover, but it can be reseeded easily. On the negative side, clover can stain clothing and shoes worse than grass does, and if it is not mowed, it will grow tall and lush, creating sprawling bunches that can crowd out lawn grasses during wet weather. Ecolawns must be hand-weeded; they cannot be treated with herbicides.

If you want your lawn to stay green in dry weather, soil depth is important. For a lush green lawn of bluegrass, for example, soil at least 4 inches (10 cm) deep is the minimum considered necessary to avoid the need for daily watering. My own lawn has less soil than that in several places, and although these areas brown first in summer, the grasses do survive. An application of about half an inch (1 cm) of compost sifted over the lawn every fall will gradually increase the soil level. Fall is also the best time to apply other fertilizers, should you wish to use them.

Sodding or Sowing

Large lawns, such as those around newly built homes, are usually grown from sod, which is delivered in rolls like carpet and laid directly on cleared ground. Different grass mixtures are available in sod form, just as they are in bags of seed, so if you have any say in the matter, ask for a drought-tolerant easy-care mixture. Even if the grass mixture is drought-tolerant, however, it must be watered regularly until the sod roots into the soil underneath it.

A lawn growing from seed requires regular watering too. James Willmott of Cornell Cooperative Extension in New York advises: "While low-maintenance grasses may require fewer inputs once they are established, they should not be neglected in the seedling stage." The soil should be enriched with compost, rotted manure or fertilizer, and a small amount of extra nitrogen should be applied six weeks after germination. This was determined in experiments at the extension department, where eight low-maintenance grass mixtures were compared.

Lawn seed is best sown during the last two weeks of August. Temperatures then are still warm enough for fast germination, and fall usually brings

To help maintain good soil quality, grass clippings can be left in place rather than raked after the lawn is mowed.

the cool, rainy weather that gets the grass off to a good start before a winter's rest and the cool, moist conditions which allow rapid growth in spring.

Thoroughly weed, smooth and rake the ground, apply seeds according to package directions, then roll or press the area under boards. Water thoroughly and frequently to maintain the surface moisture. Keep traffic off the lawn until the grass is well established, usually about two months after sowing. Don't mulch the area if you use an ecolawn mixture, because some of these seeds need light to germinate.

If you are starting a lawn from seed, look for fescues and perennial ryegrasses that include endophytes—fungi that make grass not only more drought-tolerant but also more resistant to sod webworms, chinch bugs, armyworms, billbugs, nematodes and perhaps Japanese beetle grubs. These cultivars, recent arrivals on the market, are a boon to organic growers. Storing the seed at high temperatures and humidity can destroy the endophytes, so buy fresh seed, and sow as soon as possible.

Mowing

Lawn grasses develop deeper, more drought-resistant roots if they are kept at a height of about 2½ inches (6.3 cm). Grass clippings can be raked or gathered for use as mulch in other areas of the garden, or they can be left in place if you have a mulching mower or the clippings are small. Grass clippings do not contribute to thatch (a layer of stems and roots that decomposes slowly) but instead help maintain soil fertility and quality. According to Dr. Martin Petrovic, a turf-grass expert at Cornell University, leaving grass clippings in place can reduce nitrogen-fertilizer requirements by as much as 30 percent below the applications for lawns from which clippings are removed.

Pest Problems

The worst lawn pest in many northern areas is the fat white grub of the European chafer, which feeds on roots, creating brown spots in the lawn. Also, raccoons and skunks may dig holes looking for the grubs. Their digging begins in early spring, even

Never watered, weeded or fertilized, this lawn easily survives summer droughts because it is a mixture of different plants.

before the grubs are actually feeding. According to the Guelph Turfgrass Institute in Ontario, spring attempts at grub control with pesticides are rarely successful and are generally not recommended. The institute advises helping the turf recover by seeding damaged areas and applying a little fertilizer where the grass is thin. The best time to treat for grubs is in the late summer or early fall, when they are at a more vulnerable stage of growth. If you are seeding a new lawn, use seed treated with endophytes. Another benign cure is BioSafe, a treatment of beneficial nematodes that must be applied on warm, moist soil according to package directions. Also useful is a solution of insecticidal soap or pure dish soap mixed at a rate of 1 teaspoon (5 mL) to 1 quart (1 L) water, then poured over the lawn.

Small rodents can also be pests. Moles make snaking ridges under turf, leaving mounds of soil at tunnel exits. Vole damage looks like runways that have been eaten down to ground level. Fill runways with compost, and reseed if necessary.

Fertilizing

In places where summers are dry, little or no fertilizer is recommended in spring. Certain grasses, especially buffalo grass and wheatgrass, should not be fertilized at all. If overfertilized, some grasses become lush and more susceptible to damage by drought, diseases and pests. In experiments conducted by the Rodale Institute (publishers of *Organic Gardening* magazine) and Garden Way Incorporated, lawn clippings left on the lawn provided the equivalent per acre (0.4 ha) of about 235 pounds (106 kg) of nitrogen, 77 pounds (35 kg) of phosphate and 210 pounds (95 kg) of potassium. Weed populations gradually diminished, and lawns "greened up" quickly in spring. No additional fertilizers were applied.

Weeds

Lawn grasses compete poorly with most weeds. Weeds will quickly colonize empty spots, whether the spots are the result of pest damage, weather damage or grasses at the seedling stage. In very hot, dry weather, cool-season turf grasses go dormant while weeds flourish. Crabgrass, for instance, can grow almost half an inch (1 cm) a day during a drought severe enough to cause Kentucky bluegrass to go dormant. Soon, weedy grasses predominate.

A thick, healthy lawn that includes not only grasses but a mixture of different groundcovers to fill in the empty spaces is therefore the best defense if you are opposed to herbicide use, as I am, and don't want to spend your life on your knees. Perennial ryegrass sprouts quickly and is thus a good choice to fill in empty spots in a lawn. When weeds do appear, hand-digging is the most environmentally friendly remedy. The definition of a weed, of course, is in the eye of the beholder.

Hardscape Groundcovers

The ultimate solution to a groundcover problem may be no plants at all. A stone, concrete or brick patio, for instance, can be beautiful and requires no mowing, no fertilizing, no watering. Maintenance? If the patio is made properly, weeding, even between patio stones, should be minimal. Other than that, all you may need to do is sweep off the fallen leaves once in a while.

Installing a patio can be expensive or not, depending largely on whether you do the work yourself and whether the materials are freely available or must be purchased. Slabs of stone are often piled at the edges of farm fields or along highway excavations, or you can buy concrete pavers relatively inexpensively. Purchased patio stones may be cheap or very pricey, depending on what you want and how scarce the supply is. An easy and effective patio or path that needs no instruction manual can be made simply by laying stones that are as flat as possible (so as not to trip anyone), placing them just far enough apart to allow you to set small plants in the crevices. Before you begin, remove all sod and weeds, and level the area. If you spread a shallow bed of builder's sand next, setting the stones will be easier. If they are not of about equal thickness, you will have to lay some more deeply than others to even the surface. When you're done, gently water the stones to settle them in, then pack soil between them.

The best plants to go in the cracks include any of the creeping sedums, sempervivums and hardy thymes, such as *Thymus serpyllum*, *T. herba-barona* and *T. pseudolanuginosus*. Small dianthus, such as creeping dianthus or cottage pink (*Dianthus plumarius*), and the thrifts *Armeria maritima* and *A. juniperifolia* are also good. If such a patio or path is edged by lawn, expect the lawn grasses to need occasional cutting back to prevent them from invading the cracks between the stones.

Lawn Grasses

The following species are the types you are most likely to encounter when you buy a grass mixture for a frost-hardy lawn, either as seed or as sod.

Agropyron cristatum
Crested wheatgrass

Impressed by the ability of this native grass to survive as long as 88 weeks without rain, scientists in both the United States and Canada have developed varieties that stay green in summer's heat with only about one-third the water requirements of other lawn grasses. Crested wheatgrass, which is related to the weedy quack grass, grows slowly; therefore, it requires relatively little mowing and fertilizing. But like quack grass, it spreads by rhizomes and can invade adjoining flowerbeds. It is pest-resistant and should not be fertilized.

Buchloe dactyloides
Buffalo grass

Since 1982, the University of Nebraska has been the center for the study of buffalo grass, a North American native that is a promising candidate for low-maintenance prairie and midwestern lawns. Buffalo grass requires only one-quarter the water that the standard cool-season grasses do, which translates to a watering about once a month in dry weather. In the climatic areas where it grows best, it requires little or no mowing; it slowly reaches a height of 4 to 8 inches (10-20 cm). It spreads rapidly by profusely branching stolons but is not competitive. It should not be fertilized or watered, because too much of either weakens it and gives weeds an advantage. It can be grown

If not watered regularly, grasses that are green in spring may turn brown temporarily in summer.

from seed or, where available, plugs, sprigs or sod. Unlike other lawn grasses, buffalo grass has male and female flowers on separate plants. The female flowers are so small, they are invisible from a distance, while the male flowers are showier. Buffalo grass does not do well in shade but thrives in places that are sunny and hot in summer.

Most buffalo grass cultivars are gray-green, but 'Mobuff,' from the University of Missouri, stays bright green. Unfortunately, while there are types suited to the prairies and to the South, none, at the time of writing, are suited to the wetter parts of Canada and the northern United States.

Additional grasses for dry lawns: *Phleum pratense* (timothy) is a common pasture grass included in some mixtures. It offers great winter hardiness. *Puccinellia distans* (fults, spreading meadow grass) is used for reclaiming salty prairie soil. It stays low and can be maintained without mowing. Under assessment are *Elymus angustus* (Altai wild rye) and *Bromus inermis* (smooth bromegrass),

both able to survive drought. Cultivars of Bermuda grass and centipede grass have high drought resistance too, but they are meant for southerly climates. Zoysia grass, also happiest in a temperature range of 80 to 95 degrees F (27-35°C) year-round, is difficult to establish but then difficult to eradicate. It stays green in summer, even during dry weather, but turns the color of straw in cool weather.

Festuca species
Fescue

Deep-rooted grasses that tolerate cold winters, dry summers, full sun or partial shade and infertile soils, fescues have long been regarded as cattle fodder. Recently, so-called fine fescues (at least four types of fescue that have fine, tough, bristly leaves) have undergone considerable improvement and are now recommended for low-maintenance turf. The four types are Chewings, tall, hard and creeping red fescue. The last one is a sod-former, as is a new variety of tall, whereas the others grow in bunches. All have good drought tolerance but will not survive in wet, poorly drained soil. Because tall fescue is the least cold-hardy and is likely to suffer from snow mold, it is not recommended for places with cold or variable winters.

Fescues are slow-growing and therefore demand little fertilizer. They can be kept at 1½ inches (3.8 cm) or less. On the other hand, if you want a meadow, fescues can be left unmowed or cut just once. In experiments at the Cornell extension department in Rochester, New York, mixtures containing fine fescues exclusively required mowing only every nine days, whereas mixtures that also contained perennial ryegrass and Kentucky bluegrass needed mowing twice a week.

In 1996, two of the most highly recommended types were 'SR 3000' hard fescue and 'SR 5000' Chewings fescue. Both contain high levels of endophytic fungi, which give the grasses inbred resistance to several pests. At the University of Nevada at Reno, the lowest water-use cultivars were 'Shademaster' creeping fescue, 'FRT-30149' fine fescue and 'Aurora' hard fescue.

If not watered in summer, fescues will become dormant and turn brown—the chief reason they

Provided they are not too plentiful, grass clippings and fallen leaves can be left on the lawn to contribute to soil fertility.

are often blended with other grasses—but they green up again as the weather cools in fall. Because most fescues lack underground runners, they are less aggressive than bluegrass or ryegrass, so they are more easily kept out of adjoining flowerbeds. This also means, however, that fescues can be crowded out by bluegrass, are less tolerant to foot traffic and are slower to recover when damaged, so do not use fescues in heavily trafficked areas.

Lolium perenne
Perennial ryegrass

Seeds of perennial ryegrass are often included in mixtures that are predominantly Kentucky bluegrass and fine fescues. Perennial ryegrass sprouts quickly and is much deeper-rooted than bluegrass, but it grows even faster and therefore likes steady watering and frequent mowing. Perennial rye is lighter green and forms bunches rather than sod, so it will gradually give way to Kentucky bluegrass as the latter gains strength. Some perennial ryes are now bred with endophytes for pest resistance.

Perennial rye grows best in sun and is useful for seeding into existing patchy lawns.

Poa pratensis
Kentucky bluegrass

Given fertilizer and water, Kentucky bluegrass is cold-hardy and remains dark green and luxuriantly soft if summers are not too hot. On the negative side, it grows fast and requires frequent mowing; it invades neighboring flowerbeds, is susceptible to diseases and bugs and turns brown if allowed to dry out in summer, although it will probably survive and green up again in fall. It is quick to dry out because it is shallow-rooted, with almost all its roots in the top 5 inches (13 cm) of soil. Its dense growth means that it may form a thick layer of wiry roots and stems (called thatch) when it is overfertilized. Kentucky bluegrass looks best when kept only 1½ to 2 inches (3.8-5 cm) tall and when grown on deep, fertile, well-drained soil with a pH close to neutral.

There are over 20 cultivars, some more

drought-tolerant than others. 'Challenger' has come out best in drought-tolerance trials in Colorado and Nevada.

Poa compressa (Canada bluegrass, wire grass) is a tough, invasive "poor sister of Kentucky Blue," says a Canadian seed company. It will grow where other grasses fail—in salty, poorly drained or dry ground. It is difficult to get rid of and difficult to control, so it is best used, if at all, on road banks or in other places where its aggressive creeping rhizomes will not cause problems.

Ornamental Grasses

Ornamental grasses are not lawn grasses. Some are not even groundcovers, because they spread slowly. They're simply a unique group of flowering plants. Whether groundcover or not, all of the hardy, drought-tolerant perennial types are listed in this chapter, the annuals in Chapter 6. The term ornamental grasses includes true grasses as well as grasslike plants with slender, upright foliage. The true grasses are generally plants for sun and dry ground, while other grasslike plants will put up with shade and even wet ground and are thus not within the scope of this book.

A few ornamental grasses do act as groundcovers, and some are invasive—blue lyme grass (*Elymus arenarius*) and ribbon grass (*Phalaris arundinacea*), to name two. Other grasses that have become invasive in certain parts of North America include *Arundo donax, Cortaderia jubata, Festuca arundinacea* and *Miscanthus sinensis.*

Tall grasses must be positioned carefully so that their vertical, airy form becomes a focus but doesn't block the view of other plants. The rule of thumb is that grasses should be planted as far apart as their eventual height. This helps prevent overcrowding, a frequent problem. They can be grown on the windward side of the garden to collect snow and act as wind protection in winter, when, although dry and brown, they are among the most attractive plants in the landscape. Smaller grasses can be used as spacers between other perennials. All grasses flower, though the flowers range from insignificant to graceful and feathery.

Most grasses need plenty of sun and well-drained soil. Given too much shade or dampness, they bloom less and may fall over, a habit called lodging. Like other perennials, they should be watered well during their first year, but after that, those in this chapter are drought-tolerant. Many will not survive the winter in damp soil. If you mulch grasses, do not tuck the mulch up against the plants. Ornamental grasses do not need fertilizing—it will weaken them and reduce their winter hardiness.

Do not cut back the tops until late winter or early spring, before new growth begins. Then, cut the dead stems back to 4 to 6 inches (10-15 cm) above the ground. If you have large stands of grasses, use a hedge trimmer. Division is best done in spring as soon as growth begins.

Fully 85 perennial grasses grew successfully in a six-year study of 165 ornamental varieties at the Minnesota Landscape Arboretum, zone 4, where winter temperatures were as low as minus 30 degrees F (–34°C). The following list also includes ornamental grasses found to have excellent drought tolerance in the fields of Limerock Ornamental Grasses, Inc., Port Matilda, Pennsylvania. All are hardy to zone 4 or colder areas, unless noted.

Andropogon gerardii (big bluestem) is a North American clump-forming prairie native that grows about 4 to 7 feet (1.2-2 m) tall.

Andropogon virginicus (broom sedge) forms a bunch as tall as 3 feet (1 m). It is light green in summer and turns a tan color in fall.

Calamagrostis x *acutiflora* 'Karl Foerster' (Karl Foerster feather reed grass). The Plant Selection Committee of the Ohio Nursery and Landscape Association chose this as one of its most highly recommended plants for 1994. It grows 3 to 4 feet (1-1.2 m) tall in dry soil and about 6 feet (1.8 m) in wet ground. Its purplish June flowers turn into buff-colored seedheads by August. It does best in full sun and should be pruned back in early spring. It is strongly vertical, even when brown in winter.

Calamagrostis arundinacea 'Overdam' (Overdam feather reed grass), from Denmark, is similar to 'Karl Foerster' but even more attractive, with variegated green-and-white leaves. It is a little less hardy than 'Karl Foerster,' although it survives in my zone-4 garden.

Just a foot (30 cm) or so tall and perfect for the front of a border, the ornamental fescues contribute several shades of blue.

Carex morrowii 'Variegata' (variegated Japanese sedge) is evergreen to zone 5. It has a thin white leaf margin and eventually reaches 1 foot (30 cm) in height. It is excellent for pots and borders.

Carex nigra (black sedge) forms tufts 6 to 8 inches (15-20 cm) tall. The grass is blue-green, the seedheads black. It can be used as a groundcover.

Deschampsia caespitosa (tufted hair grass) grows 2 feet (60 cm) tall and has delicate beige panicles that are attractive all season. The cultivar 'Bronzeschleier' grows 3 feet (1 m) tall.

Elymus arenarius (blue lyme grass), which grows 2 feet (60 cm) tall, has invasive rhizomes and must be grown in a container if it is among other garden plants. Otherwise, it can be used to stabilize sandy slopes.

Erianthus ravennae (ravenna grass) can grow as tall as 14 feet (4.3 m), making it the pampas-grass substitute for gardens in zone 5. The seedheads resemble feather dusters.

Festuca species (fescue). Festuca names are somewhat confused (see also the lawn types on pages 44 and 45), because their color is variable. There are many ornamentals on the market with lovely blue, green or silver foliage, hardy to zone 4 or 5. One of the most drought-tolerant at Limerock Ornamental Grasses in Pennsylvania is 'Elijah Blue.' *F. ovina glauca* 'Skinner's Blue' is a hardy form from Saskatchewan. One of the best at the Minnesota Landscape Arboretum is *F. amethystina* 'Bronzeglanz' (bronze luster fescue), 1 foot (30 cm) tall, with fine, blue-green foliage. *F. cinerea* 'Silberreiher' (silver egret fescue) grows just 6 inches (15 cm) tall.

Helictotrichon sempervirens (blue oatgrass) grows to 2 feet (60 cm) and has distinctive blue-gray foliage.

Miscanthus floridulus (giant miscanthus) grows 7 to 8 feet (2-2.4 m) tall and has dark green blades as wide as 2 inches (5 cm). The lower leaves die early, exposing the stem.

Miscanthus sinensis (eulalia grass) can grow taller than 7 feet (2 m) when conditions are suitable. It has long been a popular ornamental in the

Panicum virgatum *'Heavy Metal,'* at left, is a native North American prairie grass that tolerates both wet and dry ground.

Orient. There are dozens of cultivars in various heights and colors. All form a dense clump and are not invasive by rhizome, although in gardens in zone 6 and warmer, many spread by seed. They are not the most drought-tolerant grasses and do not grow as tall in dry conditions. However, certain cultivars will put up with dry places to zone 4. These include 'Condensatus,' green with a white midrib; 'Gracillimus' (maiden grass), with a white midrib; 'Graziella,' with a silver midrib; 'Malepartus,' a weeping form 5 to 6 feet (1.5-1.8 m) tall; and 'Purpurascens,' with burgundy foliage in fall.

Drought-tolerant cultivars hardy to zone 5 include 'Adagio,' 'Arabesque,' 'Dixieland,' 'Grosse Fontaine,' 'Kleine Fontaine,' 'November Sunset,' 'Positano,' 'Rotsilber,' 'Sarabande,' 'Silberpfeil,' 'Silberspinne,' 'Sirene,' 'Strictus,' 'Undine,' 'Variegatus,' 'Yaku Jima' and 'Zebrinus.'

Panicum virgatum 'Heavy Metal' has vertical, bluish foliage about 4 feet (1.2 m) tall topped with airy seedheads in late summer. It spreads by underground rhizome, especially in moist soil, so it should be given a spot away from other perennials. 'Rehbraun' (red switchgrass), also strongly upright, has seedheads and foliage that turn red in fall.

Pennisetum alopecuroides (fountain grass) forms a wide fountain shape as tall as 3 feet (1 m). There are several cultivars. Zone 5.

Phalaris arundinacea (ribbon grass) is an old-fashioned favorite that is quite invasive but useful for places where little else will grow. With its striped green-and-white foliage, about 2 feet (60 cm) tall, it makes an attractive groundcover in sun or shade. The cultivars 'Feesey's Form,' with pink shading, and 'Luteo-Picta,' with yellow variegation, are less invasive.

Schizachyrium scoparium (little bluestem) is a native grass with slender, bluish or greenish blades 2 feet (60 cm) tall.

Sesleria autumnalis (autumn moor grass) has yellow-green foliage 8 to 10 inches (20-25 cm) tall. Zone 5.

Sorghastrum avenaceum (Indian grass) can reach 6 feet (1.8 m). *S. nutans* 'Sioux Blue'

(Sioux blue Indian grass) has blue foliage. Zone 5.

Spodiopogon sibiricus (silver spike grass), which resembles bamboo, grows 3 feet (1 m) tall in sun, taller with some shade. It has dark green foliage.

Themeda triandra japonica (Japanese themeda) has unusual fuzzy stems and grows 3 to 5 feet (1-1.5 m) tall, with flower heads well above the foliage.

Groundcovers

Groundcovers are plants that spread outward, usually forming a sufficiently dense cover to prevent annual weeds from sprouting. While groundcovers could be any height, the plants in this chapter are mostly under 1 foot (30 cm) tall. All can be considered substitutes for lawn in places where there is little or no foot traffic, but only lawn grasses can take frequent trampling. If there is to be foot traffic through an area planted with other groundcovers, install a path. An even more important consideration is hardiness for your climate.

Acaena species
New Zealand bur

These fast-spreading carpeters tolerate poor, dry soil and can overwhelm small plants, but they are good under shrubs or in the spaces between paving stones. All have unusual spherical, spiked, burlike flowerheads. The most available and possibly the hardiest species, to zone 3, is *A. microphylla*, which has bronzy green foliage that forms a 4-inch (10 cm) mat decorated with orange-red bur flowers in summer. The cultivar 'Blue Haze' is similar, with bluish foliage and brown burs, while 'Copper Carpet' ('Kuperferteppich') has bronzed foliage and greenish red burs. *A. caesiiglauca* has silky, silver-blue foliage and reddish burs.

Achillea tomentosa
Woolly yarrow

This creeping spreader will live in very dry, even sandy, ground but resents prolonged wetness. It grows about 8 inches (20 cm) tall

COVERING GROUND

Groundcovers are meant to cover the ground densely, providing a weed-free mat. But in their first year or two— or three or four, for some of the slow-growing types—there will be gaps that invite weeds to take root. During this inevitable period of waiting, there are several things you should do:

• Make sure the ground is absolutely weed-free before you plant.

• If you intend to cover a large area in a hurry, buy enough plants at the outset so that they will be touching by the end of the second season of growth.

• Water the plants when necessary to keep them growing strongly.

• Give them enough space so that they can spread without touching their neighbors the first year. The next year, they may be too crowded; remove some.

• Pull out weeds as soon as you see them. The smaller and airier ground-covers never become impenetrable, especially to rhizomatous weeds such as quack grass.

• Herbaceous groundcovers should be divided as soon as they are big enough. Two small plants will cover an area faster than one large plant. With any groundcovers, including woody perennials, you may speed up the multiplication process by starting plants with cuttings taken from new growth. See page 28.

Thymes, sedums and daylilies form a checkerboard pattern in a northern garden.

Artemisia *'Silver Brocade' and* Sedum spurium *make excellent color and texture companions in sun.*

and has grayish woolly leaves and 2-inch (5 cm) bright yellow flowers that last for weeks. There are several cultivars. In a trial of achilleas at the Chicago Botanic Garden, 'Maynard's Gold' was considered a better choice than 'Aurea' because of a longer bloom time. Remove the flower stalks when the flowers fade.

Aegopodium podagraria
Goutweed, bishop's weed

There is a plain green form of this easy groundcover, but the variegated form, 'Variegatum,' is far better known. It is a handsome 1-foot-high (30 cm) plant, whose green-and-white-patterned leaves brighten areas that offer anything from full sun to deep shade. In the part of Ontario where I live, it often grows along the edge of house foundations and is only discouraged in its spreading tendencies by a wall behind it and a mowed lawn in front. Another place where goutweed excels is under maples and other deciduous trees

that cast heavy shade. Umbels of flowers that appear on long seed stalks in midsummer can be cut back; it is the leaves that look best. In good soil, goutweed can be a ruthless spreader that chokes out smaller plants and is almost impossible to remove. Keep it out of mixed perennial beds, and confine it to containers or places where few other plants will grow.

Ajuga reptans
Bugle

This woodland native is capable of surviving fairly dry conditions and a considerable amount of neglect. Spreading by aboveground runners and by seed, it forms a solid cover of somewhat metallic-looking leaves. Most varieties have showy blue flowers in spring, although 'Treneague' does not flower. Bugle will be better able to tolerate drought if you add plenty of organic matter to the soil where it will grow. When content, it can be somewhat invasive, even moving into surrounding lawns.

Alchemilla mollis
Lady's mantle

Lady's mantle is best known for its leaves, which are roundish and uniquely pleated and can hold drops of water upright like pearls. Sprays of greenish yellow flowers in early summer are prized by flower arrangers. Lady's mantle loves deep, rich soil but will survive, though stay smaller, in poor, dry soil if given some shade and watered occasionally. It spreads modestly, forming rounded clumps 1 foot (30 cm) tall, so it can be considered a suitable groundcover for small areas on the shady side of large rocks or under shrubs.

Antennaria species
Pussytoes

These native plants of the North American prairies have small, fuzzy leaves that form a solid ground-hugging carpet which can be less than 1 inch (2.5 cm) high. They spread slowly but surely, filling in the spaces between paving stones or between the rocks in a rock garden. I've seen *A. dioica* in a mowed Saskatchewan lawn forming gradually expanding circles of gray leaves. As is the case with many ground-huggers, flowering is a surprise. Pussytoes erupts into what, considering its diminutive size, are gigantic seed stalks 4 to 6 inches (10-15 cm) tall. They have white daisy flowers and, soon afterward, woolly seedheads. The variety *A. dioica rosea*, which has silvery foliage and pink spring flowers, is less tough and spreading than some of the wildlings. Pussytoes must have well-drained ground; my own died out after a soggy spring.

Set rooted pieces 6 inches (15 cm) apart; the plants will fill in the spaces between them within a season. Pussytoes should be planted in an absolutely weed-free area, unless you are not bothered by seeing grass grow through it.

Arctostaphylos uva-ursi
Bearberry

This handsome broad-leaved evergreen, whose leaves are about half an inch (1 cm) wide, produces a summer crop of beautiful red berries that last through fall. It needs organically rich, well-drained soil and some sun. It grows slowly at first but may eventually cover a circle 5 feet (1.5 m) wide and 1 foot (30 cm) deep.

Artemisia species
Mugwort, sagebrush

Known for their attractive, fragrant grayish leaves and their tolerance for heat, drought, sand and gravel, artemisias are a rugged group perhaps best represented by a few species native to the prairies and rangelands—pasture sage (*A. frigida*), prairie sage (*A. ludoviciana*) and big sagebrush (*A. tridentata*). These plants perfume the air of western cattle country on breezy summer days. Sagebrush is one group among hundreds of artemisias, only a handful of which have been tamed for the garden. But even the elegantly named cultivars are tougher than they look, provided the ground is well drained. No matter how hot and dry the weather, artemisias look respectable. It is wetness and rich soil that can cause discoloration from mildew.

Some of the best winter-hardy artemisia groundcovers for dry soil are:

A. ludoviciana, especially 'Silver King,' about 2 feet (60 cm) tall, and 'Silver Queen,' which is a little smaller. They are shrubby-looking plants that make excellent spacers between greener things. While they are short-lived, they are easy to multiply by division or from cuttings. 'Silver King' is often grown for its flowerheads, which are used in dried wreaths.

A. pontica forms an attractive cloudy mound, 2 feet (60 cm) tall, of pale bluish green, very finely divided foliage. It is hard to find, perhaps because of its invasiveness, but its spreading habit is an advantage on poor ground where little else will grow, even under trees or next to buildings, and it is easily rooted out if it goes too far. It looks best if the flowering stems are cut back, and it can be clipped once or twice during the season to form a low hedge.

A. schmidtiana, especially 'Silver Mound,' also known as 'Angel's Hair,' forms a neat rounded clump of finely divided bluish foliage about 1 foot (30 cm) tall. Divide plants or take cuttings every three years or so; otherwise, they eventually die out in the center.

A. stelleriana has bright white foliage. One of many plants known as dusty miller, it is good at the front of a border or as a groundcover in small areas. 'Silver Brocade,' a beauty, grows about 6 inches (15 cm) tall and has deeply indented almost pure white leaves. 'Broughton Silver' is similar but taller.

All artemisias are easy to multiply by cuttings (see page 28). Two artemisias—French tarragon and wormwood—are listed with the herbs on page 130.

Aurinia saxatilis 'Compacta'
Basket of gold, gold dust

Formerly called *Alyssum saxatile* and still sometimes known as gold dust alyssum, this hardy perennial bears only a slight resemblance to its cousin sweet alyssum. It has brilliant yellow flowers in late spring or early summer, an expression of its love for full sun, and is one of the favorites at the xeric garden of the Denver Botanic Gardens, though other gardeners may find it finicky. Where it is happy, it spreads into a mound of gray-green leaves on slender 1-foot-long (30 cm) stems that drape nicely over rocks or a wall. However, if the soil is not perfectly well drained, preferably sloped, the roots may not survive winter, although seedlings may sprout the following May. By late summer, it will form a good groundcover. There are several cultivars.

Bergenia crassifolia
Heartleaf bergenia, elephant's-ear

Bergenia is usually considered a plant for damp ground, and although it is not the best choice for a hot, dry, windy spot, it will survive almost anywhere if given a bit of shade and shelter. Bergenia's large leathery leaves resemble dwarf rhubarb and grow into a clump about 18 inches (45 cm) tall. Its pink flowers appear in spring. It looks best growing near large rocks, taller plants or anything else that balances its heavy appearance. If the snow cover is good or the winter is not too harsh, this plant is evergreen, but otherwise, the leaves turn brown in fall and new ones emerge in spring, the best season for dividing it. It is hardy to zone 3.

Calluna vulgaris
Scotch heather

Think of the Scottish Highlands when situating this plant. Cool, misty mornings and perfectly drained acidic soil on a slope or in a raised bed in sun suit it perfectly. Where it is happy, heather thrives, and it looks its best when various flower colors are grown close together. If it is not content, it soon perishes. The summer flowers bloom in shades of white, pink and lavender on the tips of shrubby plants about 1 foot (30 cm) high. It is hardy to zone 5 and has become naturalized in parts of the United States.

Campanula species
Bellflower, rampion

Campanula means bell, and all the members of this genus have lovely bell-shaped flowers, characteristically blue or purple, though there are also whites and pinks. Groundcover types range from tall to small and from the delicate to the aggressively weedy.

C. carpatica (Carpathian bellflower) forms a 6-inch-tall (15 cm) mat of delicate leaves topped by 1-inch (2.5 cm) blue flowers in midsummer. Give it

well-drained soil in sun or, if your garden is hot and exposed, semishade. It is easy to divide in spring.

C. glomerata (clustered bellflower) is somewhat coarser than Carpathian bellflower but is a better groundcover, spreading a little faster without being invasive. Blue flowers top 18-inch (45 cm) stems in midsummer.

If you live in an old farmhouse, you may have inherited a patch of *C. rapunculoides*, called creeping or rover bellflower, a plant that will survive decades of neglect and no watering at all and will rebound and spread as soon as the perennial beds are weeded by an unsuspecting newcomer. It grows about 2 feet (60 cm) tall and is topped in summer by spires of smallish purple bells. *C. rapunculoides* is almost impossible to get rid of—roots break when you are digging, and the smallest bits will resprout. It spreads by underground rhizome and by seed. If you have fallen heir to *C. rapunculoides*, be ruthless to keep it within bounds. Mowed lawn will contain it, as will pavement. This is not a plant to share with a friend.

Cerastium tomentosum
Snow-in-summer

Best in sun, this invasive plant is not suitable for growing among small, delicate things, but given a place where little else will grow and where it can be contained by paving or lawn, it is beautiful all year and a lovely contrast to plants that have green or maroon foliage. It is one of the best for tumbling down rock walls. Midwinter thaws reveal sterling-silver foliage as eye-catching as it is in spring. Snow-in-summer forms a mat about 6 inches (15 cm) high topped by pure white flowers in June. After blooming, it should be clipped back. The seedpods are unattractive and contribute to the spread of the plant. It can be divided in spring or fall.

Convallaria majalis
Lily of the valley

Although its waxy little bells look delicate and smell ethereal, lily of the valley can be a pest in rich, moist soil. Too low to crowd out weeds, it can itself invade plantings around it. This attractive grasslike plant is tolerant of dry shade, however,

Unsuitable for a perennial garden because of its aggressiveness, snow-in-summer shines all year in tough climates.

and its small, fragrant spring bells are like nothing else, so it is worth growing in containers or in patches where it can be contained by a lawn or patio.

Coronilla varia
Crown vetch

You may see this legume along highway embankments, where it has been planted to hold the soil in place with its spreading underground runners. The lilac-pink summer flowers are pretty, and because it is a legume, crown vetch improves the soil by enriching it with nitrogen. The arching branches form a tangled mat about 2 feet (60 cm) high that tumbles over other plants and down hills, no matter how dry and sunny. Valuable in its place and useful as a green manure if it is plowed under before flowering, crown vetch can be too much of a good thing where less aggressive plants grow. Confine it to dry hillsides where you would otherwise have grown grass—or nothing at all. Improved cultivars include 'Penngift' and 'Emerald.' Crown vetch is not reliably hardy to zone 3.

Cotoneaster species
Cotoneaster

Cotoneasters are shrubs, plants with woody stems. Some types grow upright (see page 142), and others are reclining, but both are valued for their spring flowers, summer berries and tiny, waxy green leaves that turn red in fall. Where winters are warmish, cotoneaster is evergreen. It does best in alkaline soil in full sun. Stems can be layered—pinned down and buried—to root, then cut from the mother plant.

C. adpressus (creeping rockspray) grows about 2 feet (60 cm) tall, with short, rigid branches that may root where they touch the ground. It is hardy to zone 5. For *C. adpressus praecox*, see *C. nanshan* below.

C. dammeri (bearberry cotoneaster) is almost completely flat. Best known is the variety 'Skogholm' (Skogholm cotoneaster), which grows a little taller than the species. It forms a 1-foot-tall (30 cm) mound of small green leaves and white flowers, followed by bright red fruits. The cultivar 'Coral Beauty' has orange berries. 'Eichholz' can spread

Like most other dianthus, maiden pinks prefer to be situated in a sunny spot in well-drained alkaline soil.

wider than 10 feet (3 m). All are hardy to minus 20 degrees F (–29°C). They do best with a good snow cover. After a difficult winter, *C. dammeri* may revive from the base upward.

C. horizontalis (fishbone or rockspray cotoneaster) is a popular foundation plant, useful as a spacer between taller shrubs. It is usually deciduous but sometimes retains its leaves. The flowers are pink. It grows 2 to 3 feet (60-90 cm) high and as wide as 8 feet (2.4 m). The cultivar 'Variegatus' is prized for green leaves edged with cream that turn reddish in fall. Both types are hardy to zone 5.

C. nanshan was, until recently, labeled *C. adpressus praecox*. It is hardier (to zone 4) and more vigorous than *C. adpressus*, with especially large, dark orange fruit and bright red fall color. In the zone-4 garden of the University of Maine at Orono, this shrub suffered a small amount of winter damage. It grows 18 inches (45 cm) high and can spread 4 feet (1.2 m) wide.

Dianthus species
Pink, carnation

Pinks are among the best flowers for dry places, especially if the soil is alkaline. Almost all bloom in shades of pink, from pale to screaming, but there are also whites and purples. Some of the tall-growing types are described on page 86. Low-growing species can create cushions of narrow foliage and bright summer flowers between patio stones, in containers or near the front of perennial beds. They are easy from seed started indoors.

D. arenarius (sand pink) grows just 4 inches (10 cm) tall, forming a mat of needlelike gray-green leaves and fringed white flowers, some spotted with pink.

D. deltoides (maiden pink) is one of the easiest to find. There are many cultivars in different sizes and colors, all hardy to about zone 3, provided they are given well-drained, preferably alkaline soil in sun, although in very dry gardens, they appreciate some shade. They may self-sow. Trim plants back after flowering.

D. sylvestris forms a low tuft or mat with pink flowers on 5-inch (13 cm) stems in summer.

Duchesnea indica
Mock strawberry

Looking every bit like a strawberry until its yellow flowers identify it, duchesnea grows about 4 inches (10 cm) tall and spreads by runners and seeds. It produces inedible strawberrylike fruit. It grows best in sun and can become a nuisance in good soil. If in doubt, grow it in a hanging basket.

Erica species
Heath, florist's heather

Along with *Calluna vulgaris* (page 52), this mostly shrubby genus turns the rounded mountains of the Scottish Highlands purple in summer. It is amenable to the dry garden too, provided certain conditions are met. A sunny rock garden or raised bed of sandy, perfectly drained acidic soil suits it best. Given these conditions, there are species and varieties hardy to zone 4. Flowers bloom in late spring in shades of white, pink, rose and magenta on the tips of slender stems circled

Heathers and other natives of the Scottish Highlands can survive drought with well-drained acidic soil and mild winters.

with tiny green leaves. *E. carnea* (winter heath, spring heath) is the least finicky and one of the hardiest species. Somewhat less hardy, to zone 5, are *E. x darleyensis* and *E. cinerea*. Heaths are mostly evergreen and should be given a position sheltered from winter winds. Mulch with pine needles. Prune occasionally to keep them bushy.

Galium odoratum (Asperula odorata)
Sweet woodruff

Given shade, this delightful plant, whose leaves radiate in whorls from the stem, will put up with a surprising amount of dryness. It is one of the few groundcovers with sufficiently shallow roots to allow it to survive under certain evergreens such as eastern white cedar. In such shade, its foliage is dark green. In sun, it becomes pale. It spreads gradually by underground runners and self-sown seeds but is easily controlled in most northern gardens, though it can be pesky in milder areas such as the Pacific Northwest. It grows about 6 inches (15 cm) tall and has starry white flowers in spring.

Genista pilosa
Broom, silkyleaf woadwaxen

Most types of broom can be considered either groundcover or shrub (see page 143). *G. tinctoria* (dyer's greenweed) and its dwarf forms make decent groundcovers that are hardy to zone 4. *G. pilosa* is similar but has silky hairs on the undersides of the leaves. It forms an evergreen carpet about 1 foot (30 cm) tall. Like the closely related *Cytisus* species, also called broom, it has bright yellow flowers in late spring. 'Vancouver Gold,' developed at the University of British Columbia, is an improved selection that is now quite widely available. It is hardy to zone 4 and can be used as a lawn substitute where there will be little or no foot traffic. Give broom well-drained soil in full or part sun.

Geranium species
Cranesbill

There are hundreds of species of true geranium, or cranesbill, more and more of which are appearing in perennial catalogs as their admirers increase. There is at least one for every garden. Unlike many perennials, cranesbills have beautiful foliage that lasts all season, and some have a long blooming time as well. Many are drought-tolerant and hardy to zone 4 or even colder gardens, provided the soil is well drained. Some stay in their appointed places (see page 90), while others spread into beautiful groundcovers. Deadhead all of them after blooming to prevent excessive seeding.

G. x *cantabrigiense* is a modest clump-former just 4 to 6 inches (10-15 cm) high that can be used as a groundcover for small areas to about zone 5. The glossy green foliage turns bright red in fall. Cultivars include pink-flowered 'Biokova' and rose 'Cambridge.'

G. himalayense has blue-violet flowers in early summer. It spreads, even under shrubs and trees, and has good fall color. The cultivar 'Plenum' has double flowers.

G. macrorrhizum has become the choice groundcover for difficult areas, replacing ivy, pachysandra and several others. What it offers is fragrant, wide, softly fuzzy foliage in a weed-excluding overlapping clump about 1 foot (30 cm) tall, with pretty magenta flowers in late spring. It is easy to divide and is capable of surviving in the dry shade under deciduous trees, on a slope or alongside a driveway, where it looks good all season. There are several cultivars, including clear-pink-flowered 'Ingwersen's Variety,' magenta 'Bevan's Variety' and white 'Spessart,' which has pink stamens. It is hardy to about zone 4.

G. x *oxonianum* is a spreading hybrid. There are several cultivars. One of the best for a groundcover is the pink-flowered 'Thurstonianum,' zone 5. It grows 2 to 2½ feet (60-75 cm) tall. Also good are the 18-inch (45 cm) dark pink 'Phoebe Noble' and the slightly smaller 'Claridge Druce,' zone 4.

G. sanguineum, named bloody cranesbill for the dramatic fall color of the foliage, can spread into a clump about 3 feet (1 m) wide in a few years, making a mounding weed-smothering carpet for shade or sun in any soil. The magenta flowers are persistent, and the maplelike leaves turn scarlet in autumn. It is easy to divide. Cultivars include red-flowered 'Alpenglow,' reddish purple

'Max Frei' and bright pink 'Shepherd's Warning.' 'Striatum' (also called 'Lancastriense,' varieties *prostratum* and *striatum*) is pale pink. 'Album' is taller, about 1 foot (30 cm), with pure white flowers. All are hardy to zone 4.

G. tuberosum grows from small tubers to a height of about 1 foot (30 cm). It has showy violet flowers and spreads readily. 'Leonidas' is a taller form with bright pink flowers. Both are hardy to zone 4 or 5.

Glechoma hederacea (Nepeta glechoma)
Creeping Charlie, ground ivy, gill-over-the-ground

In its green form, this is an extremely invasive creeper that roots from its stems and can grow happily in a lawn, crowding out the grasses, or just about anywhere else short of a busy highway. It should not be intentionally introduced into a garden unless you want a lawn of it, which might not be a bad thing. Certainly, a cutting in a hanging basket trails attractively and needs minimal care. Creeping Charlie thrives in any soil. It has fragrant foliage and pretty purple flowers in late spring. The variegated and golden forms are less invasive and are sometimes grown in wild gardens. Incidentally, if your creeping Charlie has become too much of a good thing, it can be killed with a benign herbicide: household borax. Dissolve 5 teaspoons (25 mL) borax (sodium tetraborate, as in 20 Mule Team) in 1 quart (1 L) hot water, and drench the foliage. This amount will treat 25 square feet (2.3 m²) and does not harm grass. Be careful not to spray other plants, however, because many are sensitive to borax.

Hemerocallis hybrids
Daylily

Visit a daylily farm sometime, if you can, to see with your own eyes how varied these sturdy plants can be. Petals may be ruffled or plain, bi-colored or single-toned. Colors range from cream through pale and bright yellow to orange, pink, burgundy and plum, all with undertones of yellow. A few have double flowers. Height varies from a few inches to almost 5 feet (1.5 m), with flowers tiny to large, some fragrant. The average daylily

Each daylily flower lasts for just one day, but more buds may bloom in succession for several weeks.

eties need a heavy mulch where winters are colder.

Daylilies do well in full sun but will also flower in partial shade, although extended cloudiness and dampness reduce flowering. Their chief demand is well-drained soil. So tolerant of neglect are daylilies that they escaped pioneer gardens and colonized roadsides as far north as zone 3. Given plenty of water in summer, they grow tall and bloom more profusely, but they will survive drought. Most do best where summer nights are warm.

Daylilies grow not from bulbs, like true lilies, but from fleshy tuberous roots. Clumps gradually expand, making daylilies an excellent grassy ground-cover, although speed of spread varies greatly with cultivar. Fast spread is now a breeding priority, so check with the catalog or nursery. Most daylilies are best divided every four or five years to keep them blooming well and to increase plantings. Push a spade into a clump to break it into sections, or pull the roots apart. The only pest problem is slugs and snails, especially on young plants in damp areas.

Iberis sempervirens
Perennial candytuft

A relative of arabis, aubrieta and *Aurinia saxatilis*, perennial candytuft is winter-hardy and lovely in flower. A mass of bright white flat-headed flowers appears in early summer. Cut back the stems as soon as flowering is over. It is more drought-tolerant than some of its cousins but is evergreen, so it benefits from a mild winter or good snow cover. It grows as tall as 1 foot (30 cm) and looks best at the front of a perennial or shrub border, where it can form a clump about 3 feet (1 m) across. It prefers full sun and requires well-drained soil. English gardener Beth Chatto considers perennial candytuft "invaluable amongst helianthemums and grays." The cultivar 'Snowflake' has larger flowers.

Juniperus species
Juniper

There are all sizes and shapes of juniper, from trees and shrubs to spreaders. Most are described as shrubs on pages 145 and 146. Junipers lack

blooms for three weeks, but many new cultivars will bloom for six to eight weeks, from June or July until August, and a few carry on virtually the entire season. My daylily season begins with the fragrant 'Hyperion' in mid-June and ends with 'Red Magic,' which blooms until September. Individual flowers last only a day, but some varieties carry as many as 50 buds per stem.

Best known of the long bloomers is 'Stella d'Oro,' which "did for daylilies what Olga Korbut did for gymnastics," says Angelo Cerchione, executive director of the All-America Daylily Selection Council. 'Stella d'Oro,' though smaller than many cultivars, produces clear orange flowers almost nonstop from early summer until frost. Any variety with the word 'Stella' or 'Siloam' in its name can be assumed to bloom a long time. 'Stella d'Oro' and many others are hardy to zone 3 and die back to the ground in winter, but some varieties are evergreen, hardy to zone 5, or semievergreen, hardy to zone 4 or 5. These vari-

Creeping junipers may be prickly, but given sun, they are beautiful all year and require little or no maintenance.

showy flowers, and most are prickly, but otherwise, they are plants of many virtues. They complement broad-leaved groundcovers, they can be seen in winter if snows are not too deep, and they put up with very dry soil. Among the best groundcovers are *J. horizontalis* (creeping juniper) and *J. sabina* (Savin juniper), although there are also low-growing cultivars of other species, such as *J. squamata* 'Blue Carpet.'

J. sabina has a distinct resinous fragrance. Savins need plenty of room, although not necessarily when they are first planted. You can keep moving perennials farther out as the junipers widen from year to year or transplant the junipers when they outgrow their space. Savins relocate easily. In time, some can spread as wide as 15 feet (4.5 m). Popular on the prairies, Savins can suffer from winter browning in full sun but usually recover in spring. Some grow up to 4 feet (1.2 m) tall, but highly recommended lower-growing cultivars include the bright green tamarisk, or tam, junipers 'Arcadia' and 'Calgary Carpet,' only about 1 foot (30 cm) high or a little taller. The latter has soft

foliage that makes it easy to work with. 'Buffalo' stays bright green through the winter and is a good spreader. These cultivars do best with a generous snow cover. 'Blue Danube' grows taller, to about 3 feet (1 m) high, and twice as wide.

J. horizontalis is generally a little slower-growing and more modest in size than *J. sabina*, although characteristics vary with cultivar. Creeping junipers are native to the prairies and the Midwest, where they grow on dry, sandy hillsides. Cultivars recommended by Saskatchewan Agriculture, all of which grow 6 to 16 inches (15-40 cm) tall and 7 feet (2 m) wide or more, include 'Andorra,' 'Prince of Wales,' 'Wapiti' and 'Dunvegan Blue.' 'Blue Ice,' selected from the wild in Alberta and registered in 1993, is a powder-blue cultivar that grows 6 inches (15 cm) high and spreads wider than 3 to 5 feet (1-1.5 m). Its extreme hardiness, to zone 3, gives it an advantage over other prostrate junipers. 'Douglasii,' called Waukegan, is a very hardy carpet, blue in summer, plum in winter. 'Yukon Belle' has soft silver-blue foliage.

Additional excellent cultivars of *J. horizontalis* include gray-green fern-textured 'Heidi,' cream-splashed 'Variegatus,' golden 'Mother Lode' and the North Carolina release 'Lime Glow.' 'Quonset,' a Montana State University hybrid of *J. horizontalis* and *J. scopulorum*, seems immune to cedar apple rust and survives to at least minus 40 degrees F (–40°C). It has a unique mounded form with stems that cascade down from the center. It is silvery blue in winter and greenish blue in summer.

Creeping junipers are difficult to transplant. Some spring pruning may be necessary. Wearing gloves (if the variety is prickly), cut away any dead needles and trim broken branches back to the closest joint. Junipers are among the evergreen shrubs most susceptible to infection by snow mold, which develops on foliage covered by snow until late spring. Remove the gray mats of fuzzy mycelia before they turn black and tarry.

Lamiastrum galeobdolon
(Lamium galeobdolon)
Yellow archangel

This member of the mint family is a rampant groundcover with toothed nettlelike leaves and, in early summer, yellow flowers. Shear it back after flowering. There are several cultivars, the most common being 'Variegatum,' with variegated foliage. Set plants 1 foot (30 cm) apart in full sun, and they will quickly fill in the gaps. 'Variegatum' is a good groundcover under trees but is too invasive for a perennial bed. 'Herman's Pride,' which grows upright with silvery leaves, does not spread and needs more moisture. Lamiastrum prefers some shade and is hardy to zone 2.

Lamium maculatum
Spotted dead nettle

Dead nettles appreciate moisture and thrive in shade, but they are rampant enough to succeed in dry ground, provided they have some shade and protection from strong winds. With their spotted nettlelike leaves, they form a loose mat about 8 inches (20 cm) tall and flower in late spring. Ambergate Gardens of Minnesota recommends the silver-leaved, pink-flowered cultivar 'Pink Pewter' under red-fruited crabapples. Lamium may die back some winters in zone 4. It looks best in spring and fall and may become straggly in mid-summer in dry soil.

Mahonia species
Oregon grape

This group of evergreen shrubs is native to the Pacific Coast yet will tolerate dry soil and cold winters to zone 5, provided there is shelter from wind and hot sun. These shrubs spread by underground stolons.

M. aquifolium (Oregon grape) has shiny, leathery leaves that turn bronze in fall. It grows about 3 feet (1 m) tall. Fragrant yellow flowers in spring are followed by clusters of bluish black fruit; hence the common name. The fruit makes a good jelly.

M. repens (creeping mahonia) is similar but grows less than 1 foot (30 cm) tall and spreads more rapidly. It is not as attractive as Oregon grape and is harder to find.

Microbiota decussata
Russian arborvitae, Siberian carpet

Microbiota looks like flattened cedar. Bright green in summer, it spreads over low rocks and carpets the ground to form a circle that can eventually measure 10 feet (3 m) wide and 1 foot (30 cm) thick. In winter, it turns purplish brown. One of the few needle evergreens that thrives in shade, microbiota is hardy to zone 3.

Nepeta x faassenii
Faassen's catmint, Persian ground ivy

Although not a plant for really windy, dry places, *N.* x *faassenii* (*N. mussinii*) can tolerate drought for several weeks, provided it has humusy soil and some shade. This mint relative does best where spring and fall are damp. Although there are white and pink varieties, the flowers are typically lavender-blue, appearing above blue-gray foliage in late spring and early summer. Shear nepeta after it flowers, and it will probably bloom again later in the summer. It grows about 1 foot (30 cm) tall, forming a gradually spreading carpet. All the catmints are attractive to cats.

Polygonum affine 'Dimity' has leathery green leaves and flowers that fade from red to pink.

Pinus sylvestris
Scots pine

There are some low-growing pines such as *P. sylvestris* 'Repens' and 'Hillside Creeper,' which turns gold in winter. 'Albyns,' found 20 years ago in an Ohio nursery, spreads widely and is hardy to minus 50 degrees F (–45°C). Its blue-green coloring lasts through winter. For more information about pines, see page 149.

Polygonum species
Knotweed

There are several spreading forms of the common garden knotweed, or smartweed. The name knotweed and the genus name, which means "many knees," describe the bamboolike joints along the stem. Knotweeds put up with very dry, poor soil but will tolerate wetness as well.

P. affine (Himalayan fleece flower), also known as *Persicaria affinis*, grows about 6 inches (15 cm) tall and has pink flowers in summer. Shear off the spent flower stalks to keep it presentable.

P. bistorta is a little taller than *P. affine* and forms a solid mat with pink summer flowers.

P. cuspidatum (Japanese bamboo, northern bamboo) is not a bamboo at all, although its jointed stems are reminiscent of bamboo. It grows about 6 feet (1.8 m) tall and has dark green leaves. While beautiful when it produces its froth of white flowers in early summer, it is too invasive for any place other than a dry, out-of-the-way wild corner. Keep it out of a small garden and away from other perennials.

Potentilla species
Creeping cinquefoil

As well as the shrubby upright potentillas described on page 149, there are several herbaceous species, some of which make good groundcovers.

P. reptans (creeping cinquefoil), which may be hardy in gardens as cold as zone 3, forms a perennial 6-inch-deep (15 cm) mat of strawberrylike leaves with yellow flowers in summer. The cultivar 'Pleniflora,' or 'Flora Pleno,' has double flowers. It spreads quickly and invasively by long runners, forming a dense mat, so it is best confined by paving or walls. Creeping cinquefoil does best in full sun and well-drained soil. Like crown vetch, this is a good plant for dry slopes.

P. tridentata, which has white flowers, is a modest spreader suitable for a small area in a rock garden or perennial border.

P. verna (spring cinquefoil) grows into a mat as low as 3 inches (7.5 cm).

Rosa species and hybrids
Rose

On the opposite end of the rose spectrum from the tender hybrid teas are certain species that are hardy and self-sufficient, even invasive. All groundcover roses are prickly, so keep them away from places where they will be brushed against or stepped on and handle them carefully. They are best given a spot on their own, such as between a wall and a sidewalk or on the sunny south-facing side of deciduous trees. While they tolerate drought once established, they do best in decent, deep, well-drained soil amended with compost.

There are resilient roses ancient and new. Among the hybrids are the white-flowered prostrate 'Snow Carpet'; 'Nearly Wild,' 3 feet (1 m) high with pink flowers; and 'Ralph's Creeper,' 18 inches (45 cm) tall with red flowers.

R. rugosa. A few of these spread by underground runners and can be used as groundcovers. Look for 'Charles Albanel,' red flowers, 18 inches (45 cm) tall; 'Dart's Dash,' fragrant red flowers, 3 feet (1 m) tall; and 'Frau Dagmar Hastrup,' pink flowers, 3 feet (1 m) tall. Roses in the Pavement series, developed in Germany in the 1980s and 1990s, are hardy to zone 3. They grow about 2 feet (60 cm) tall and spread 3 to 4 feet (1-1.2 m). The flowers are fragrant and set hips.

R. wichuriana (memorial rose) is less hardy, to zone 5 or 6, but given light, well-drained soil and full sun, it grows so densely that it smothers weeds and can become invasive. The species, which has fragrant, pinkish white single flowers, has become naturalized in some areas. *R. wichuriana* hybrids include 'Paul Transom,' with pink flowers, and 'Red Cascade,' which is prostrate and has red flowers.

Selections of Rosa rugosa, *which spread by underground runners, make tall, prickly groundcovers.*

Saponaria ocymoides
Rock soapwort

Best in sun with well-drained soil, preferably alkaline, rock soapwort forms a carpet of green leaves about 6 inches (15 cm) deep. It has bright pink flowers in summer. Cut the flower stalks back after blooming. It is hardy to zone 2.

Sedum species
Stonecrop

There are more than 100 species of sedum in cultivation, evidence of the suitability of this genus for many gardens, not just dry ones. But it is in the dry garden that sedums take the limelight. There are upright forms (see page 103) and creepers, the latter being some of the best groundcovers for rock gardens, containers and perennial beds and for covering slopes in dry sun. They root at stem nodes, forming a fairly dense cover, and are easy to divide. Varieties may spread quickly or at a snail's pace. The starry flowers may be white, yellow or, within the pink range, anywhere from pale to brilliant magenta. Like other succulents, sedums' chief demand is well-drained soil; prolonged wetness causes root decay. In fact, in their native habitat, sedums usually grow over or between exposed rocks, surroundings easily copied in the garden.

Sedums are often mislabeled in nurseries and are easily confused. Like the sempervivums, their foliage may change color from pot to garden and from spring through summer. Foliage that is bright green in spring may turn drab green in summer; grays turn to beige, maroons to green. Another surprise with sedums, like sempervivums and artemisias, is their fundamental change of shape at flowering time. With sedums, tall flower stalks and starry flowerheads become dominant on plants best known for their foliage the remainder of the year. Shear off the flower stems when the flowers dry to show off the foliage again. Among the most commonly available are the following:

S. acre (showy stonecrop) is the smallest of all,

A mixture of sempervivums and sedums, mostly Sedum kamtschaticum, *happily colonizes a dry corner in Ontario.*

just 1 to 3 inches (2.5-7.5 cm) tall. It is a European species that spreads so easily, even in the shallow patches of soil on exposed rocks, that it can invade lawns and has become naturalized throughout much of North America. In trials at Colorado State University in Fort Collins, *S. acre* was the only tested groundcover deemed a suitable alternative to Kentucky bluegrass in terms of attractiveness and water conservation. (The other groundcovers tested were *Potentilla neumanniana* and *Cerastium tomentosum*.) *S. acre* has sunny yellow summer flowers, but the variety *aureum* (golden stonecrop, also known as the cultivar 'Aureum' and as the species *S. aureum*) has paler flowers. All should be kept away from small or delicate plants.

S. album forms a rapidly spreading mat 4 inches (10 cm) deep. 'Murale' (coral carpet stonecrop) has rounded green leaves and light pink flowers. 'Murale Cristatum' (crested stonecrop) has white flowers.

S. divergens (old man's bones) has spherical, pearl-like green leaves and yellow flowers. It forms

a rapidly spreading blanket 4 to 6 inches (10-15 cm) deep.

S. floriferum 'Weihenstephaner Gold' is a rapid spreader with variegated green-and-gold foliage that creates a beautiful solid mat about 6 inches (15 cm) deep.

S. kamtschaticum (Russian stonecrop) was described in an 1871 garden book as "pretty in hanging baskets," and indeed, all the trailing sedums are excellent choices to trail over the edge of a basket in sun. The Royal Botanical Gardens in Burlington, Ontario, considers the species one of the best sedums for use as a groundcover. It is identified by its scalloped leaves and bright orange-yellow flowers. 'Variegatum,' which spreads slowly, has green-and-white foliage and golden flowers.

S. oreganum (Oregon stonecrop) has thick, shiny green leaves that turn bright red in hot, dry weather. The flowers are yellow. It slowly forms a mat 6 inches (15 cm) deep.

S. reflexum looks like a giant version of *S. acre*. Its soft bluish stems, which resemble spruce cuttings, grow about 6 inches (15 cm) tall and are topped by bright yellow flowers in summer. It spreads quickly.

S. sexangulare (six-sided stonecrop) has tiny, tightly spiraled bright green leaves and yellow summer flowers. It spreads quickly, forming a mat 4 inches (10 cm) deep.

S. spathulifolium, hardy to zone 5, is one of the most decorative spreaders, with beautiful small rosettes of foliage that create a mat 3 to 6 inches (7.5-15 cm) deep. It has yellow flowers. 'Capa Blanca' has gray-white foliage. 'Purpureum' (purple spoon sedum) has dark purple foliage and spreads slowly. They cannot survive in soggy soil.

S. spurium (dragon's blood), hardy to zone 3, has white or pink flowers that may be pale or brilliant, depending on the cultivar. 'Ruby Mantle' has purple foliage and dark pink flowers. It is a slower spreader than the others. 'Tricolor' has pink flowers and variegated green, cream and pink foliage. Pinch out any green shoots. 'Bronze Carpet' has pink flowers and green foliage that turns bronze in fall.

S. ternatum, hardy to zone 3 and native to the eastern United States, has white flowers in spring. Give it a spot with some shade. The cultivar 'Larinem Park' has bright green foliage.

Sempervivum species
Hens-and-chicks, houseleek

Given time, hens-and-chicks can cover a large area by the charming practice of creating new offsets on shoots nestled close to the mother plant. The round rosettes of fleshy leaves are lovely in stone or terra-cotta containers or growing in the spaces between steps, on sandy slopes or between stones at the front of a sunny flowerbed. These succulents were called houseleeks in the Old World because they were raised on sod or gravel rooftops, supposedly to fend off lightning and bad spirits. The Latin name means "live forever," which they will do in perfectly drained ground. There are smooth varieties and hairy ones, in colors from pale to dark green to bluish, maroon and variegated, mostly members of the species *S. tectorum*.

The labeling can be confusing, so choose what you like by its color and size. Like sedums, however, sempervivums may change color with temperature and season. And they look like entirely different plants when in flower—which happens only when they mature and are happily growing in sun—because the stalks are ungainly, almost as wide as the rosettes themselves, topped by small bright pink or yellow flowers. After a rosette flowers, it dies, but surrounding "chicks" soon fill in.

S. arachnoideum is called the cobweb, or spiderweb, houseleek because of the fine silvery hairs that form a net over the plant. It is one of the more attractive species in flower because it has slender stems and proportionately larger flowers compared with the thick stems and small flowers of the others. Flowers are pink.

S. hirtum (*Jovibarba hirta*), known as false houseleek, is often sold as jovibarba. It has foliage arranged in rosettes and yellow flowers with fringed petals.

There are two additional genera also called hens-and-chicks: *Echeveria* species are less hardy than most sempervivums and are usually grown as houseplants; they have bluish foliage and slender flower stalks. Winter them indoors. *Orostachys*, whose members are sometimes classed as sempervivums or sedums, wither in fall to leave behind a compact bud of leaves that grow outward in spring.

Stachys species
Lamb's ears

If any plant in the garden can be described as cute, it's *S. lanata* (*S. byzantina*), whose common name suggests its endearing appearance. Lamb's ears is a favorite of children, who love to stroke the downy, silvery ear-shaped leaves. The leaves grow in rosettes on stems 1 foot (30 cm) tall. This plant does best in full or part sun in well-drained soil rich in organic matter. It is usually grown in clumps within a perennial bed, although it will spread fairly quickly to form a groundcover if grown in fertile soil with occasional watering. Small rose-colored flowers bloom on tall woolly spikes in summer. These are not especially ornamental; some gardeners lop them off like lamb's tails. The shorter 6-to-8-inch (15-20 cm) cultivar 'Silver Carpet' does not flower. 'Primrose Heron' has

A good choice between paving stones, mother of thyme forms blankets of fragrant leaves that can tolerate light foot traffic.

golden yellow foliage. After wet winters, remove mushy leaves. Plants may resprout from the roots.

S. macrantha or *S. grandiflora* (woundwort) looks quite different. It has attractive dark green foliage with scalloped edges and is very hardy and drought-tolerant.

Symphoricarpos x chenaultii 'Hancock'
Hancock coralberry

This prostrate form of coralberry, a deciduous shrub with dark blue-green leaves and persistent coral-colored fruit, forms a 2-to-3-foot-high (60-90 cm) groundcover that spreads by suckers. It originated in Ontario and is hardy to zone 4. It will grow in sun or shade in any well-drained soil.

Thymus species
Thyme

The cooking thymes (see pages 136 and 137) are joined by several groundcover types that are less esteemed in the kitchen but are wonderful in the garden. Grown between the paving stones of a patio or pathway, all thymes proffer their distinctive fragrance whenever you step on them or brush by. Thyme is easy to divide in spring or fall. Creeping thyme can also be propagated by stem cuttings (see page 28).

T. praecox (creeping thyme) forms flat mats of narrow green leaves topped with tiny flowers in early summer. Flower color may be white, red or lilac, depending on the cultivar.

T. serpyllum (mother of thyme) forms a tumbling 6-inch-deep (15 cm) groundcover of slender stems and tiny aromatic leaves. Its small, rosy lilac flowers bloom in midsummer. It can take more foot traffic than the others. Cultivars of *T. praecox* may be labeled as this species. This can be grown from seed, although it is a slow process.

T. serpyllum lanuginosus, *T. pseudoserpyllum*, *T. lanuginosus* or *T. praecox pseudolanuginosus* (woolly thyme) is well named for its fuzzy foliage. The leaves are tiny, and the entire plant grows less than 1 inch (2.5 cm) tall. It will stand a bit of foot traffic and will extend out over flat rocks.

Veronica species
Speedwell

As the common name suggests, this is a rapid spreader. Indeed, a couple of species, *V. chamaedrys* and *V. filiformis*, invade lawns. Veronicas are best known for their spikes of usually blue but sometimes pink or white flowers. They need well-drained soil in sun or partial shade.

V. incana (woolly speedwell) has grayish leaves and forms a clump 1 foot (30 cm) tall and equally wide. The flower spikes are purple.

V. pectinata (comb speedwell) grows just 2 to 4 inches (5-10 cm) tall, gradually spreading outward. It forms a dense, usually weedproof cover and has tiny, bright blue flowers for about a month in spring. Its name comes from the shape of the leaves, which are toothed like a comb. They are slightly woolly. The variety *rosea* has pink flowers. Give both types full sun to light shade.

V. peduncularis 'Georgia Blue,' a clone from the Caucasus Mountains of Russia, was released in 1996 from the University of British Columbia. About 8 inches (20 cm) tall, it flowers in early spring and again in fall. The foliage is bronze-green. It is hardy to zone 4 and does best with some shade.

V. prostrata (creeping speedwell) forms a low 4-inch-tall (10 cm) 1-foot-wide (30 cm) mat of gray-green foliage with pink ('Mrs. Holt') or brilliant blue ('Heavenly Blue') flowers in late spring. It is hardy to zone 5.

V. repens resembles moss, with half-inch (1 cm) shiny green leaves and light blue flowers in late summer. There are also pink and white varieties.

There are several additional spreading forms of veronica, including *V. austriaca* 'Trehane,' *V. daubneyi* and *V. liwanensis*.

Vinca minor
Periwinkle

Weedy in rich ground and invasive in some areas, periwinkle can be just the thing for poor, dry soil, where its evergreen foliage can carpet the ground between tall perennials and shrubs. In my garden, it dies back after harsh winters. The stems root as they grow, and blue flowers bloom in spring. Keep it away from low plants that it might otherwise swamp. It puts up with light or deep shade in dry or damp soil.

Less hardy but more decorative are the cultivars, which include 'Bowles Variety,' with blue flowers; 'Alba,' with white flowers; and 'Rubra,' with red flowers.

GROUNDCOVERS FOR DRY SHADE
The following plants will survive in dry shade once established. However, flowering will be reduced: the deeper the shade, the fewer the blooms.

Aegopodium podagraria
Convallaria majalis
Galium odoratum
Geranium macrorrhizum
Lamiastrum galeobdolon
Lamium 'Pale Peril'
Microbiota decussata
Veronica peduncularis 'Georgia Blue'

Geranium macrorrhizum *is an ideal groundcover for almost any situation.*

Bulbs

◆ *4*

"BULBOUS PLANTS ARE THE SAVING AND
VERY GRACIOUS GRACE OF MANY GARDENS."

—Louise Beebe Wilder, *Adventures with Hardy Bulbs*, 1936

Plants that grow from bulbs and similar plump underground parts are among the best candidates for dry gardens. A bulb acts something like a camel's hump, storing moisture and nutrients to help the plant survive droughts. Many bulbous plants originated in such places as semidesert grasslands that dry out in summer. These plants build strength right after blooming, usually in spring when their foliage is green and the soil is still wet. They ripen their seeds and die back to the ground, weathering the summer, fall and winter invisibly.

Not only can bulbs survive parched summers, but many *need* a dry period for survival. Their worst enemy is wet ground in summer, which causes them to rot, turning species that should be perennial into annuals which must be replanted every fall. Planting bulbs amongst herbaceous perennials can be risky for the bulbs if you intend to water the perennials all summer. The bulbs would rather dry out in a neglected spot on their own, even on a grassy slope left unmowed—or at least not mowed until early summer, when their leaves have dried out. Bulbs will take pretty

well any soil, but if it is heavy clay, they should be planted on a slope or in another well-drained area.

There are both common and uncommon flowering bulbs to consider for the dry garden. Many of them bloom in spring, but a few hardy bulbs such as lilies bloom in summer and fall, and a large group of tender-perennial summer bulbs color the garden during July, August and September but cannot be left in the garden to overwinter. In other chapters, bulbs such as chives, garlic and lily of the valley are described.

Hardy Bulbs

These are mostly spring and summer bloomers that come on the market in late summer. They can be planted from then until just before the soil freezes, although late-summer planting makes spring blooming the first year more certain. All do best in full sun, but some will put up with partial shade. Most can be divided anytime after the leaves and stems die back in late spring or early summer but before the soil freezes again. If you intend to divide them, mark their position at blooming time. Mulch bulbs during their first

The bright yellow flowers of the ornamental onion
Allium moly *complement the blue of baptisia.*

winter, especially in places where the snow cover is unreliable. In following winters, mulching helps ensure survival but may not be necessary.

Allium species
Ornamental onion

This genus presents the dry-land gardener with a beautiful selection of umbel flowers from late spring until late fall. Blues, pinks, purples and lilacs are most strongly represented, but there are also whites and yellows. Many attract butterflies. Unlike most bulbs, alliums have remarkably long-lasting flowers, sometimes colored for weeks and then fading to beige or brown stars that have their own beauty and are prized for dry arrangements. As well, stalks cut while the flowers are at the peak of color can be hung upside down in a warm, dry place to dry. Many alliums self-sow. Alliums can be grown from purchased seed too, but the seeds must be fairly fresh. Some sprout easily, but others, including *A. aflatunense* and *A. roseum*, require ex-

posure to cold and light before they will germinate.

Most grow from bulbs, much like edible onions or chives. Indeed, all are edible, although they would be expensive fare. The ornamental onions obtained as bulbs are planted in fall anytime before the soil freezes, and most do best in sun, although they will take some shade. Where winters are colder than about minus 22 degrees F (–30°C), mulch their spot after the soil freezes.

The following alliums are fairly easy to find as bulbs, plants or seeds. All are hardy to zone 3 except as noted.

A. aflatunense (Persian onion, aflatun onion) is a Chinese species with stiff stems as tall as 3 feet (1 m) topped with 4-inch (10 cm) lilac-purple flower balls in late spring. It is usually sold as 'Purple Sensation.'

A. albopilosum, or *A. christophii* (star of Persia), is a Middle Eastern native with amazingly big silvery starlike umbels as wide as 1 foot (30 cm); very eye-catching in early summer. The stiff stem is just 1 to 2 feet (30-60 cm) tall.

A. caeruleum, or *A. azureum* (blue globe onion, azure onion), comes from Siberia. Its 2-to-3-inch (5-7.5 cm) sky-blue umbels bloom on 1-to-3-foot (30-90 cm) stalks in early summer. The narrow leaves wither by the time the flowers bloom. Zone 5.

A. carinatum pulchellum, *A. flavum pulchellum* or *A. pulchellum* (keeled garlic), from southern Europe, is a late-summer bloomer with loose clusters of dangling purplish winged flowers on 2-foot (60 cm) stems. The foliage is bluish, and the plant self-sows. There is also a white form.

A. cernuum (nodding onion) is a North American species with pale purple early-summer flowers on 12-to-18-inch (30-45 cm) stems.

A. flavum (small nodding onion, small yellow onion) has flat, sweetly scented loose yellow flower-heads 2 to 3 inches (5-7.5 cm) across in mid-summer. Stems are about 1 foot (30 cm) tall, and foliage is bluish. There are several cultivars.

A. giganteum (giant onion) is an Asian species often pictured in seed catalogs beside and at eye level with a standing child. A single bulb may set you back a couple of dollars, but 4-foot (1.2 m) or taller stems bear 4-to-5-inch (10-13 cm) flower

Allium sphaerocephalum *has numerous small flowers that are grouped into showy umbels on self-supporting stems.*

balls of deep violet in early summer. Zone 4.

A. karataviense, from central Asia, is just 6 inches (15 cm) tall, with unusually wide, purplish leaves, sometimes twisted, and a pale pink or rose-colored flower ball in spring. It is excellent in a rock garden or a border's edge in full sun.

A. moly (yellow onion, lily leek, golden garlic) is a southern European species with flat, bright yellow early-summer flowers 2 to 3 inches (5-7.5 cm) wide on 6-to-12-inch (15-30 cm) stems. The leaves are narrow and gray-green. In full sun, the leaf tips may scorch, so give it a bit of shade.

A. nutans (steppe onion) has 2-foot (60 cm) stems with soft lilac globe flowers in midsummer. It spreads by seed.

A. ostrowskianum (*A. oreophilum*) is a Turkish species with 6-inch (15 cm) stems and loose pink or purple umbels in late spring. It needs sun but will tolerate a bit of shade cast by other plants. The cultivar 'Zwanenburg' has carmine flowers.

A. ramosum (Siberian fragrant onion, fragrant-flowered garlic) has 2-foot (60 cm) stems that bear umbels of fragrant white flowers in midsummer.

A. rosenbachianum has 2-foot (60 cm) ribbed stems bearing starry violet flowers in early June. *Album* has white flowers. Zone 5.

A. schoenoprasum (chives) makes a good garden flower, and of course, the young foliage can be snipped off anytime for salads (see pages 129 and 130). The ornamental cultivar 'Forescate' has bright pink flowers.

A. senescens, or *A. montanum* (pink curly onion), is a Eurasian species, sometimes with unusual twisted leaves. In late summer, it produces many small rose, lilac or pink umbels on 6-inch (15 cm) stems compact enough to suit it to the cracks between paving stones.

A. sphaerocephalum (roundheaded leek, ballhead or drumstick onion), from Europe and the Middle East, has tightly compacted oval purple-red heads, just 1 inch (2.5 cm) wide, on slender 2-foot (60 cm) stems. It blooms throughout the summer, produces many offsets and self-sows well. There are several subspecies.

Species crocuses such as Crocus ancyrensis *may be smaller than Dutch crocuses, but many are also earlier and brighter.*

Anemone species
Windflower

These small daisylike flowers held over deeply divided foliage do well in dry shade. The following species are surprising in the early-spring garden, where they contrast with the more usual cup- or bell-shaped spring bulbs. Anemones grow from corms that are best planted in fall.

Most common is *A. blanda*, about 5 inches (13 cm) tall, available in several cultivars in shades of white, pink, red and blue. *A. ranunculoides*, named for its similarity to buttercups (*Ranunculus*), has bright yellow 1-inch-wide (2.5 cm) flowers on 4-to-8-inch (10-20 cm) stems, while *A. nemorosa* (wood anemone) has white or blue flowers on stems up to 4 inches (10 cm) tall.

Chionodoxa species
Glory of the snow

This flower, given its common name because it blooms so early in spring, looks best planted in masses. It grows about 6 inches (15 cm) tall, with white, blue or lilac flowers. Plant wherever the soil is well drained, in either sun or partial shade. After blooming, leave the flowers in place to allow them to set seed to increase the colony.

Crocus species
Crocus

Large-flowered hybrid crocuses in Easter shades of white, yellow and lilac mean spring in much of the North, but there are many additional types known as species crocuses, some of which bloom even earlier.

C. ancyrensis, with brilliant yellow flowers, is one of the earliest bulbs in my garden.

C. chrysanthus, a parent of many garden hybrids, is also very early. Among cultivars are 'Cream Beauty,' creamy yellow; and 'Blue Pearl,' soft blue and bronze inside, darker violet outside. The variety *fusco-tinctus* is golden bronze.

C. tommasinianus has been grown in gardens for almost two centuries. It naturalizes well and blooms early. Its silvery gray petals are pale lavender inside, and its stems are about 6 inches (15 cm) tall. The grassy foliage looks untidy for weeks after blooming, so situate them carefully.

C. vernus, another garden heirloom, is one of the first to bloom. The 3-inch (7.5 cm) flowers may be white or purple, striped or feathered. 'Joan of Arc' ('Jeanne d'Arc') is all white.

There are also hardy fall-blooming crocuses, notably *C. speciosus*, with blue or white flowers on 6-inch (15 cm) stems. Crocus bulbs are a favorite food of mice and squirrels. Where these rodents are a problem, dip corms in bitter-tasting Ro-pel or another predator repellent before planting. Also, spray the planted area with the same substance, or sprinkle it with cayenne pepper.

Eranthis species
Winter aconite

Brilliant golden buttercup flowers just a few inches above the ground—or the snow—are the gift of this very early hardy bulb, which blooms around the same time as crocuses and snowdrops. The leaves appear after the flowers, and no trace of either is left by late spring. Plant the little tuberous roots in masses at the front of a border in late summer or early fall, as soon as they become available. They need well-drained soil and prefer dappled or partial shade.

Fritillaria species
Fritillaria

The standard-bearer of this genus is the showy crown imperial (*F. imperialis*), but it is fussy, and experimenting is expensive—a single grapefruit-sized bulb can cost more than $20. Many of the charming but smaller fritillarias are easier, and you can buy a bedful of bulbs for the same price. Give them well-drained soil with some sun. All of these are hardy and bloom in spring.

F. meleagris (purple snake's-head fritillary, checker lily) has interesting checkered foliage on nodding bells atop 10-inch-tall (25 cm) stems. There is a white version, *F. meleagris alba*.

F. michailovskyi has maroon-purple petals

BEGINNING STRATEGIES

Clumps of bulbs generally look better than bulbs grown singly, and given time and contentment, all bulbs will form clumps. If the bulbs are not too expensive, buy at least three of the same variety and color to avoid a sparse look, and plant them close together. An exception is lilies, which are expensive and begin to form clumps by the second season. When clumps become too crowded, dig them up after flowering and transplant a few elsewhere.

Spring bloomers are planted in fall and summer bulbs in spring. For planting bulbs in a garden bed, I use a regular trowel. (Some gardeners swear by special bulb planters—tubes that remove a plug of earth or sod.) The bulb is dropped into the hole, and the soil is firmed in around it. For naturalizing bulbs in a lawn or field, I lift the sod

Large bulbs may be too expensive to buy in quantity, but division is easy.

with a spade and tuck the bulbs underneath, with the flat side down. The general rule for hardy bulbs is to plant to a depth of at least twice the diameter of the bulb. They can go as deep as 1 foot (30 cm), however, which encourages stronger growth in windy places and permits survival in colder winters. Emergence and blooming will be somewhat later if bulbs are planted deeper.

with a bright yellow edge and grows 8 inches (20 cm) tall. This is rated to zone 7 but sailed through winter in my zone-4 garden.

F. pallidiflora grows clusters of greenish yellow bells on 1-foot-tall (30 cm) stems.

F. persica is a good substitute for those who can't grow the crown imperial. It reaches heights of up to 2 feet (60 cm) and has narrow grayish foliage and fragrant, dark purple flowers. "I let mine lean against euphorbia," writes English gardener Beth Chatto.

Galanthus species
Snowdrop

Snowdrops are among the hardiest, most dependable spring bulbs. They also may be your earliest—April here, in zone 4—sometimes pushing buds through the snow. *G. nivalis*, the common snowdrop, grows just 3 to 4 inches (7.5-10 cm) tall and multiplies into colonies fairly quickly. The cultivar 'Flore Pleno' has double flowers. A little taller and less well known are *G. elwesii* and *G. caucasicus*, both about 6 inches (15 cm) tall.

Snowdrop bulbs do not tolerate drying out before planting. If you buy bulbs, plant them immediately. In your own garden, divide plants and move bulbs after blooming but while the foliage is still green.

Lilium species
Lily

Lilies of many species, sizes and colors are among the most fabulous and reliable flowers for a dry garden with cold winters. Given water, they will grow bigger and more lush, but they will survive and bloom in very dry soil. At the Devonian Botanic Garden near Edmonton, Alberta, a lovely plot is dedicated solely to lilies developed by Canadian breeders. Any gardener could do likewise—or assemble lilies of a certain type or color.

Lilies are categorized in several divisions. Listed below are the ones that are appropriate in dry northern gardens. Unless otherwise noted, all include the full spectrum of colors—red, pink, yellow, white, orange. In general, the whites,

reds and pinks predominate early in the season, while the yellows and oranges come later. Within each division described are varying blooming times. Lily catalogs identify the bloom time of their offerings, so select accordingly for lilies from June through late summer. These divisions include the hardiest lilies.

Division 1: Asiatic lilies, often the first to bloom, starting in June, are the most prevalent in my garden. They grow about 3 feet (1 m) tall, with plain, bicolored, spotted or striped petals. They are not fragrant but are hardy to zone 2.

Division 2: Martagon lilies and hybrids are erect, up to 6 feet (1.8 m) tall, and have whorled leaves and as many as 50 little Turk's-cap flowers on each stem in late June and early July. Best in alkaline soil with some shade and hardy to zone 2, these are among the oldest lilies in cultivation. They resent division. "We apply old, very well-rotted manure to our clumps in mid-May to act as a mulch and to provide nourishment," notes the catalog from Alyssa's Garden in Fort Saint John, British Columbia. "This seems to produce fabulous results."

Division 6: Trumpet lilies, hardy to zone 5 but possible with winter mulch in colder areas, have waxy, fragrant, usually outward-facing flowers in July or August on 3-foot (1 m) or taller stems. The Aurelians are an especially easy group of trumpet lilies.

Division 7: Oriental lilies, fragrant August bloomers up to 6 feet (1.8 m) tall, have the biggest flowers and are a little more difficult to grow, preferring acidic, moist soil and mulch over winter. In its zone-1 garden, Alyssa's Garden overwinters Orientals and Trumpets in a deeply mulched raised bed whose acidic soil includes plenty of peat.

Division 8: Longiflorum Asiatics, shortened to L.A. hybrids, have big flowers with some perfume and are hardier than the Orientals but also should be mulched over winter in zone 4 or colder. *L. longiflorum* is the Easter lily, a fragrant white species that occasionally overwinters in my zone-4 garden. The so-called Orientpets, also in this division, are Oriental-Trumpet hybrids and Aurelian-Asiatic hybrids.

Division 9: This division covers the species, or

Most of the hardy hybrid lilies are termed Asiatics, a huge group that is self-reliant and blooms in a range of colors.

wild, lilies and their varieties. The catalog of The Lily Nook of Neepawa, Manitoba, lists the following species as hardy on the prairies: *L. amabile, L. amabile luteum, L. davidii, L. henryi, L. michiganense, L. tigrinum flaviflorum* and *L. tigrinum splendens.* According to Honeywood Lilies of Saskatchewan, the Korean *L. dauricum* also grows easily on the prairies. It "sets huge crops of seed almost annually and will naturalize readily, even in meadows of established grass." *L. formosum,* one of the rare late-blooming white lilies, grows 6 feet (1.8 m) tall and produces clusters of fragrant trumpets in August and September. It will survive zone-5 winters, but in colder places, gardeners should save seeds to replant outdoors early in spring. It blooms the first year from seed.

Lilies are generally grown from bulbs or plants, either of which can be planted in fall or spring. Most can tolerate freezing without harm. Plant them three times as deep as the height of the bulb or as deep as 1 foot (30 cm), because roots grow from the stem as well as the bulb. The Madonna lily (*L. candidum*) is an exception. It must be planted very shallowly in August or September, with just 1 inch (2.5 cm) of soil over the bulb. It prefers alkaline soil. Give lilies deep organic soil, but make sure it is well drained. A surrounding groundcover such as periwinkle or perennial oregano will help keep the bulbs cool, which they prefer. Give them plenty of space when planting—about 2 feet (60 cm) apart. They will soon create a clump that fills the spaces between. Deadhead flowers as they fade; otherwise, they set seed, which draws energy from the bulb. Pull out dead lily stems in fall.

Lilies are easy to divide almost anytime. Dig out entire sections of a clump, or plant stem bulblets, or bulbils (the aerial beads along the stems of some varieties), or scales (healthy outer sections of a bulb, similar to cloves of garlic). Scales can be rooted in plastic bags filled with damp peat moss or vermiculite, tied and kept in a warm place. Bulblets will grow on the scales and can be detached and planted.

Where conditions suit it, grape hyacinth will multiply to form a lovely low-lying carpet of color in spring.

Lilies are vulnerable to rot and fungus caused by wet soil or prolonged wet weather. Botrytis produces pinhole spots on the leaves, which enlarge to form patches and may destroy all foliage and flowers. Apply a spray of 1 teaspoon (5 mL) baking soda in 1 quart (1 L) water as a preventive measure or to limit the spread of the disease.

Muscari species
Grape hyacinth

Resembling tiny bunches of grapes held aloft on the tips of 4-to-6-inch (10-15 cm) stems, muscari is an excellent edging for a bed in sun or partial shade. Flowers bloom in early spring in shades of white, blue and purple. Foliage appears in late summer, then dies back. There are several species, and most spread fairly quickly.

Narcissus species
Daffodil, narcissus, jonquil

These spring bulbs—technically corms—are loved for their trumpets in shades of yellow, orange, pinkish and white. Aficionados divide them into 12 categories, including everything from the common daffodil (Division 1) through various shapes of narcissus whose trumpets (correctly, coronas) may be large or small. There are doubles, tiny *N. cyclamineus* cultivars, fragrant jonquils and a scattering of wild, or species, narcissus. A few, such as the paper-whites purchased for forcing indoors, are not winter-hardy, but most are—although they will not survive in soggy ground.

Where daffodils, or narcissus, are content, especially in acidic soil, they will form gradually widening clumps that can be easily divided after the foliage fades. They can even be coaxed to naturalize in grassy areas, provided the grass is not cut until the foliage fades, around mid-June. The best survival approach is to grow several types in different spots to find out what suits your own garden.

The narcissus bulb fly infests bulbs in some areas. The fly lays its eggs at the base of the foliage. When the eggs hatch, the grubs move into the soil and burrow into the bulbs to feed. In spring, the grubs emerge as flies. Covering the plants after they bloom with a fabric cover such as Reemay excludes the flies. Also, bulbs growing through a groundcover are less likely to be attacked; the flies prefer bare soil. The biological control BioSafe is also effective.

Some of the less common narcissus species have been harvested from the wild, endangering the natural supply. If you buy unusual narcissus, make sure they are labeled "cultivated."

Tulipa species
Tulip

There are tulips large and small for the dry garden. Some of the smaller species begin blooming soon after the snow melts, while the tall hybrids, especially the doubles, continue into early summer. A wide variety is available in all colors except blue. Like lilies and narcissus, tulips are grouped into several divisions.

Earliest to grow are the species, or botanical, tulips. Some of these are only about crocus height and begin to bloom soon after the hybrid crocuses. Hybrid tulips are labeled early, midseason and late. Midseason tulips, which bloom around mid-May in zone 4, include the Mendels and Triumphs. Later come the popular Darwins, some as tall as 2 feet (60 cm), the Cottage tulips, the Rembrandts, with their "broken" colors, the feathery Parrot tulips and, finally, the Double Late, or Peony-Flowered, tulips, which have so many petals that they scarcely look like tulips at all. In my garden, the white double 'Schoonord' is finished by July 1, closing the tulip season. Consider varieties with variegated foliage for more interest. 'Garant,' for instance, is a Darwin hybrid whose leaves have a yellow edge, and *T. greigii* and its cultivars have striped or mottled leaves.

Certain tulips are reliably perennial, provided the soil is very well drained. Tulips planted in my garden generations ago bloom every year, no matter what the weather, although the flowers are smaller than those of some of the new hybrids. On the other hand, many new hybrids I have planted died out after a winter or two. In trials at North Carolina State University, only about one-quarter

Certain tulips are reliably perennial, provided the soil is well drained. Others need frequent replacing.

of more than 100 cultivars proved to be perennial.

Among species and cultivars with a proven record as perennials are a host of small early tulips and several heirlooms, including the following:

T. fosteriana grows about 1 foot (30 cm) tall, with gray-green foliage and wide-open flowers. Dependable hybrids include 'Candela,' 'Red Emperor,' 'Orange Emperor,' 'Princeps' and 'Purissima.'

T. greigii is 10 to 12 inches (25-30 cm) tall, with large flowers and gray-green striped or mottled foliage. Dependable cultivars include 'Plaisir' and 'Red Riding Hood,' both more than a century old.

T. kaufmanniana (water-lily tulip) has starry flowers that resemble water lilies and open flat. Most are bicolored. Dependable cultivars include 'Giuseppe Verdi,' 'Heart's Delight,' 'Shakespeare,' 'Showwinner' and 'Stresa.'

T. praestans has been cultivated in Holland since the 1600s. It is tall, to 16 inches (40 cm),

Agapanthus will bloom in the northern summer but is too tender to spend the winter outdoors.

with abundant foliage and from one to four red cup-shaped flowers per stem.

T. tarda is a midseason bloomer whose bright yellow petals have white tips. It suits naturalized settings.

T. turkestanica has 8-inch (20 cm) stems bearing creamy white star-shaped flowers that are yellow-orange at the base.

Where squirrels are a problem, dip bulbs in bitter-tasting Ro-pel or another predator repellent before planting. Also, spray the planted area with the same substance, or sprinkle the ground with cayenne. Grow bulbs through a groundcover.

Tender Bulbs

Increasingly available from large nurseries in spring—or from mail-order specialists such as Jacques Amand (for bulbs) or Thompson & Morgan (for seeds)—the tender bulbs, corms or rhizomes are tropical or subtropical plants that need to be grown as annuals where winters are harsh

or overwintered indoors. A few are hardy only to zone 9, some to zone 7 or 8. They can be kept in large pots year-round and moved indoors after the first fall frost, or if grown in the garden, they should be cut back almost to the ground after a fall frost. Then carefully dig up the bulbs, let them dry, and dust them off before bringing them indoors.

These bulbs need to be overwintered in conditions that will prevent them from desiccating or rotting. They can be stored in cardboard cartons under layers of newspaper or buried in dry peat moss or vermiculite. The best storage temperature is above freezing but under 50 degrees F (10°C). They can go into the garden around the last spring frost date, but if you want a head start in spring, plant them in pots about a month before the last spring frost date, and fertilize with houseplant fertilizer. Many tender bulbs, such as begonias, callas and dahlias, need steady moisture, but the following are some of the better choices for dry places. They should be given full sun and well-drained soil.

Agapanthus umbellatus, or *A. africanus*, *A. orientalis* (blue lily of the Nile), has as many as 30 funnel flowers, usually blue, on a stem 3 feet (1 m) tall with straplike leaves. There are also white and pink forms. Agapanthus is drought-resistant enough to grow into weedy clumps along roadsides in hot places in zone 8. In the North, it needs a long season of hot sun to bloom and should be fed once a month and watered once a week or so. Grown permanently in a large pot, it will need repotting about every three years. The species *A. campanulatus*, recommended by Beth Chatto for dry gardens, is hardy to zone 7.

Alstroemeria aurantiaca (Peruvian lily) is a hardier yellow- or orange-flowered cousin of the alstroemeria favored by florists. It grows from thick tubers that must be handled carefully. In places colder than zone 7, they are best grown year-round in pots of compost. Mulch heavily in zone 6.

Crinum moorei has large 4-inch (10 cm) or wider pink or white flowers and strap-shaped leaves as long as 3 feet (1 m). *C. x powelli* is a *C. moorei* hybrid. They are both hardy to zone 7 with winter mulch.

Crocosmia species (montebretia) form graceful

Crocosmia *will overwinter with mulch in zones 6 and 7, but in colder areas, the corms must be wintered indoors.*

clumps of grassy foliage and 18-inch (45 cm) stems bearing orange, pink or red flowers. It will overwinter with mulch in zones 6 and 7.

Dietes vegeta, or *Moraea iridioides* (African iris, butterfly iris, Natal lily), resembles a 2-foot-tall (60 cm) iris whose white flowers are marked with purple. It grows from a corm. Zone 9.

Gladiolus species are best known as cut flowers. Hardy to zone 9, they are remarkably easy in the garden, although their thick stems usually settle into obtuse angles that look awkward. If I grow them at all, they are relegated to a back corner of the vegetable garden where I can cut them for a vase when needed. *G. callianthus*, or *Acidanthera murieliae* (butterfly flower, peacock orchid), is an elegant cousin whose white purple-centered flowers have an intoxicating fragrance. They grow as tall as 2 to 3 feet (60-90 cm). Offsets from either species can be wintered indoors and planted out in spring to grow into blooming size in about three years.

Rhodohypoxis baurii is a tender flower that can be bought in spring as a tuber or a potted plant. Plants grow just 4 inches (10 cm) tall, with grasslike leaves and dozens of small, starry white, pink or red flowers. Rhodohypoxis is a good candidate for a 2-to-4-inch (5-10 cm) pot or for the front of a border or rock garden in full sun.

Sparaxis tricolor (wandflower) has a broad fan of leaves at the base, with a 1-foot (30 cm) stem bearing funnel-shaped flowers in warm shades of yellow, orange and red, as well as white. J.L. Hudson recommends planting six corms to a 6-inch (15 cm) pot. This species should be watered while growing but allowed to bake dry after blooming. It is hardy to zone 8.

Perennials and Vines

◆ 5 ◆

"YOU MAY BE ONE OF THOSE PEOPLE WHO...CAN PICK OUT A PIECE OF
FURNITURE OR A PICTURE AND TAKE IT HOME KNOWING EXACTLY WHERE TO
PUT IT SO IT WILL LOOK LIKE AN HEIRLOOM. I TRY TO DO THIS WITH PLANTS.
THEY NEED A BACKGROUND, A MIDDLE GROUND AND A FOREGROUND. THERE
WILL BE STAR PERFORMERS, BUT THERE MUST BE A SUPPORTING CAST. ALL
WILL CONTRIBUTE TO THE SCENE, MAKING HIGHLIGHTS AND SHADOWS."

—Beth Chatto, *The Dry Garden*, 1978

The theater metaphor has often been used to describe a perennial garden. Look at it anytime from April to October, and you can easily pick out the stars from the supporting cast, although their roles keep changing. The dry garden has a somewhat lesser-known cast than you may be used to. Call it off-Broadway, if you like, or maybe Toronto rather than Hollywood. But these are long-term players that will keep the dry-summer, cold-winter garden blooming season after season.

Achillea species
Yarrow, milfoil, sneezeweed

Yarrows ranging from aggressive to unassuming deserve places in almost any garden, but it is where the soil is poor and dry that they take on star status, whether in full sun or partial shade. All have aromatic foliage, and most have long-lasting flat umbels of tiny flowers whose color fades as they age, so a single plant may have several colors at once. Common yarrow (*A. millefolium*) grows on prairie roadsides and into the mountains where little else will survive. It is one of the white-flow-

ered types, with flower stems as tall as 3 feet (1 m), and may be the toughest and pushiest of the lot. But some of its cultivars are tamer and bloom in beautiful shades of pink, rose and red. Other achillea species flower yellow or orange. The groundcover *A. tomentosa* is described on pages 49 and 50.

A landmark study of yarrows took place at the Chicago Botanic Garden from 1989 to 1993, when 42 species and cultivars were tested for ornamental value, ease of cultivation and distinctiveness. Another characteristic that was noted was the habit of flopping. Some cultivars flopped so badly that all the fallen stems had to be removed, leaving nothing but a patch of brown stubs and bits of leaves. The only species without sufficient cold hardiness for this book was *A. ageratum*, with an estimated hardiness rating of zone 7. Of the 42 types tested, here are the best 10:

A. 'Citronella' has creamy flowers that fade to grayish brown and last a full month on stems which usually stay upright. There is some repeat blooming.

A. 'Coronation Gold' bears dense clusters of large, long-lasting golden flowers on relaxed 3-foot (1 m) stems. It has silvery green foliage

While many achilleas bloom in the white to yellow palette, the flowers of Achillea millefolium *are pink, lilac or red.*

and a nonspreading habit. There is no repeat bloom.

A. 'Hoffnung' produces a solid mass of yellow flowers on spreading upright plants. Repeat bloom is good.

A. millefolium 'Lilac Beauty' and the similar 'Sawa Sawa' are the only two cultivars given the Chicago trial's top rating of "excellent." Both have upright stems and lavender flowers that fade to pink or white. 'Sawa Sawa' is the taller of the two, with darker flowers. Its stouter stems remain more erect than those of other cultivars.

A. millefolium 'Rosea' has large, loose clusters of reddish flowers and a better growing habit than the similar 'Nakuru' and 'Rosy Red.' The stems usually remain upright, and repeat blooming is good. In a different trial, the similar cultivar 'Fire King' was found to be one of the best perennials for long bloom, about 15 weeks from July to October.

A. 'Parker's Yellow' is similar to 'Coronation Gold,' although it differs in its greener foliage and greater height, about 4 feet (1.2 m).

A. 'Peach Blossom' produced the clearest pink flowers in the trial. It reblooms well, and the stems are mostly erect.

A. ptarmica 'The Pearl' was the best of the whites in the trial. This species is quite different from the others, with dark green foliage, relaxed stems and double pure white button flowers that are not borne in flat heads. The stems grow as tall as 3 feet (1 m), somewhat taller than most other types. 'The Pearl' can be invasive, but it blooms for a full six weeks in July and August and puts up with almost anything, even wet ground—although that encourages floppiness. It is easy from seed. Similar cultivars are 'Ballerina' and 'Perry's White.' Synonyms are 'Boule de Neige' and 'Schneeball.'

A. 'Snow Taler' produces bright white flowers for a full two months on stems that usually remain upright. There is little reblooming, but deadheading is not needed until late in the season.

Although a popular choice among gardeners because of its luminous pale yellow flowers, *A.* 'Moonshine' did not make the top-10 list because of occasional flopping.

All these achilleas, except for 'The Pearl,' must be purchased or grown from divisions or cuttings. Other species and cultivars can be grown easily from seed, but they did not rate as high and may be invasive or variable. It is important to note that since this trial concluded, additional excellent cultivars have come on the market. 'Fireland,' whose red flowers fade to gold, is one of these.

Set plants 18 to 24 inches (45-60 cm) apart, preferably in full sun and well-drained soil. By the second season, most should fill in the empty spaces. After three or four years, established clumps should be divided. Flowerheads fade soon after they bloom and turn brown or black; they should then be removed. In the Chicago trial, deadheading had little effect on encouraging repeat blooming. Stems of achillea can be cut in full flower for drying; hang them upside down in an airy place.

Fungal disease may strike achilleas, especially if plants are watered or fertilized. At Chicago, *A. ageratum* and *A. ptarmica* were the species most likely to suffer from powdery mildew.

Aconitum napellus
Monkshood, wolfsbane

One of the taller elements for the background of the dry garden, monkshood is a plant of ancient reputation that can reach 6 feet (1.8 m) or more and has deeply divided foliage, similar to that of delphiniums. It sends up spires of purple or bicolored flowers that resemble monks' hoods and are acutely poisonous. The tall, slender stems usually require staking. Flowers bloom in July and August. When flowering is over, remove stalks to the base before they turn black and ragged-looking. Monkshood is easy from seed or division. It is best planted in spring rather than fall.

Althaea species
Marshmallow

These eastern European cousins of hollyhocks (*A. rosea* or *Alcea rosea*) were favorites of the pioneers, not only because they produce a lavish crop of lovely silky flowers for weeks with almost no effort on the part of the gardener but also because they are entirely edible. The flowers still make lovely edible garnishes. Furthermore, the roots of *A. officinalis* have been used to make a soothing mucilaginous paste, *pâté de guimauve*, to treat coughs and sore throats. It bore little more than a textural resemblance to today's marshmallow confections. *A. taurinensis* (*A. armeniaca*) has showier rose-pink flowers and is somewhat taller, at about 4 feet (1.2 m), than the similar *A. officinalis*, whose flowers are usually white, although there are also pink and rose versions. Unlike other mallows, these plants have velvety leaves. Both species are hardy only to about zone 5 and may otherwise act as self-seeding annuals. They are easy from seed sown directly in the garden anytime in spring, in sun or partial shade.

Anemone patens (Pulsatilla patens)
Prairie crocus, pasqueflower

Not a crocus at all, although it blooms around the same time and is also suited to dry summers and to the front of the border, the prairie crocus is a native North American anemone that produces its flowers before its foliage—unlike the European anemones, which yield their foliage first (see page 70). Purplish blue flowers bloom in early spring on 6-inch (15 cm) stems. This species has a fibrous root system and thus needs more coddling than bulbous anemones, both at the outset and in transplanting. It is fairly difficult from seed, which should be kept fresh until sowing and may then need a winter to germinate. The soil for prairie crocus must be well drained, preferably sandy or gravelly, and in sun or partial shade. The common name pasqueflower is more accurately applied to a close relative, *Pulsatilla vulgaris* (see page 101).

Anthemis tinctoria
Golden marguerite, chamomile

This vigorous plant is valued for its tolerance of dry ground, where it produces attractive ferny foliage and several weeks of small yellow daisies on relaxed 2-foot (60 cm) stems in summer. It spreads well to fill empty areas while slower plants are gathering steam. Writing in the 1992 edition of *The Prairie Garden*, Ann Stacey of Manitoba calls this and *Salvia* x *superba* 'Rose Queen' the most dependable plants in her garden for rampant self-sowing. "I confess there are days when they weary me, but in our climate, it's rather nice to have such reliable, if unruly, performers." Cultivars include 'Kelwayi' and the smaller 'Grallagh Gold.'

Golden marguerite is easy from seed. Although it is sometimes called chamomile, it is not the herb grown for tea, *Matricaria chamomilla* (see page 133). The species *A. sancti-johannis* has orange flowers.

Aquilegia species
Columbine

Although columbines are natives of deciduous woods, they will tolerate dry ground, especially if they are given a little shade and lots of compost. One of my own, the native *A. canadensis*, with its distinctive red-and-yellow flowers, was rescued from a dry hayfield where it had somehow taken root—evidence of its tenaciousness. There are several additional species of columbine native to the North, and although they are not widely available as plants, they are not difficult from seed. *A. alpina*, for instance, is a small blue species. The cultivated varieties, most commonly the McKana hybrids, have larger flowers on taller stems, about 3 feet (1 m), in a wider color range. All columbines have beautiful, distinctive, deeply lobed bluish foliage.

Columbines are hardy perennials, but they tend to be short-lived, seldom reappearing for more than three years. It is not worth trying to divide them; it is better to buy new plants or seeds. Columbines often self-sow, but seedlings of hybrids may not look like the parent plant.

Armeria species
Thrift, sea pink

The common name, thrift, for *A. maritima* attests to the ease with which pieces of this low-growing perennial will root. From a cushion of thin, grassy leaves (often weeded out by mistake) grows a slender 1-foot-high (30 cm) or shorter stem bearing a 1-inch-wide (2.5 cm) pompom of pink or white petals in early summer. *A. juniperifolia* (Spanish thrift) is a 3-inch-tall (7.5 cm) version that is perfect for the spaces between patio stones or for other spots where it will be displayed well. Both armerias form neat, round cushions of foliage in well-drained soil in sun. Both are unhappy in shade or if crowded by other plants. They are easily grown from seed.

Asclepias tuberosa
Butterfly weed

Anything with "weed" in its common name should do well in stressful conditions, yet I have found butterfly weed as flighty as the first part of its common name. Once established, this milkweed cousin is tenacious in zone-4 or warmer gardens—it was one of the most successful perennials at the Xeriscape Demonstration Garden in Plainview, New York, after the 1995 drought—but it does not have the aggressive nature of many weedy plants. Also known as pleurisy root, a name that suggests its use as a medicine, the species has brilliant orange flowers in late summer. It is easy to grow from seed, although it may not flower for two or three years. Eventually, where it is content, it makes a large eye-catching clump of stems as tall as 3 feet (1 m). Butterfly weed emerges late in spring, so mark its spot with a label to prevent damage.

There are cultivars of butterfly weed, the most popular being the 'Gay Butterflies' mixture, in shades from yellow to red. All milkweeds attract monarch butterflies; they lay their eggs on milkweeds, and the larvae feed on the plants. Other butterflies are attracted to the flower nectar.

Baptisia species
False indigo, wild indigo

B. australis forms a pleasing clump, 3 to 4 feet (1-1.2 m) tall, of pealike foliage and intensely blue lupin flowers. It looks too exotic to be a low-maintenance perennial that puts up with poor soil in full sun, yet it was one of the most successful perennials during the 1995 drought at the Xeriscape Demonstration Garden in Plainview, New York. Discovered at the North Carolina Botanical Gardens, the cultivar 'Purple Smoke,' hardy to zone 4, has spires of violet flowers on dark-colored stems. The species *B. leucantha* is a white-flowering North American native. All baptisias resent transplanting, so situate them carefully from the start.

Boltonia asteroides
Boltonia

On thread-thin but upright branching stems as tall as 3 to 4 feet (1-1.2 m), boltonia has narrow, grayish leaves and flowers that are disproportionately small, only 1 inch (2.5 cm) wide, giving the plant a little of the airy quality of baby's-breath, although boltonia is more drought-resistant. The daisy flowers of the species are white or pinkish with a yellow center. You may want to stake it. Blooming begins in July and continues until fall.

Campanula persicifolia
Peach-leaved bellflower

Despite their pampered English-cottage-garden appearance, certain bellflowers are extremely tough. Some are described on page 52. Peach-leaved bellflower, too, will prevail in the driest ground. It has wiry but floppy 2-to-3-foot (60-90 cm) stems that need staking if you want them to do anything but lean. Nevertheless, the stems are strong and wind-resistant. They grow from a clump of basal foliage that is easily divided. The usual flowers are blue, but there is also a white version.

Carlina acaulis
Stemless thistle

This 5-inch-wide (13 cm) daisy with papery silver petals can be used in dried-flower arrangements. The large flowers, which bloom in late summer above a rosette of spiny, thistlelike 6-inch (15 cm) leaves, can apparently be eaten like artichokes. The variety *caulescens* has a 4-inch (10 cm) stem. Carlina grows in sun or partial shade, preferably in alkaline soil, and it is hardy to zone 4. It is easy from seed, but the seeds need light to germinate so must be scattered on the soil surface.

Cassia hebecarpa (Senna hebecarpa)
Wild senna

Many of the best plants for dry places are members of the pea family, Leguminosae. This North American native, which is suited to the back

Baptisia is a lupin relative that resents transplanting but is drought-tolerant once established.

of a sunny border, forms a shrubby mound of lacy dark green foliage that grows 3 to 5 feet (1-1.5 m) tall and almost as wide, topped with clusters of bright yellow pea flowers in summer. In a way, wild senna can be considered the yellow-flowered version of baptisia. Give it well-drained soil in sun or partial shade. It is hardy to about zone 4.

Centaurea species
Cornflower, bachelor's button, basketflower

There are both annual (see page 115) and perennial members of this sometimes weedy genus. The weediest, called knapweeds, are notorious invaders of pastureland. Basketflower, the common name for some centaureas, indicates a method of identifying all centaureas by the basketlike arrangement of sepals below the petals. The perennials are not commonly available from plant nurseries but are easy from seed sown directly in the garden in spring or in pots indoors. They will bloom the first year from seed and are hardy to zone 2 or 3.

Perfect for the dry garden, Shasta daisies are available in tall and dwarf selections that bloom from spring through summer.

C. dealbata (Persian cornflower) has purplish red flowers on 2-foot (60 cm) stems with grayish foliage. It blooms in early summer.

C. macrocephala (globe centaurea) has golden yellow flowers as wide as 4 inches (10 cm) on strong stems 3 to 4 feet (1-1.2 m) tall. English gardener Beth Chatto says that this beauty can be planted near trees and shrubs, as it is strong enough to compete with their roots.

C. montana (mountain bluet, perennial bachelor's button) resembles the common annual bachelor's button (*C. cyanus*), with flowers that are usually bright blue, although there are also whites and pinks. Stems grow 2 to 3 feet (60-90 cm) tall, topped by flowers in early summer and again later if the stems are cut back. Once established, *C. montana* will survive, like the annual form, in little more than dry sand. After a couple of years, it can be divided in spring.

C. scabiosa forms multiple branches 3 to 4 feet (1-1.2 m) tall, with large, purple flowers that resemble scabiosa.

C. uniflora nervosa is "one of my favorites," writes Kristl Walek of Gardens North, "with very long interest in the garden from bud to flower stage." It grows 1 to 2 feet (30-60 cm) tall and has feathery buds followed in summer by large, purple flowers.

Centranthus ruber
Red valerian

Much like valerian (see page 137) in leaf and flower shape, red valerian blooms in shades of white, pink and rose. The 1-to-3-foot (30-90 cm) stems are self-supporting. The flowers are fragrant and long-lasting, excellent for bouquets. It puts up with very dry soil and full sun, and although it is not known for its longevity, it often self-sows.

Chrysanthemum (Dendranthema) species
Chrysanthemum, Shasta daisy, pyrethrum

There are chrysanthemums and chrysanthemums. The oxeye daisies that decorate roadsides almost everywhere on the continent and are considered invasive weeds in most areas are at the opposite end of the plant spectrum from the fussy potted plants sold for Mother's Day. Then, too, there are the hardy fall-blooming chrysanthemums in every shade but blue that can survive northern winters. These are usually called garden chrysanthemums. No wonder taxonomists sometimes group garden species under a different genus name, *Dendranthema*. During the 1990s, however, *Chrysanthemum* was officially approved as the genus name for all the garden mums.

Although not necessarily the most drought-tolerant—again, there is a great variety of choices, some tougher than others—garden chrysanthemums are valued for their late bloom, September and October in most gardens. The plants build their strength during the hot, dry weather of summer, when they need only an occasional watering. They can be planted in full sun or a little shade. There are dwarf, medium and tall types, as well as different kinds of flowers, from the simple daisies that recall their wild forebears to complex pompoms, some with threadlike or spoon-shaped petals. In my own garden, an irrepressible and completely self-reliant chrysanthemum with pinkish purple flowers, its name unknown, came from the local horticultural society.

If you have any doubts about the hardiness of your garden chrysanthemums, mulch them heavily after the soil freezes. A safer way to overwinter marginally hardy chrysanthemums is to dig them up after the leaves and flowers have been killed by frost, taking a good-sized rootball, and store them in boxes in a garage or other unheated building. Water the soil about once a month. As the weather warms in spring, growth will begin and plants can be divided and planted out. Discard the older middle of the plant, and use the new shoots emerging around the edges. Water thoroughly after planting, and continue to water until new growth is evident. Plants can also be multiplied from rooted cuttings (see page 28).

When you order garden chrysanthemums by mail, you will receive rooted cuttings in spring. After the last spring frost date, plant them in fairly rich soil, and water them until growth resumes. Pinch the plants back at least once, starting when they are about 6 inches (15 cm) tall, to encourage bushiness. Stop pinching back in early July.

Additional chrysanthemum species include:

C. coccineum (painted daisy or pyrethrum) has wide early-summer daisies, usually pink or red but occasionally white, on 18-to-24-inch (45-60 cm) stems. The type of chrysanthemum used to make the insecticide pyrethrum, incidentally, is *C. cinerariifolium*, which is not winter-hardy in zone 5.

C. maximum (Shasta daisy) looks like a larger version of the common oxeye, with white-petaled yellow-centered daisies on stems that may be tall and floppy or short and stiff, depending on the cultivar and strain. Some bloom in June, while others don't begin until August. The larger the flowers, the more likely this species is to fade in dry weather and suffer in cold winters.

Coreopsis species
Coreopsis, tickseed

Eye-pleasing companions for the Shastas, these daisies are mostly sunny yellow with orange or yellow centers. They are easy, bloom for an extended period and are drought-resistant, making them suitable for poor soil. The following are all North American wildflowers and their cultivars:

C. grandiflora, with branching stems as tall as 3 feet (1 m), has bright yellow flowers with yellow centers. It is easy from seed. It should be staked.

C. rosea (pink-flowered coreopsis) has pink flowers but otherwise resembles 'Moonbeam' (see below), with a cloud of wiry 1-foot-tall (30 cm) stems holding small daisies. In moist soil, it is invasive, but in dry soil, it spreads slowly.

C. tripteris can grow twice as tall as *C. grandiflora*, with small, pale yellow daisies much like those of 'Moonbeam' (see next entry). Stems are self-supporting. It is easy from seed.

C. verticillata has wiry stems, small, narrow leaves and starry daisies that last for weeks. The best-known cultivars are 'Golden Shower,' 2 feet (60 cm) tall, with orange flowers; 'Zagreb,' similar but just half as tall; and 'Moonbeam,' the most famous of the lot, because it was Perennial Plant of the Year for 1992. Its 1-inch (2.5 cm) pale yellow daisies combine well with most other colors in the garden. It should be mulched in zone-3 or colder gardens. It is sterile, so it cannot be grown from seed, but once you have let the plant spread for a year or two, it is easy to divide in early spring or in fall. Because 'Moonbeam' is slow to appear in spring, you should mark its spot to avoid damage. Tip cuttings are also easy to root (see page 28) and are best taken before the plant begins blooming.

Crambe cordifolia
Heartleaf sea kale

This member of the mustard family needs plenty of space. It has huge kalelike leaves a little reminiscent of rhubarb, but bigger—about 5 feet (1.5 m) tall and 4 feet (1.2 m) wide. Give it a spot on its own, or grow it next to a pond, as Gardens North does near Ottawa, Ontario. It can take full sun or light shade but should be sheltered from strong winds. In summer, tiny white flowers bloom on stalks tall enough, at about 8 feet (2.4 m), to be broken by the wind. *C. cordifolia* and its vegetable-garden cousin *C. maritima* (sea kale) are easy from seed.

Dianthus species
Pink, carnation

The long-stemmed florist's carnations are far more delicate than the varieties that thrive in dry soil. Some dianthus species and hybrids are among the best perennials for parched alkaline ground, whether in sun or light shade. Most flowers are shades of pink, from light to shocking, pale to dark to purple, some bicolored. There are also whites. Look for the mat-forming groundcover types described on page 54. Also good are biennial sweet William (*D. barbatus*) selections and cultivars and their winter-hardy hybrids (*D. barbatus* x *chinensis*), some of which are biennial and some perennial. The Ideal and Telstar series, for instance, are advertised as annuals but act like short-lived perennials for me. They will bloom the first summer from seed.

The Festival series resembles the Ideals, but all are bicolors or picotees (petal edges are white). Floral Lace, a new series in 1995, with lacy-edged petals, has excellent heat tolerance and the habit of the Telstars. Stems are generally recumbent or curve upright. Other hardy and drought-tolerant dianthus species include:

D. 'Allwoodii Alpinus,' also called *D. alpinus* and *D.* x *allwoodii* (alpine pink), grows about 6 inches (15 cm) tall, with broad silver foliage.

D. amurensis (Amur pink) grows 1-foot (30 cm) tall, with 2-inch (5 cm) pink flowers that bloom for weeks. Because of its large flowers, this species is very showy.

D. 'Berry Burst' was chosen in 1996 as the best modern cultivar by The American Dianthus Society of Santa Fe. It grows 1 foot (30 cm) tall, with fragrant purplish pink flowers splashed with red. It is drought-resistant and hardy to zone 4.

D. carthusianorum (clusterhead pink), 2 to 3 feet (60-90 cm) tall, with grasslike foliage and clusters of small magenta flowers, is recommended for wildflower meadows.

D. gratianopolitanus (Cheddar pink) is an old-fashioned garden favorite that forms a cushion of grayish or bluish foliage with sweetly scented flowers on stems 8 to 12 inches (20-30 cm) tall. There are many cultivars.

D. plumarius (cottage pink) grows 6 to 18 inches (15-45 cm) high and has narrow gray foliage and fragrant flowers. There are many cultivars. 'Ursula Le Grove,' which has maroon-eyed white petals on 10-inch (25 cm) stems, was chosen as the best antique cultivar of 1996 by The American Dianthus Society. It is drought-tolerant and hardy to zone 4. Another award winner was 'Rose de Mai.'

D. superbus (superb pink), 1 to 3 feet (30-90 cm) tall, has feathery, fragrant lilac or rosy purple flowers. 'Rainbow Loveliness' is an American Dianthus Society winner.

Dianthuses are easy from seed. Although the usual procedure is to start them indoors in March, I have started seeds in pots outdoors in early summer and had plants in bloom from midsummer on. Dianthus plants can be multiplied by layering stems and keeping the buried stems moist until they root. Clump-formers can be divided after about three years.

Popular for its beauty as well as its medicinal attributes, echinacea is likely to spread by seed in gardens that suit it.

Dictamnus albus

Gas plant, burning bush

Both common names for this perennial come from the flammable gas given off by its flowers. Classy but dependable, gas plant forms a shrubby mound, eventually 3 feet (1 m) high and wide, of leathery, deep green lemon-scented foliage. It blooms in late spring or early summer, around the same time as peonies. Flowers bloom for two to three weeks, pure white on the species, pink on the variety *purpureus.*

Gas plant should be confined to a protected area out of strong winds and left in place, not moved around. Position it carefully in full sun and well-drained soil. It will take a year or so to become established, but once settled in, it is long-lived. Trim the flower stems back after blooming.

Echinacea species

Purple coneflower

Coneflowers are native North American plants long used medicinally by indigenous peoples. Again, these plants are as well known for their healing properties as for their beauty in the garden. The most common and tallest form, *E. purpurea,* is not especially drought-resistant. It survives high temperatures and full sun but wilts when the ground is parched, so it needs occasional watering during dry periods. Because of its unusual purple daisies on stems often taller than 3 feet (1 m), however, it is worth including in the dry perennial border. While the species is beautiful, with down-curved magenta petals and a protruding dark center, the cultivar 'Magnus' (also called 'Bravado' and 'Ovation'), Perennial Plant of the Year for 1998, is showier because the petals lie flat. 'White Swan,' 'White Luster' and 'Alba' are shorter, with white petals. 'Leuchtstern' ('Bright Star') is rose-pink.

E. angustifolia (western coneflower) is more drought-tolerant and is smaller, about 2 feet (60 cm), with slender foliage and narrow white, pink or rose-purple petals.

E. pallida is a taller pink-flowered form, to 40 inches (100 cm).

E. paradoxa has yellow flowers on 2-to-3-foot (60-90 cm) stems.

Echinacea is easy from seed and often self-sows, although it generally does not bloom until the second year. The roots and aboveground parts of all four species are used to make medicinal extracts and tinctures especially valued for strengthening the immune system.

Echinops ritro
Globe thistle

With its grayish, thorny foliage and distinctive, slate-blue metallic-looking spiny flowerheads, globe thistle should be represented in almost any sunny garden that has well-drained soil. Flower stems may grow as tall as 5 feet (1.5 m) above 3-foot (1 m) clumps of foliage. The flowers hold their color into September and can be used in dried arrangements. Echinops spreads by seed or underground rhizome, so situate it carefully. It can be used as an everlasting. There are additional echinops species for the adventurous gardener. All are easy from seed and may self-sow.

Epilobium species
Fireweed, willow herb

Fireweed, the towering rosy flower that seems to appear from nowhere to color parched ground after a forest fire, also frequently shows up in open meadows and on riverbanks in sun. It blooms in summer. The usual flower color is pink to reddish purple, and the flower shape is similar to that of the related evening primroses. *E. latifolium* grows to about 18 inches (45 cm). *E. dodonaei* has foliage resembling that of rosemary and dark pink flowers on 30-to-36-inch (75-90 cm) stems.

Erigeron species
Fleabane, Spanish daisy, blue-fringed daisy

E. canadensis is a North American native that grows on roadsides and has even become a noxious weed in Europe. Much like asters, the flowers are pink or lilac daisies. The toughness of this species is an indication of the drought tolerance of more desired species, such as *E. karvinskianus* 'Profusion,' a white-flowered 6-inch-tall (15 cm) type

The sunny-colored petals of gaillardia persist for weeks and are followed by attractive seedheads.

popular for pots and hanging baskets. It is hardy to zone 5.

E. compositus (alpine fleabane) grows just 4 inches (10 cm) tall and has silvery foliage and lavender flowers.

E. speciosus is the most common garden species. There are several cultivars, most about 2 feet (60 cm) tall, such as the Jewel series, 'Blue Beauty' and violet-blue 'Darkest of All.' They may need staking, especially if the soil is rich. Cut the flower stems back after blooming to promote a second flowering. They are hardy to zone 2.

Eryngium species
Sea holly

Sea holly, so named for its prickly, waxy holly-like leaves and love of sand dunes, has a thick taproot that enables it to survive in hot, dry, even salty soil. The unique spiny flowers are excellent for drying. The most common species, *E. alpinum* (alpine sea holly) and *E. giganteum* (Miss Willmott's ghost), have beautiful steel-blue flowers but are not the most drought-tolerant and need watering in dry weather. The former is a perennial to zone 4, the latter a self-seeding biennial. Better for the no-care dry bed is *E. amethystinum* (amethyst sea holly), which grows about 3 feet (1 m) tall and bears big crops of metallic-blue flowers in summer. It should be grown in well-drained soil in sun and is hardy to zone 2. Another good choice, equally hardy, is *E. planum* (blue sea holly), with smaller flowers. Unlike most drought-tolerant perennials, sea holly will also survive in wet ground.

Erysimum x allionii (Cheiranthus x allionii)
Siberian wallflower

There is some confusion between the genera *Erysimum* and *Cheiranthus* (see page 115), both members of the mustard family known as wallflower. Erysimum may be biennial or perennial, while cheiranthus is biennial or annual. Both generally have flowers in clusters, typically yellow or orange. There are several erysimum species for the garden, but some are tender perennials that must be grown as annuals in the North. Siberian wallflower, hardy to zone 3, generally produces a rosette of foliage in the first year and 1-foot (30 cm) stems of fragrant orange or yellow flowers in the second. Sown early in spring, however, it may bloom the first year, and it will self-sow.

Euphorbia species
Spurge, milkweed

There are euphorbias from tree size to prostrate, including the houseplants poinsettia and crown of thorns, all with distinctive, long-lasting colored bracts. Some euphorbias will grow in little but sand and so are among the best and most self-reliant members of the dry garden. A few are suited to the cooler parts of North America. All of these have foliage that is attractive all season, and all are easy from seed sown indoors in spring. They bloom in their second year. Be careful when pruning euphorbia, however, because its milky sap can blister skin.

E. corollata (flowering spurge) grows 3 feet

(1 m) tall, with pretty white bracts in summer and wine-red foliage in fall. Ambergate Gardens of Minnesota suggests this plant as an easy drought-tolerant alternative to baby's-breath.

E. griffithii, hardy to zone 2, forms a 2-to-3-foot-tall (60-90 cm) mound of green leaves with orange bracts. Most commonly available is 'Fireglow,' with bright orange bracts and fall coloring of yellow and red. It does well in good soil in partial shade.

E. myrsinites (donkey-tail spurge) forms a mound of reclining 6-inch (15 cm) burrow tails of waxy bluish leaves topped with greenish yellow flowers. It is hardy to zone 5.

E. polychroma (cushion spurge), hardy to zone 2, forms a 1-foot-tall (30 cm) mound covered with brilliant golden flowers in late spring. The green foliage turns reddish in fall.

Gaillardia species
Blanket flower

G. aristata grows wild along roadsides in the dry hills of central British Columbia and across the prairies, flaunting its Mexican-skirt flowers decorated with bands of dark orange and yellow. This is one of the most cheerful flowers for the dry, sunny garden, and blooming lasts several weeks. Seedheads the size of ping-pong balls are also appealing. Cultivars of *G.* x *grandiflora*—hybrids of *G. aristata* and the annual *G. pulchella*—are the usual perennial-garden choices, hardy to zone 2. Stems of taller cultivars, such as 'Burgundy' and 'Torchlight,' are 2 to 3 feet (60-90 cm) tall, and their 3-inch-wide (7.5 cm) flowers have raised brown centers. The smaller 'Goblin' grows about half as tall, although the flowers are just as big. 'Golden Goblin' has solid yellow petals.

Gaillardia does not divide well, but it may self-sow, and seedlings can be dug up and moved.

Gaura lindheimeri
Whirling butterflies, butterfly gaura

This native of the southern United States needs well-drained soil and thrives in sunny, droughty situations. The common name comes from the freely moving delicate white flowers tinged with pink. It has an unusually long season

In the author's garden, the flowers of Geranium *'Johnson's Blue' decorate their spot throughout the month of June.*

of bloom, from June to October. The leaves are gray-green, as are the self-supporting wiry stems, which grow about 3 feet (1 m) tall. It is hardy to about zone 5 but should be mulched in marginal winter areas. If it does not survive the winter, self-sown seedlings often keep it going. It is quite easy from seed sown indoors in spring.

Geranium species
Cranesbill

Many of the cranesbills, or hardy geraniums (not to be confused with the tender pelargoniums, also called geraniums), spread well enough to be classified as groundcovers, listed on page 56. Many others generally stay neatly in one place. All have beautiful deeply divided foliage that remains handsome throughout the season. Following are a few that are hardy and drought-tolerant:

G. cinereum, hardy to zone 5, forms a 4-to-6-inch (10-15 cm) mound of grayish foliage and large flowers on trailing stems. It needs well-drained soil and prefers full sun. Cultivars include

'Ballerina,' 'Lawrence Flatman' and 'Giuseppi.'

G. dalmaticum (Dalmatian cranesbill), hardy to zone 3, has glossy green leaves that form a 4-inch (10 cm) mound topped by beautiful pink flowers in late spring. The fall foliage is bright red.

G. 'Johnson's Blue' has long-blooming purplish blue flowers above green leaves. It forms a mound about 1 foot (30 cm) tall and twice as wide that is lovely at the front of a border. It is hardy to zone 2.

G. maculatum is a North American native that grows about 18 inches (45 cm) tall, with slightly hairy leaves and 1-inch-wide (2.5 cm) rosy to pink flowers. Fraser's Thimble Farms of British Columbia recommends this one for naturalizing in woodlands. It is hardy to about zone 4.

G. phaeum (mourning widow) grows 3 feet (1 m) tall, with reflexed maroon to purple flowers. Hardy to zone 3, it tolerates shady ground, whether moist or dry.

G. renardii has nubbly, grayish foliage different from the others. The flowers, which are white striped with purple, bloom in clusters. It is hardy to zone 4.

Geraniums have long, beaked fruits (hence the name cranesbill) that split suddenly when ripe to fling out their seeds. Seedlings may crop up in unexpected places. If you intend to gather the seeds, check the plants frequently to collect the pods before they burst. Germination can be slow and erratic. Some seeds must be stratified—given a period of cold in moisture—to sprout.

Gypsophila paniculata
Baby's-breath

Fragile though it may appear, with its thread-thin stems and sprays of tiny white or pink flowers, this florist's favorite can put up with dry soil so well that it is a pest of the dunes around the Great Lakes. As its genus name suggests, it is a lover of gypsum—in other words, alkaline soil. It is less tolerant of acidic ground and soggy winters and springs. The species has small single white flowers on 3-foot (1 m) stems and can be grown from seed. 'Bristol Fairy' has double white flowers. 'Pink Fairy' is the double pink form. 'Rosy Veil,' or 'Rosenschlier,' grows 18 inches (45 cm) tall, with pinkish flowers, as does 'Viette's Dwarf.' In the garden, baby's-breath looks best when squeezed between other plants, much the way it's used in bridal bouquets. Its stems are too fragile for it to stand on its own. It resents being moved or divided. The creeping form is *G. repens.*

Helianthemum nummularium
(H. mutabile)
Rock rose, sun rose

Helianthemum can be considered a perennial, an annual, a modestly spreading groundcover or a shrub, depending on where and how you garden and what species you choose. No matter how long-lived it is, this is one of the loveliest and most distinctive small flowers for the dry garden. *H. nummularium* is most dependable in places colder than zone 6, although it demands well-drained soil, preferably alkaline, for survival and does best in full sun. Flowers that resemble single or double roses in shades of white, yellow, orange, pink or red bloom on stems 1 foot (30 cm) or so tall. The flowers begin blooming in June and continue sporadically through the summer. Helianthemum forms a gradually spreading mat as the stems root where they touch the ground. It is evergreen, so it needs protection in and beyond zone 4 but does well where there is a good snow cover.

Helianthemum can be difficult to find as a plant, but it is easy to grow from seed started eight weeks early indoors. Set the plants outdoors while they are still small, as large plants do not transplant easily. Other species and hybrids can be worth growing as annuals in colder places. A winter mulch and a cover of evergreen boughs may bring them through the winter.

Helianthus species
Sunflower, Jerusalem artichoke

The best-known sunflowers are the annuals described on page 120. Most of the perennials prefer moist ground, but one that will grow almost anywhere is *H. tuberosus* (Jerusalem artichoke), which is a sunflower above the ground and a perennial root crop underground. It is one of the few vegetables native to North America. Jerusalem artichoke easily survives neglect; in fact, it shows its familiarity with this climate by claiming the status of weed in many areas. On the plus side are its crop of edible tubers, tasting vaguely like artichoke, and its summer bounty of 4-inch (10 cm) yellow sunflowers on stems 3 to 9 feet (1-2.7 m) tall.

Jerusalem artichoke rarely reproduces by seed—more often by strongly spreading rhizomes. Plants will grow from almost any piece of rhizome or tuber left in the ground after the plants are tilled.

If Jerusalem artichoke becomes too much of a good thing, the Ontario Ministry of Agriculture recommends tilling it several times during the season—spading would do in a small plot. Then remove or mow the top growth frequently, starting in May. There are a couple of related species, also tolerant of drought, that lack the edible tubers.

Heliopsis helianthoides scabra (H. scabra)
Sunflower heliopsis, false sunflower

Heliopsis is shrubbier than sunflowers, about 3 feet (1 m) tall, with several stems and bright green leaves. It tends to slump; either let it grow that way, to form a mound of flowers, or stake it. The 2-inch (5 cm) golden daisies with yellow centers are borne steadily throughout summer and into fall. The most common cultivar is the golden semidouble 'Summer Sun.' Heliopsis seeds can be sown directly in the spring garden. Choose a sunny spot with well-drained soil. Divide plants every two or three years to keep them blooming. It is hardy to about zone 3.

Hesperis matronalis
Dame's rocket, sweet rocket

This wild form of phlox is a common sight along field edges and roadsides in eastern Canada and the United States in early June. It has fragrant flowers that bloom white through light to dark pink on spires about 3 feet (1 m) tall. A lover of dry, alkaline soil, it will survive almost anywhere and is invasive in some areas, spreading gradually by seed and sometimes acting like a biennial. It is easy to grow from seed and hardy to zone 2.

Iris species
Iris, flag

Old-fashioned bearded irises (*I. germanica*) will survive for many years in neglected farmyard gardens, a testament to their toughness. Their flowers are only about half the size of some of the modern hybrids, but they don't need staking. The usual colors are yellow, cream, brown and blue, sometimes bicolored. Newer selections—there are hundreds—may have flowers as big as an outstretched hand, in shades of pink, rose, burgundy and brown, bicolored and plain, ruffled and lacy. Stems may reach 3 feet (1 m), making them vulnerable to toppling in heavy rains or strong winds unless they are staked. Dwarf varieties 10 to 15 inches (25-38 cm) tall and the even smaller miniatures do not require staking. For all of them, blooming may last little more than a week if the weather is hot, but the fanlike foliage persists until late summer, gradually turning browner and more ragged. Grow bearded irises behind something that will camouflage the foliage late in the season, as it should not be cut back until it has yellowed.

Plant bearded irises in late summer or early

fall in loamy soil in full sun or a little shade. Dig a shallow hole wide enough to accommodate the roots, then prepare a mound of soil in the middle and arrange the roots so that they extend out and downward. Fill in the hole with soil so that the tops of the rhizomes are slightly exposed. Water thoroughly after planting, and continue to water whenever the soil is dry until growth commences. When dividing irises, which should be done about every three years to keep clumps from becoming overcrowded, discard any unproductive or damaged rhizomes, and make sure each piece of planted rhizome has an eye, the spot from which leaves emerge.

If you are growing large-flowered hybrids or if you garden in a place with harsh winters, cover the rhizomes with a 4-inch (10 cm) mulch as soon as the ground freezes. Plants often bloom the first year after planting and certainly by the second year, unless conditions are wrong. Deadhead spent flowers, and remove the stems when all blooming has finished.

The iris borer, the larva of a small gray moth, may invade bearded iris rhizomes, leaving them perforated and hollow. Eggs laid on bearded iris foliage in fall overwinter to hatch in spring, then the larvae tunnel down into the rhizomes. The larvae may carry fungal spores that cause rhizome rotting and plant death. To combat iris borers, BioSafe—a liquid containing beneficial nematodes—can be applied over the rhizomes when the soil is moist and has warmed to 55 degrees F (13°C) in late spring. Water the soil after the application.

Not troubled by iris borers and tougher in many other ways are irises with attractive grassy foliage, especially *I. sibirica* (Siberian iris). The blooming period may be even briefer than that of bearded irises, but the flowers are delicate and lovely. Siberian irises thrive in damp sites, where they may grow taller than 4 feet (1.2 m), but they will survive in dry places too, although they will not grow as tall. As they become more popular, the Siberians are appearing in a wider range of colors, including purple, blue, white and pink. All bloom in late spring or early summer, about the same time as the bearded types, and are very hardy. Elaine

The bearded iris has a larger flower than the Siberian iris (see page 78), which is valued for its long-lasting foliage.

Peek of Peek's Perennials in Edson, Alberta (zone 2), says that not all Siberian irises do well for her, but she recommends the Sino-Siberian hybrid 'Puget Polka,' "dainty but drought-tolerant," and the Siberian cultivars 'Augury,' with pink-lavender flowers, and 'Sparkling Rose,' red-violet.

Plant Siberian irises in fall in full sun or some shade. Divide them every three or four years, because the crown gradually widens, leaving an empty spot in the center of the plant. Dig down with a spade and remove sections in spring when the leaves appear.

Jasione perennis
Shepherd's bit

This small edging perennial forms a mat of grassy leaves and produces 18-inch (45 cm) flower stems topped with 2-inch (5 cm) light blue flower balls in summer. Give it sun or partial shade in well-drained acidic soil. It is easy to divide in spring or fall but can also be grown from seed. One supplier suggests growing it alongside heathers.

Knautia macedonica
Crimson scabious

On the sandy south-facing slope of the zone-3 alpine garden at the Devonian Botanic Garden near Edmonton, Alberta, *K. macedonica*—also known as *Scabiosa macedonica* and often confused with *K. lyrophylla* (*S. lyrophylla*)—displays its flat, purple scabiouslike flowers in midsummer. The thin stems are about 2 feet (60 cm) tall, although Thompson & Morgan says that they can grow to twice that height. 'Melton Pastels,' a Thompson & Morgan cultivar, blooms in shades of pink, mauve, salmon and crimson. Plants form low clumps of deep green leaves. Flowers bloom on wiry stems the second year from seed, starting in late spring and continuing for weeks. Knautia may self-seed and perform as a biennial. Give it full sun or a little shade.

Lewisia species
Lewisia

These relatives of portulaca have similar fleshy foliage and love similar conditions: well-drained,

Liatris spicata 'Kobold' won the highest praise in a trial of liatris species and cultivars in Chicago in the early 1990s.

even sandy, acidic soil and no winter sogginess, although the lewisias appreciate moisture when their foliage and buds are developing in spring. They go dormant and disappear during summer, so they should be treated much like spring bulbs, with their spot camouflaged by later foliage. Flowers bloom in the white through pink to red range. *L. rediviva*, known as bitterroot because the roots were eaten by the indigenous peoples, is a low-growing plant with 1-inch (2.5 cm) pink flowers. It prefers full sun. *L. tweedyi* has pink flowers that are twice as large, so it is the usual garden choice. It is evergreen and should be given some shade.

Liatris species
Gayfeather, blazing star

Like goldenrod and rudbeckia, liatris is a North American wildflower that was accepted into European gardens before it was considered worth cultivating in its home territory. There are about 40 species, although most are not yet available to gardeners. The garden selections, excellent for cutting and widely used in the florist industry, attract butterflies and bees. All bloom in late summer, when many other perennials have finished. Another distinction is their habit of blooming from the tip down. Give all of them well-drained soil in full sun. They are very drought-tolerant, but most will also survive in moist, well-drained ground, although too much winter wetness can kill them. All varieties are susceptible to powdery mildew.

In a four-year comparison of 21 liatris species and cultivars at the Chicago Botanic Garden, zone 5, the top rating of "excellent" went to only two varieties: the mauve-purple *L. spicata* cultivars 'Kobold' and 'Floristan Violet.' Both grow about 2 feet (60 cm) tall, although 'Kobold' is the taller of the two. Both received the top rating because of their uniformity, erect stems, robustness, floral quality and length of time in bloom. The next highest rating, "good," went to the white-flowered *L. spicata* cultivars 'Alba' and creamy 'Floristan White.' Both grow 3 to 4 feet (1-1.2 m) tall. *L. spicata* is easy from seed. Also rated "good" were:

L. callilepis and *L. pycnostachya*, both rose-purple. The former is about 2 feet (60 cm) tall; the latter grows very tall, up to 5 feet (1.5 m).

L. pycnostachya 'Alexander,' bright lavender, and 'Alba,' white. This species is native to moist prairies and woodlands, so it is less drought-tolerant than the dry-ground native *L. spicata* but therefore less likely to suffer winterkill from wet ground. The prairie natives *L. ligulistylis* (meadow blazing star), which was not included in the trial, and *L. punctata* (dotted blazing star), judged "fair" in the trial, are also good garden plants for dry places but will die in wet ground.

Limonium latifolium
Sea lavender

This unusual plant, named for its ability to grow on sandy beaches, produces a rosette of leathery, dark green leaves out of which emerge slender 2-foot-tall (60 cm) stems holding clouds of delicate violet-blue flowers resembling baby's-breath. Sea lavender has a long taproot, so it resents being moved and is difficult to divide. It is easy from seed, however. Give it well-drained soil in full sun. It is hardy to about zone 2.

Linum species
Flowering flax

Sky-blue flowers on graceful stems that move with every breeze are the hallmark of *L. perenne*, one of the best perennials to fill the spaces between other things, in the manner of baby's-breath, although these flowers are much larger. Stems grow about 18 inches (45 cm) tall, covered base to tip with slender gray-green leaves and topped with flat, blue 1-inch (2.5 cm) flowers that continue to open for weeks. There are also dwarf and white-flowered forms. Although listed as a perennial to zone 2, flowering flax resents wet winters, so the roots may not survive. However, it generally drops enough seeds to ensure a crop of seedlings for next year's flowers, provided you do not weed them out. While small, these can be moved into preferred positions, either in full sun or partial shade. Flowering flax is easy from seed, which can be scattered directly on the garden soil in early spring.

L. flavum 'Compactum' grows 1 foot (30 cm) tall, with bell-shaped yellow flowers and dark green foliage. It is less hardy, to about zone 5.

Lupinus hybrids
Lupin

Lupins sometimes establish a colony sustained by self-sowing where they are happy—that is, in well-drained acidic soil, where they can grow big and healthy, even in mostly sand. Lupins have become naturalized along roadsides in the Atlantic Provinces and northern Ontario. Cool spring weather suits them, and they prefer to grow in peace and not be moved. Lupins bloom in late spring to early summer, then should be camouflaged behind showier plants while they fade. The 3-foot (1 m) Russell hybrids bloom in shades of yellow, blue, pink, rose, white and bicolors.

Lychnis species
Campion

Four-petaled "cross" flowers, generally in shades of red through orange, have inspired the common names of several of these perennials, such as Maltese or Jerusalem cross. Catchfly, another common name, refers to stems that are sticky enough to trap small insects. There are several species and cultivars. The following are drought-tolerant and hardy to at least zone 3. All are easy from seed, which can be scattered in the spring garden.

L. alpina (arctic campion) forms a 4-inch-tall (10 cm) clump of slender gray leaves. The flowers are bright pink. Although short-lived, it often self-sows.

L. coronaria (rose campion) has rigid, gray 2-foot (60 cm) stems holding bright magenta flowers. Before it flowers, the plant forms a clump of downy leaves that look much like lamb's ears. It may act as a biennial, dropping enough seeds each year to keep itself going. There are also white and bicolored forms.

L. 'Dancing Ladies' is a silver-leaved release with violet, pink and white flowers first year from seed.

L. flos-jovis (Jove's flower) is similar to rose campion, but the leaves are lance-shaped and the flowers deep pink.

L. miqueliana, although difficult to find, is an impressive Japanese species with purplish foliage and bright red flowers. It grows about 8 inches (20 cm) tall and self-sows. It tolerates dry ground but may go dormant in summer's heat.

L. viscaria (German catchfly) is as tall as 3 feet (1 m), with purple or bright magenta flowers borne singly on 18-inch (45 cm) stems. There are also white and dwarf forms.

Lysimachia species
Loosestrife

Purple loosestrife (*Lythrum salicaria*), an invader of wetlands in large areas of North America, has given a bad name to all loosestrifes, but several cousins are still approved for gardens, although they, too, can be domineering. Both yellow loosestrife (*Lysimachia punctata*) and gooseneck loosestrife (*Lysimachia clethroides*) are aggressive plants that spread quickly by underground stolons, but they have the virtues of dependability and beauty that endeared them to pioneer gardeners. The former forms a clump of stout vertical stems about 2 feet (60 cm) tall, topped with a spire of bright yellow flowers in early summer. The latter grows 3 feet (1 m) tall, with lovely swanlike, tapered white inflorescences from summer till fall. Both prefer moist soil but are tough enough to weather weeks of drought with nice-looking foliage and pretty flowers in sun or partial shade. They are hardy to zone 2. Don't use them in mixed borders with modest plants, however, as they will crowd them out. These plants need a spot on their own, perhaps surrounded by lawn or paving.

Malva moschata
Musk mallow

This native of Europe and North Africa has become naturalized in some parts of North America, a sure sign of a plant that survives neglect. It is self-supporting, about 2 feet (60 cm) tall, with silky pink or white flowers. It has become naturalized in some places and easily renews itself by self-seeding. Mallow quickly forms a deep taproot that enables it to grow rapidly and survive dry weather but makes it difficult to transplant. Sow directly outdoors, or transplant when young, then leave the plants in place. Most self-sow in any case, and seedlings can be left to grow or weeded out.

Oenothera species
Evening primrose, sundrop

This genus for the dry garden has many members, of which there are two groups: day-blooming sundrops and evening-blooming evening primroses. Best known in the North and the most widely available from nurseries, although not especially drought-tolerant, is *O. tetragona* (*O. fruticosa*), a day-bloomer hardy to zone 4 and usually misnamed evening primrose. Its brilliant yellow flowers bloom for about six weeks, from June to August, on 1-foot (30 cm) red stems. It will wilt if dry weather lasts for more than a week or so but, even if left unwatered, will generally recover when the rains return. It forms a gradually spreading groundcover with new rosettes that can be removed for propagation. All are easy from seed.

O. biennis (common evening primrose) can grow as tall as 6 feet (1.8 m) and produces hairy foliage and fragrant, pale yellow flowers that bloom in the evening. This species often self-sows.

O. missouriensis (Ozark sundrop) is a sprawling plant with 3-inch (7.5 cm) bright yellow flowers. It is very drought-tolerant and blooms all summer.

O. speciosa (showy primrose), hardy to zone 5, has 2-foot (60 cm) stems topped with pink flowers that bloom by day. It spreads by underground runner, so it is invasive and should be given a spot on its own. It blooms for about six weeks in May and June and will self-sow.

Opuntia species
Cactus, prickly pear

The direction "do not water" in a package of mail-order opuntias is the gardener's first indication that cacti are not like other plants. My shipment also brought the typed warning: "We suggest using barbecue tongs to unpack and handle *Opuntia*." True enough; the merest brush against these long spines is painful.

Plants exclusive to the western hemisphere, cacti were unknown in Europe and Asia before Europeans arrived in America. Taken back to Europe, these odd plants caused a sensation and were given the Greek name *kaktos*, meaning cardoon or thistle. In his *Herbal* of 1597, John Gerard described "Thistle of Peru": "It doth much resemble a fig in shape and bignesse, but so full of sharpe and venomous prickles, that whosoever had one of them in his throat, doubtlesse it would send him packing either to heaven or to hell."

Cacti are supremely adapted to drought. The stem—the body of the cactus—is enlarged to hold water. It shrinks and withers after prolonged dry periods or in overly wet ground but stretches out full, like a balloon, when the plant is again content. The leaves are reduced to mere thorns or hairs that do not lose precious water and, at the same time, help shade and protect the stem. The skin is leathery or waxy, the sap thick or milky. The root system is usually fibrous and shallow to take advantage of rainfall over as wide an area as possible. All cacti have unique structures called aureoles on their stems and branches. The aureole has two buds: the lower usually makes spines; the upper produces new branches or flowers.

Some species of prickly pear cactus are remarkably cold-hardy, but they demand soil that is perfectly drained.

Northerners generally think of cacti as houseplants, but there are a few species hardy to temperatures as low as minus 40 degrees F (−40°C). What these hardy types have in common with their frost-tender kin is the need for full sun and perfectly drained soil, preferably sandy. Rotting is a greater danger than drying out. Cacti of the genus *Opuntia*, the prickly pears—also called bunny ears, beaver tails, cactus pears and Indian figs—are the best-known hardy types. These have stems flattened into large pads with smooth skin and prickles that can be formidable. Deceptively soft-looking fuzzy patches are covered with stickers called glochids, which easily penetrate the skin but can be scraped off with a sharp knife. Pads can produce several flowers apiece, and each flower yields one fruit called a prickly pear. The fruit of all species is edible and high in ascorbic acid, but only a few are tasty and sweet. If you want to try them, scrape off the glochids, then, using tongs, twist the fruit from the pad to avoid tearing the plant. It can be eaten either raw or cooked. The sap from the pads can also be applied topically to

sooth burns and cuts, much like aloe vera, and is used in some areas as a mosquito repellent.

Cacti gradually spread by growing new pads from the edges of the old, like cartoon mouse ears. It is easy to multiply plants from pads that are at least six months old. Using tongs and a knife, slice off a pad where it joins the parent, set it in a dry, sunny place for a couple of weeks to form a callus, then insert the callused end about 1 inch (2.5 cm) deep in sandy soil, holding the pad upright with stones or toothpicks. Do not water it for about a month. Space plants 6 to 12 inches (15-30 cm) apart.

Cacti are best treated as conversation pieces in the garden. Keep them away from passing hands and feet and from competition from grasses or plants that might shade them. One of the best ways to show off cacti is in a small area of sand or gritty soil in a rock garden or in large terra-cotta pots or containers with drainage holes. Pots should be at least 2 feet (60 cm) wide to accommodate the plants. Purchase special cactus mix, which is available in garden stores, or mix your own soil

A gift from generations past, this sweetly perfumed unidentified herbaceous peony still blooms every year for the author.

with 20 to 50 percent sand. Be sure to keep the pot weeded, but otherwise, do nothing; cacti need little or no fertilizer—at most, a small amount once in spring. A mulch of gravel or stone chips will help reflect heat and light onto the plants. In zone-5 or colder gardens, overwinter cacti in a protected place near a south-facing wall where cold winds will not damage them.

Opuntias often wither or turn limp in winter, looking as though they are at death's door. This happens because they eliminate water from their cells to prevent damage from freezing. Some varieties also lie close to the ground to escape winter winds. In spring, pads lying on the soil may root. Flower buds then develop and open in June or July.

Cacti grown as houseplants can move outdoors for the summer too, but like any other plant, they need hardening off between moves indoors and out. Put them in shade at first, and of course, bring them back indoors if frost threatens. Prolonged temperatures of 41 degrees F (5°C) or colder can damage many indoor species.

Paeonia species
Peony

Peonies look far too lush for dry gardens, yet they are among the toughest of plants, capable of surviving considerable neglect. Some of the ones I inherited, planted beside a dusty driveway, untended for years and infested with weedy grasses, bloomed every spring. This is the herbaceous peony (*P. lactiflora*), the type that dies back to the ground in winter. Another hardy type, although not nearly as tough, is the tree peony (*P. suffruticosa*, *P. moutan*), which retains a woody stem where winters are sufficiently warm. Rarer and quite different in appearance are the yellow-flowered *P. mlokosewitschii* and the fernleaf peony (*P. tenuifolia*), which has early bright red flowers and does not like really dry soil, where it grows slowly. There are also hybrids of herbaceous and tree peonies, sometimes called Ito hybrids.

The easiest peony for dry gardens is *P. lactiflora*. Fortunately, limiting yourself to herbaceous peonies hardly limits the range of possibilities.

From heirlooms to hybrids, fragrant doubles—some with flowers as big as cabbages—to graceful singles, in shades from white and pink through red and purple, there is a herbaceous peony for every garden, provided it is given well-drained soil. The most common reason herbaceous peonies fail to bloom is too much water at their roots. The flowers bloom for a couple of weeks in spring, and the attractive foliage lasts until late fall, when it turns rusty red before it blackens.

Cut the flower stems back when blooming is finished, but leave the foliage in place to help collect snow in winter. Cut the dead stems back in early spring before the new growth appears. A week or so after the buds appear, surround the young stems with a tomato cage or a circle of sticks and twine—it will be camouflaged as the plant grows—to support the flower stems later. Peony flowers, especially the doubles, are so heavy that they may bow to the ground after a rain. All are excellent cut flowers. Cut just before the buds open, and they will last for weeks in a cool room.

Peonies are often grown as specimen plants, but they look best in midborder surrounded by other plants. Give them full sun or a little shade in well-drained soil. The growing point, or eye, should be no more than 2 inches (5 cm) below the surface. Once established, they resent dividing or moving and may take a couple of years to revive. They spread very slowly and can be left in place indefinitely. If you do want to divide a herbaceous peony, take a piece with at least three eyes from a well-established plant soon after it sprouts in spring.

Papaver species
Poppy

There are both annual and perennial poppies for the dry garden. All have short-lived flowers with silky petals in the crystal colors of a stained-glass window. The color palette is warm, from cream and yellow through pink, orange and red. Stems are slender but do not need staking. All poppies are similar, too, in their dislike of being transplanted; but all are easy from seed. The best plan is to sow seeds in fall directly where the plants will grow. Most poppies also spread by self-seeding.

The showiest of the perennials, *P. orientale* (Oriental poppy), is also one of the toughest. It may grow taller than 3 feet (1 m) and is fabulous during its brief late-spring season of bloom. Like the peony, however, its huge pink or white flowers often fall victim to heavy spring rains and gusty winds. The foliage dies back by midsummer, leaving a gap in the garden that should be camouflaged with bedding annuals or a screen of more durable perennials. Division or moving is best done during dormancy in late summer. If you dig close to the crown and leave some lateral roots in the soil, both the crown and the remaining roots may develop into flowering plants.

P. nudicaule (Iceland poppy) is a lovely but short-lived perennial about 1 foot (30 cm) tall. It does best where summers are cool, as its common name suggests, and in hotter places, it may wait for the arrival of cool fall weather to bloom.

Many small species, known collectively as alpine poppies, are suitable for a rock garden or the front of a dry border.

Penstemon species
Penstemon, beardtongue

Just a decade ago, penstemons were largely the property of garden connoisseurs, but with the ranking of 'Husker Red' as Perennial Plant of the Year for 1996, the genus hit the garden mainstream in a big way. Now, the durability and variability of penstemons have brought them to the forefront of home gardening, especially in areas that are subjected to droughts. There are hundreds of species native to rocky slopes and semidesert regions of North and Central America, and it has been estimated that 75 percent of them will do fine in unimproved clay soil with little water, summer temperatures as hot as 100 degrees F (38°C) and winters as cold as minus 40 degrees (−40°C) with no snow cover. Most penstemons do best in full sun in well-drained soil, even sand or gravel. There are evergreen species, but the hardiest types die back to the ground in winter.

Their kinship to foxgloves and snapdragons is evident in the shape of the flower, which often has a hairy throat or lip; hence the common name beardtongue. Most bloom in shades of blue, lilac, pink and scarlet, but there are also whites and yellows. Heights vary from creepers to 6 feet (1.8 m) tall. They may bloom in spring or summer. They are short-lived perennials but can be renewed every few years if the gardener takes cuttings (see page 28) or grows new plants from seed. The named cultivars must be grown from cuttings or divisions. Among the best drought-tolerant penstemons, hardy to about zone 3 except where noted, are:

P. angustifolius produces 1-foot-tall (30 cm) stems with blue flowers in late spring.

P. caryi, a 1-foot-tall (30 cm) spring bloomer, with blue flowers and glossy green foliage.

P. cyananthus, with blue flowers in late spring, similar to *P. caryi*.

P. digitalis, named for its resemblance to the flowers of foxglove (*Digitalis*). Perennial Plant of the Year for 1996 was 'Husker Red,' released from the University of Nebraska. It grows 30 inches (75 cm) tall, with green foliage burnished with bronze and masses of white flowers in July and August. 'Albus' is a taller form. Both will flower in light shade.

P. fruticosus 'Purple Haze,' native to British Columbia, forms a mound of mauve flowers as tall as 2 feet (60 cm). Zone 4.

P. nitidus (shining or smooth penstemon) has blue flowers in early spring on 10-inch (25 cm) stalks above a rosette of fleshy leaves.

P. ovatus (broadleaf penstemon), 3 feet (1 m) tall, with pale blue flowers in June.

P. palmeri, as tall as 7 feet (2 m), with pinkish or white flowers in late spring over a 1-foot-wide (30 cm) clump of leaves.

P. 'Prairie Fire,' from the University of Nebraska, grows 2 feet (60 cm) tall. Its bright red flowers, like small lipsticks, attract hummingbirds.

P. strictus (Rocky Mountain penstemon), 2 feet (60 cm) tall, with purple-blue flowers in spikes over evergreen foliage.

Perovskia atriplicifolia
Russian sage

Russian sage was named Perennial Plant of the Year for 1995 by the Perennial Plant Association because of its long season of attractiveness and its

The variegated form of Polygonatum odoratum *is an excellent foliage filler in the author's garden.*

adaptability to most conditions, especially heat and drought. It requires well-drained soil and is best in full sun. This is not a showy plant, however. Gardeners who grow Russian sage, attracted by all its advance publicity, are sometimes disappointed by a modest gray-green plant with small flowerheads in summer.

What Russian sage can provide is a background for midborder. This native of Afghanistan and Tibet can grow as tall as 4 feet (1.2 m), with self-supporting stems soft enough to bend attractively in light breezes. The finely divided leaves smell of sage when crushed. The long flower spikes, blue to lavender, may bloom from July until September. The foliage persists through winter, although stems should be cut back to the ground in spring when new growth begins.

There are several cultivars. 'Blue Mist' is the earliest to flower and has pale blossoms, as does 'Blue Haze.' 'Blue Spire' has deep purple flowers. 'Longin' has stiff, upright stems. 'Filigran' is more compact, about 2 feet (60 cm) tall, with deeply cut foliage and bright blue flowers. All can be easily propagated from tip cuttings taken in early summer (see page 28).

Petrorhagia saxifraga
Tunic flower

Sometimes called tunica, this unusual perennial for the front of a border or a rock garden forms a low mound of tiny green foliage about 6 inches (15 cm) high. On the tips of wiry stems, little pink or white flowers that resemble pinks bloom in summer and form an airy mass. Give it well-drained soil in sun. It is easy from seed and can be divided in spring.

Platycodon grandiflorus
Balloon flower

Beautiful in every way, this elegant perennial forms a 2-foot-tall (60 cm) clump of graceful stems with shiny gray-green leaves. From early until late summer, the buds swell into spherical balloons that pop open into 2-inch (5 cm) or larger single flowers. The species is blue, but there are also white, pale pink and purple cultivars. Give balloon flower well-drained soil in full or part sun. It is well suited to the middle of the perennial border. Mark the plant's spot, as it is late to emerge in spring and thus can be easily damaged with early cultivating. Balloon flower is difficult to divide and may resent transplanting. It is best planted in spring. There is a dwarf form, about half as tall.

Polygonatum odoratum
Solomon's seal

Solomon's seal is a plant for moist woodlands, yet it looks splendid all summer in a sunny, dry border, where it persists while other plants wilt around it. The variegated form, with white-edged green leaves, is especially beautiful all season and excellent in flower arrangements. Arching stems ascend about 2 feet (60 cm) and are decorated with small, white dangling bells in late spring. It spreads slowly by underground rhizome and is easy to divide and move but can be difficult to get rid of, so situate it carefully. Give it sun or partial shade.

Pulsatilla vulgaris (Anemone pulsatilla)
Pasqueflower

This British wildflower, hardy to zone 5, is sometimes called prairie crocus, although it is not a crocus—nor is another plant more commonly called prairie crocus, *Anemone patens* (see page 81). An early-spring bloomer, pasqueflower cheers up the garden with feathery foliage and large 2-to-3-inch (5-7.5 cm) saucer-shaped flowers that are usually blue to violet-purple, although there are also white, bluish white, pink and red cultivars. Graceful, airy seedheads follow. Pasqueflower needs well-drained soil in full sun and will naturalize where it is content. A slightly hardier species, but difficult to find except as seed, is *P. alpina sulphurea*, with fernlike foliage and wide yellow flowers later in spring. Plants resent transplanting.

Ratibida species
Coneflower, Mexican hat

This prairie wildflower has only begun to make its way into home gardens. Its delightful small daisies, with their long conical centers, bloom on and off from late spring to early fall in dry soil. *R. columnifera* (Mexican hat) has recurved petals that make it look like a floppy Mexican hat. Petals may be all yellow or red tipped with yellow. Curving, slender stems grow as tall as 3 feet (1 m). J.L. Hudson (see Sources) says that the flowers and leaves were once made into tea by the Dakotas. *R. pinnata* (yellow coneflower) can grow as tall as 5 feet (1.5 m), with larger leaves than *R. columnifera* and yellow flowers. Both species are easy from seed and will bloom the first year. They should be given full sun or a little shade. They may self-sow.

Rudbeckia species
Black-eyed Susan

There are annual, biennial and perennial types of rudbeckia suitable for the no-care garden. All have daisy flowers with green to black centers and yellow to orange rays. Flowering takes place from mid-July until fall. Some rudbeckias like moist soil, such as *R. nitida* (usually 'Herbstonne,' 'Autumn Glory' and 'Viette's Little Suzy') and *R. laciniata* (one variety, the heirloom 'Golden Glow,' grows 6 feet/1.8 m tall). Although in the Chicago Botanic Garden's four-year evaluation of 10 perennial types, *R. fulgida sullivantii* 'Goldsturm' was rated best, it, too, requires regular watering. Other rudbeckias, however, are superlative for dry places.

R. hirta (gloriosa daisy) generally acts as a self-seeding annual or biennial but may also be perennial. Flowers bloom in shades of reddish brown, gold, yellow and bicolors. It is easy from seed, which can be scattered directly in the spring garden. It grows about 2 feet (60 cm) tall and needs watering only after a week or so of hot, dry weather.

R. maxima is given a high rating by Kristl Walek of Gardens North, near Ottawa, Ontario. It grows about 8 feet (2.4 m) tall and is "fabulous with ornamental grasses. I have planted it in spots where no other tall plant would remain standing because of strong winds. Prefers full sun and tolerates a wide range of wet or dry soils. Easy from seed."

R. triloba (three-lobed coneflower) has bright yellow flowers in late summer. The winner of the 1997 Georgia gold medal for herbaceous perennials, it is tolerant of drought, heat and pests. It grows about 3 feet (1 m) tall.

Ruellia strepens
Wild petunia

This little-known North American wildflower, native as far north as Pennsylvania and Wisconsin, is not, as the common name suggests, a petunia at all but a member of the acanthus family. It does best in dry, sandy soil or anyplace with excellent drainage and puts up with sun or shade, rewarding the gardener with blue flowers all summer on prostrate plants that look best on a rock wall or at a border's edge. Stems grow 1 to 3 feet (30-90 cm) long. It self-sows freely, and seedlings are easily removed where they are not wanted. Other species of ruellia are becoming more common in seed catalogs, and although some are not cold-hardy, all are worth a try in the dry garden.

Salvia species
Salvia, sage

There are both annual and perennial forms of salvia in great number. Some of the annuals are described on pages 124 and 125, and kitchen sage is described on page 135. Most have flowers in the spectrum of pink and rose through lilac to blue, light or dark. Salvias can be grown in full sun or light shade but do best out of strong wind. Many self-sow, ensuring a crop of flowers even if the plants do not survive the winter. Leave some flower spikes for seeds, but otherwise, trim them off after flowering to encourage more flowers.

S. x *superba* (*S. nemorosa*) has deep blue, purple or pink flowers on 18-to-30-inch (45-75 cm) spikes that do not need staking and may retain their color for as long as 12 weeks. Cultivars include dark purple 'Lubeca,' violet-purple 'East Friesland' ('Ostfriesland'), medium purple 'Rose Queen' ('Rosakonig'), pale blue 'Blue Hill' ('Blauhugel') and white 'Snow Hill' ('Schneehugel'). 'East Friesland' was one of the most outstanding survivors of the 1995 drought at the Xeriscape Demonstration Garden in Plainview, New York. *S.* x *superba* cannot be grown from seed but must be grown from a cutting or a rooted plant. It is one of the most cold-hardy salvias, to about zone 3 if grown in well-drained soil and mulched. 'May Night' ('Mainacht'), which blooms almost steadily from June until September, is the Perennial Plant Association's Perennial Plant of the Year for 1997. It has dark blue flower spikes 2½ feet (75 cm) tall.

S. verticillata 'Purple Rain' (lilac sage) is hardy to zone 5 and has 18-inch (45 cm) arching spires of smoky purple flowers over a rosette of fuzzy green foliage.

Santolina chamaecyparissus
Cotton lavender

Santolina is hardy only to zone 6, although it may survive mild winters in colder zones if the soil is well drained. Its value in the garden is that it forms an airy shrub of eye-catching, fragrant, silver-blue foliage. Only 12 to 18 inches (30-45 cm) tall, it can be clipped to edge a herb garden, a perennial border or a pathway. In places where it does not survive winter, it can be grown as a bedding annual in the manner of dusty miller and other gray-foliage plants.

Sedum species

Stonecrop

Most garden sedums are spreaders—these are listed as groundcovers on pages 61 to 63—but there are a few upright and reclining forms for the perennial border or for dry containers. All bloom in late summer, contributing to what is often a sparse time in the garden. Cut stems for a vase just as the flowers begin to open, and they will bloom indoors for weeks. *S. spectabile* will eventually root in the vase water; others do so less frequently. Rooted stems can be planted out in spring. Clumps eventually die out in the center but are easy to renew with divisions taken from the edge.

S. alboroseum 'Medio-variegatum' has a confusing list of names, including *S. spectabile* 'Variegatum' and *S. spectabile aureum*, but is easy to identify. It is much like the well-known 'Autumn Jo,' but a little smaller, with variegated white-and-green foliage that contributes to the plant's interest all season and makes it a perfect candidate for a large container. It forms a clump about 1 foot (30 cm) tall and has pale pink flowers. Give it some shade.

S. spectabile 'Autumn Joy' ('Herbstfreude') is an upright plant, about 1 foot (30 cm) tall, crowned with long-lasting rose or dark pink flowers from late summer to fall. Buds begin to color pink in August and remain bright until October.

S. telephium 'Atropurpureum' has dark purple foliage on stems about 2 feet (60 cm) tall. Flowers are pink. 'Hester' is also upright, with large, shiny purple-and-green leaves and pink flowers.

Several hybrids also offer variously colored foliage. All have an extended bloom time, generally starting in late August and continuing for about a month, until the flowers finally turn brown and can be snipped off. 'Bertram Anderson' has 8-inch (20 cm) stems of deep purple foliage and bright red flowers. 'Mohrchen' is dark bronze-red, with pink flowers on stems 18 to 24 inches (45-60 cm) tall. 'Vera Jameson' forms a neat 1-foot-high (30 cm) clump of maroon-and-green leaves topped by medium pink flowers. 'Ruby Glow' is similar but only 6 inches (15 cm) tall, with gray foliage and pink flowers. 'Sunset Clouds' is recumbent, with pink stems, bluish green foliage and bright pink flowers.

Upright forms of sedum for late-summer bloom include 'Vera Jameson' (foreground) and 'Hester' (background).

Solidago species

Goldenrod

Considered one of the most unappealing weeds in its native North America and burdened with an unwarranted reputation for triggering allergies—the culprit is more often ragweed—goldenrod is prized as one of the most beautiful perennials in Europe, where many cultivars have been developed, including 'Crown of Rays,' 'Lemore' and 'Praecox.' Wild goldenrod can be invasive, but the cultivars are not. Goldenrod is valued for its hardiness, drought tolerance and flowers that bloom from late summer to fall. Usually golden, the flowers have been hybridized into pale yellow as well. Unfortunately, many varieties suffer from mildew and rust, although the *S. rugosa* cultivar 'Fireworks' is disease-resistant. It grows 3 feet (1 m) tall and is hardy to zone 4. Goldenrods were among the most outstanding plants during the 1995 drought at the Xeriscape Demonstration Garden in Plainview, New York.

Tradescantia x andersoniana (T. virginiana)
Spiderwort

A real trouper, spiderwort hangs in there when other plants fail—in wet ground or dry. In this way, it is similar to many other monocots, such as lilies and daylilies, all plants with grasslike foliage and weather-resistant root systems. In the driest weather, tradescantia stops blooming, but its foliage remains decent-looking, and the blooming that stopped in early summer may resume with the cooler fall weather. The three-petaled triangular flowers are distinctive and may be purple, blue, red, pink or white. Stems grow 18 to 36 inches (45-90 cm), all slightly shorter in drier soil. If it grows tall, it may need staking. Where it is content, tradescantia spreads quickly enough to need dividing every two years. It is too invasive to grow alongside modest plants.

Verbascum species
Mullein

Mullein is best known for the weedy *V. thapsus*, but many species and cultivars are appearing on the North American garden scene. All tolerate poor conditions, and once established, some will survive extreme drought and wind. The best garden species and the cultivated varieties stay in flower longer than the wild species, and they bloom in the familiar yellow as well as white, pink, purple, rose and orange. A rosette of foliage, usually downy, forms at the base, then the self-supporting flower spike grows up above it, sometimes taller than 10 feet (3 m). Verbascums are excellent at the back of a sunny border or along a fence. Some are easy from seed, but hybrids such as the rose-colored 'Pink Domino' and 'Cotswold Queen' must be grown vegetatively. These and *V. phoeniceum* (purple mullein), which has white or purple flowers, prefer some moisture in the soil. The following are drought-tolerant and hardy to zone 3 or 4:

V. blattaria (moth mullein) grows 1 to 3 feet (30-90 cm) tall, with green foliage and white, pink or yellow flower spikes.

V. bombyciferum (giant silver mullein, Turkish mullein) is one of the most spectacular, as tall as 6 feet (1.8 m), with felted leaves and yellow flowers.

V. chaixii produces slender 3-foot-tall (1 m) spikes of small yellow flowers. The white version is 'Album.' It often self-sows.

V. nigrum grows 4 feet (1.2 m) tall and has dark green leaves and branching spikes of yellow flowers with brown centers. 'Album' is the white-flowered version.

V. olympicum (Olympic mullein) has grayish foliage and bright yellow flowers. It can grow taller than 6 feet (1.8 m).

Veronica species
Speedwell

Veronica, available in several species and cultivars, is one of the best sources of the color blue in the dry garden, although there are also pink, rose and white selections. There are small and tall types—creepers are described on page 65—all with attractive foliage and spikes of flowers. The taller types may need staking. Some are easy from seed.

V. allionii (alpine speedwell), hardy to zone 2, grows 6 inches (15 cm) tall, with 1-foot (30 cm) spikes of violet flowers in summer.

V. daubneyi (pink speedwell) is similar, with pink flowers and bright green leaves.

V. longifolia is easy from seed and, at 2 to 4 feet (60-120 cm), a good height for the back of the border, with blue or white flowers until fall frosts.

V. spicata (spike speedwell) is the type most often available. The flower spikes of the species grow 1 to 2 feet (30-60 cm) tall, but there are compact types as well. 'Goodness Grows,' which originated at a Georgia nursery of that name, has deep blue flowers from May until October and is now considered one of the best varieties. 'Sunny Border Blue,' Perennial Plant of the Year for 1993, has 2-foot (60 cm) spikes of dark blue flowers from June until frost. The foliage is bright green. 'Icicle' has white flowers and gray foliage.

Veronicastrum virginicum
Culver's root

This North American native is a dramatic showpiece of prairie-restoration gardens, with its 4-to-6-foot (1.2-1.8 m) spires of white or pale

The three-petaled tradescantia's roots are so persistent that the plant can be somewhat invasive, even in dry ground.

lavender flower spikes above whorled dark green leaves. Culver's root is suited to the back of a dry border in sun; it is easy in any well-drained soil and does not need staking.

Yucca species
Adam's needle

About 30 species of yucca are native to North and South America. Like the agaves of the New World and the aloes of the Old, they form spiky rosettes of fleshy leaves, lending the dry garden the look of the Wild West. The leaves may grow as tall as 6 feet (1.8 m). In early summer, a long flower stalk topped by white or violet-tinted bell flowers emerges from the center of the rosette of a mature plant. Yuccas are easy from seed, but it may be several years before they form a sizable clump. They enjoy heat and perfectly drained soil and should be mulched in winter. The young plants and their flowers are edible. Most species are frost-tender, but the following are hardy to about zone 4:

Y. filamentosa (*Y. smalliana*), known as Adam's needle, has slender 30-inch (75 cm) leaves whose margins have long, curly threads (straight threads indicate a similar species, *Y. flaccida*).

Y. glauca (*Y. angustifolia*), called Spanish bayonet or soapweed, has even narrower, sword-shaped 2-foot (60 cm) leaves, with pale margins and fine filaments along the edge.

Vines
All vines can be tattered by strong winds, so grow them in a sheltered place, preferably with the root run shaded by rocks or perennials and the tops in sunshine. Perennial vines that can be considered for the dry garden include the following:

Celastrus scandens (bittersweet) has shiny, waxy green leaves on shoots that rapidly grow to a height of 10 feet (3 m) or so. Stems quickly grow straight up, twining their way through a support, so if you want this plant to cover a trellis, it must be coaxed to grow more horizontally. It can overwhelm nearby plants and should be pruned heavily. It is hardy to zone 2. The females produce

Small-flowered clematises, including 'Blue Bird' and 'White Swan,' thrive in an unwatered garden in central Ontario.

decorative crimson berries, but a male is needed for pollination.

Clematis species. The large-flowered species and hybrids need regular watering, but there are smaller-flowered species, such as *C. alpina, C. macropetala, C. paniculata* and *C. serratifolia,* that survive in dry soil, although all need occasional watering. *C. serratifolia,* incidentally, spreads by rhizomes and can thus be somewhat weedy. Many of the species sometimes self-sow. Clematises are divided into three groups according to their pruning needs, and most of the above-mentioned species belong to group two: The year after they are planted, group-two clematises should be cut back very early in spring to just above the lowest pair of strong, healthy buds. A year later, cut back the main shoots to half their height. Every summer thereafter, cut back all stems that flowered that year to nearly their base. If the vines become too tangled, they can be cut back almost to the ground, but always prune back to just above a pair of healthy buds. All clematises need training

as the vines grow. After the flowers fade, lovely silky seedheads remain decorative until winter.

Humulus species (hops) are aggressive, fast-growing twiners. Among the hardiest cultivars of *H. lupulus*—the plant that gives characteristic flavor to lagers and ales and grows 12 to 20 feet (3.7-6 m)—are 'Cascade,' bred at Oregon State University and hardy to zone 4, and the even hardier 'Old Early Cluster,' or 'Old Cluster,' brought to North America by European settlers. 'Tettnang,' a German type favored for lagers, is hardy to about zone 5. The cultivar 'Aureus' (golden hop) should be kept out of full sun to prevent scorching but is otherwise hardy and dependable, with beautiful golden foliage on 10-foot (3 m) stems. *H. japonicus* (Japanese hops) is an ornamental species, also about 10 feet (3 m). The variety 'Variegatus' has green leaves splashed and spotted with white. It is neither as hardy nor as tall as the species. Hops spread underground and can be invasive. In cold places, they die back to the ground in winter. The stems quickly grow vertically, so you must train them sideways if you want them to cover a trellis.

Hydrangea petiolaris (climbing hydrangea) can take a couple of years to start growing, but then it puts up with considerable dryness, especially if the soil is acidic. Its shiny green leaves and white summer flowers can cloak almost any wall beautifully. It climbs as high as 30 feet (9 m) or more by aerial holdfasts that can cling to a vertical surface.

Lathyrus latifolius (perennial sweet pea), hardy to zone 3, climbs by tendrils to a height of about 9 feet (2.7 m). It does best in part shade and appreciates a loamy soil. Flowers are white or pink.

Lonicera x *brownii* 'Dropmore Scarlet Trumpet,' a vining honeysuckle hardy to zone 2b, bears orange-scarlet flowers from June to November. A selection from Dropmore, Manitoba, it was one of the varieties found to be aphid-resistant at North Dakota State University.

Parthenocissus species. These green-leaved clinging plants are ivy substitutes for climates too severe for the real thing. Especially hardy is *P. quinquefolia* (Virginia creeper), which was judged one of the best perennial climbing plants by the Devonian Botanic Garden, near Edmonton, Alberta. *P. tricuspidata* (Boston ivy) is a little more refined and a bit more demanding of good soil. There are several cultivars. Both species cling to walls with holdfasts.

Polygonum aubertii (silver fleece vine) is fast-growing, to about 20 feet (6 m), and will overwhelm neighboring plants where it is content. The foliage is bright green. Lacy flowers appear in large masses in summer. It should be pruned severely at the end of the season. Hardy to zone 5.

Rosa species. See pages 151 to 153.

Vitis species (grape). Grapes grown for fresh eating or wine need regular watering, but wild grapes, such as *V. riparia*, will stay green in dry soil and can grow into a weedy tangle unless they are severely and frequently pruned. Although wild grape needs to be given something to hang onto, it can be used to clothe a television aerial or telephone pole.

BEGINNING STRATEGIES

The object in a perennial bed is to have plants just touching or slightly overlapping, but the first year after they are planted, perennials may not bloom at all, and it could be three or four years before you have a satisfying clump. In the beginning, there will be tiny plants here and there with gaping spaces between. It makes sense, in the first year or two, to fill these spaces with annuals that will give the border an overall impression of completeness, even though those plants may not be there again the following season. What works best in this role is a long-acting annual that stays fairly low, such as coleus or Virginia stocks for partial shade and portulaca or dusty miller for sun. Toward the back of the border, choose tall-growing annual daisies,

These high-reaching Shasta daisies make a perfect back-of-border selection.

bachelor's button, cosmos or whatever you prefer.

If you find that when the perennials do start to bloom or grow larger, they are growing in the wrong places, make a note to move them in the fall or the following spring. It is best not to disturb them in summer.

Vegetables and Annual Flowers

6

"WATCHING THE ENTIRE PROCESS OF SEED GERMINATION UNFOLD WITHIN
A MATTER OF DAYS IS ONE OF THE AWE-INSPIRING EVENTS TO WHICH
ONLY PLANTS-PEOPLE ARE PRIVY."

—Brian Capon, *Botany for Gardeners*, 1990

If you plant seeds in your garden or start seeds indoors, chances are fairly good that you are growing annuals. To call a plant an annual is to define it by its brief life span— from seed to maturity in one growing season. Such rapid growth means that annual plants are relatively desperate for all the necessities of life, including water. Roots don't have much time to reach for underground moisture, so annuals are often the first plants in the garden to wilt in a hot wind and the first to die after a few dry days. The annuals that continue to look perky under these conditions have developed such tactics as quickly descending taproots and fuzzy hairs which shade foliage.

Vegetables

Almost all the common garden vegetables are either true annuals or biennials or tender perennials grown as annuals. The few that are hardy perennials —asparagus, rhubarb, Jerusalem artichoke—are among the most dependable vegetables for dry gardens because they are able to take advantage of the wet ground of early spring. There are a couple of lesser-known perennial vegetables. One is sea kale (*Crambe maritima*), which is especially drought-tolerant, with edible young shoots that are generally blanched under pots and beautiful big leaves ornamental enough for a flowerbed. Another is Good King Henry (*Chenopodium bonus-henricus*), which produces a huge crop of somewhat spinach-like spring greens and edible seeds on stems sometimes taller than 9 feet (2.7 m).

But the vegetables almost everyone wants to grow are more demanding of water and care. The National Gardening Association estimates the following season-long water requirements for vegetables:
- 9 inches (23 cm): spinach and leaf lettuce
- 12 inches (30 cm): cabbage family
- 18 inches (45 cm): cucumbers, onions, pole beans, beets, carrots, eggplants, peas, peppers, squashes, muskmelons, sweet potatoes
- 24 inches (60 cm): tomatoes
- 25 to 30 inches (64-75 cm): potatoes, celery

Although vegetables require adequate water throughout their growth and a soil-moisture deficiency at any time will reduce yield or quality or both, there are certain critical growth stages that are most susceptible to water stress. The Nova

Unless they receive 18 inches (45 cm) of water during the growing season, beets may become pale and woody.

Scotia Department of Agriculture and Marketing has published the following list of vegetables and their critical period for watering:

- Asparagus during fern growth.
- Beans and peas during flowering and pod-setting.
- Broccoli and cabbage during head formation and enlargement.
- Carrots and radishes during root enlargement.
- Cauliflower throughout the season.
- Celery during all hot periods.
- Sweet corn during tasseling, silking and ear-filling.
- Cucumbers, eggplants, melons, squashes, pumpkins and tomatoes during flowering and fruit development.
- Head lettuce during head development.
- Onions during bulb formation and enlargement.
- Peppers after they have been transplanted

and during fruit-setting and development.

- Watermelons from blossoming to harvest.

The general rule for the vegetable garden is that it needs 1 inch (2.5 cm) of water per week, which translates into 64 gallons (240 L) per 100 square feet (9.3 m^2). This general rule is only a guideline, however. A vegetable garden will survive with considerably less, provided it is mulched, the soil is high in organic matter and spot-watering is done on certain plants at their neediest times.

Too little water at critical growth periods can mean undersized plants, fallen blossoms, fallen fruit or small, tough, bitter-tasting fruit. Vegetables with edible stems, such as celery, and vegetables with edible leaves, such as lettuce, are also best if they are juicy, which means thoroughly watered. Deprived of water, onions and radishes become hot and ornery, potatoes develop hollow hearts, and beets, radishes and carrots are small, pale and woody.

All this may mean that if your garden is dry and apt to be neglected, you will be better off buying vegetables from the supermarket or at a pick-your-own farm. But if you have any water at all —enough, at any rate, to get seedlings under way early in the season and to water sporadically—you can grow most vegetables. You probably have at least one thing going for you: Dry gardens are often sunny gardens, and most vegetables thrive in sun. Desert areas like California's Imperial Valley are among the most productive places for vegetables, provided the ground is irrigated.

Vegetables From Seeds

Vegetables grown from seeds sown in the garden, including carrots, radishes, beets, peas, beans, sweet corn and perhaps cucumbers, squashes and cabbages and their relatives, should, if the weather allows, be seeded while the ground is still holding some spring moisture. Don't plant too early, however. Frost-hardy vegetables should not go in until the soil is workable—when you squeeze a handful of soil and release it, it should fall apart and water should not ooze out between your fingers. Frost-tender vegetables should not be planted until after the last average spring frost date for your area.

If the soil is already dry at seeding time, water

the rows thoroughly before sowing, sow the seeds, press soil over them and water them in. Water every couple of days if there is no rain; drying out at germination time will kill the emerging roots. Seeds can be kept damp until they germinate if seeded rows are covered with boards or black plastic, but you must check daily for sprouting and remove the covering as soon as there are signs of life. Once the seedlings are tall enough, they can be mulched. Most seed-grown crops develop deep roots quickly and are able to fend for themselves during all but the driest weather, especially if you have given them a windbreak and can do some spot-watering during very dry weather.

Vegetables From Transplants

Long-season tender plants, such as tomatoes and peppers, are best grown from transplants, whether purchased or homegrown. Many other vegetables, too, can be purchased as transplants or started indoors, where they can be coddled until they are almost at the blossoming stage and the weather is warm enough for planting out. Any blossoms that appear before planting are best pinched off.

Water the hole where the transplant will grow before you set it in the ground. Plant it at the height it was growing in its pot (except for tomatoes, which can be planted much deeper), and make a dish shape in the soil directly around the stem to hold water. Then water again, preferably using water that is approximately the same temperature as the air. Boards or leafy twigs set into the ground on the sunny side of the transplants will give them a little shade for their first week or so.

No Raised Beds

While raised beds can be attractive and easy to tend, they are not practical for vegetables in a dry

---

SAVING SEEDS

The most common annuals and vegetables can be purchased as transplants in spring, but if you want to grow anything unusual, you will have to obtain seeds. You seldom need all the seeds in a packet, but because almost all seeds last for more than a year, you can save the leftovers. Some seeds that should be purchased fresh every year are members of the onion genus (*Allium*) and of the dill family (Umbelliferae), which includes carrots, dill and several other herbs. Many daisy seeds do not last for more than a year either.

To store leftover seeds, write the year of purchase on the packet, tape it shut, and keep the packet in a closed glass jar or cookie tin in a dry, cool, dark place such as a basement cupboard.

Many annual flowers self-sow, but where their seedlings appear is at the whim of nature. If you prefer to choose where they grow, you can deadhead all the flowers before they go to seed

The gardener must grow unusual plants such as globe artichokes from seed.

and save a few seedheads for your own supply. Make sure these seeds have fully dried, either on the flower or on a cookie sheet, before storing them the same way as purchased seeds. A few petals or bits of leaf in with the seeds will not hurt germination.

The saved seeds of hybrid flowers and vegetables may not grow into plants exactly like the parent, but if you are willing to take a chance, growing them can be an interesting adventure. Flower seeds, even those that are not hybrid, do not always reproduce the color of the parent but may, instead, recall the color of a former generation.

Vegetable-garden beds should be flat rather than raised, and the soil should be improved with compost.

garden, because raised beds quickly dry out. Instead, vegetables should grow in flat or slightly hilled ground, in soil improved with as much compost as possible and mulched about 4 inches (10 cm) deep as soon as the plants are tall enough, usually early June, and preferably after a good rain or watering.

In a small garden, the ring method, in which plants are grown in a circle around a central cage filled with compost, helps concentrate water and nutrients in one spot. Watering is done into the compost reservoir.

Make sure you walk only in pathways, even if these are nothing more than indentations in the soil between beds of vegetables. Leave the area directly around the plants untrampled; loose soil aids root growth and holds water better.

Also, keep up with weeding, because weeds can grow faster than vegetables and are good at grabbing whatever water is available. When you pull out weeds, leave them in the pathways as extra

mulch. Remember, too, that some common garden weeds, including purslane, lamb's-quarters, pigweed and nettle, are drought-tolerant and as edible as lettuce or spinach.

Flowers

Among the flowers best suited to drought survival are the hardy annuals that self-sow. Their seeds remain dormant in the winter garden, awaiting their favored germination temperature, then sprout while the soil is still damp. Their roots are already deep in the soil by the time it begins to dry out. Sowing these seeds anytime between fall and early spring has the same effect as self-sowing.

Among the flowers to try are annual species and varieties of *Anthemis, Antirrhinum, Argemone, Calendula, Calliopsis, Centaurea, Cleome, Consolida, Coreopsis, Cynoglossum, Dianthus, Eschscholzia, Gaillardia, Helianthus, Iberis, Linaria, Lobularia, Nigella, Papaver, Petunia, Portulaca, Rudbeckia* and *Salvia*. A mixture of these in color-coordinated cultivars sown in early spring in a sandy area can create a lovely "wildflower meadow" that will bloom and self-sow all summer.

Other drought-tolerant annuals can be grown from seed started indoors, or they can be purchased as transplants (see Chapter 2 for information about sowing and transplanting). If you have favorite annuals that are not drought-tolerant, consider growing them in a container close to a water source so that you can give them a drink as often as they need it—in many cases, once a day (see information about containers on page 35).

Arctotis hybrids
African daisy

This is one of a group of native South African daisies that bloom not only in the common daisy shades of yellow and orange but also in some unusual pinks, reds, creams and purples. Stems are about 18 inches (45 cm) long, with finely divided grayish foliage. Arctotis is usually grown from transplants but will bloom in about 11 weeks from seed sown early indoors. Hybrids are the types most widely available, but there is also a blue-flowered species.

Brachycome is most valued for its contribution of the colors blue and purple to containers, window boxes and borders.

Argemone species
Prickly poppy

These beautiful but well-armed New World poppies thrive in dry places and often self-sow to reappear next year. Because of the prickly leaves, they are best grown away from tended places, and you should weed the area well at planting time to avoid having to handle them later. There are many species, all easy from seed sown directly in the spring garden. Thin seedlings to about 6 inches (15 cm) apart.

The Devonian Botanic Garden near Edmonton, Alberta, displays *A. grandiflora* and *A. platyceras*, both with 4-inch (10 cm) white tissue-paper poppy flowers on 14-inch (35 cm) stems with prickly bluish foliage; *A. ochroleuca*, with yellow flowers above more slender, greener foliage; and *A. subfusiformis*, with pale yellow 3-inch (7.5 cm) flowers and more slender leaves. J.L. Hudson also sells *A. hispida*, white with yellow centers, whose seeds were collected at an altitude of 5,500 feet (1,675 m) near Boulder, Colorado. All parts of argemones are poisonous.

Brachycome iberidifolia
Swan River daisy

A popular container and window-box annual for sun and also appropriate to edge a border or pathway, brachycome is most appreciated for its shades of blue and purple, although there is also a white cultivar, 'White Splendor.' The daisies are only about 1 inch (2.5 cm) wide but are produced in great numbers on slim 1-foot (30 cm) stems. Spring transplants are fairly easy to find, or you can start seeds indoors six weeks early.

Calandrinia grandiflora
Rock purslane

This member of the portulaca family has 1-inch (2.5 cm) magenta primroselike flowers and long, gray-green, hairy, somewhat succulent-looking foliage. The species has trailing stems as long as 3 feet (1 m), but a couple of dwarf forms and a few additional species, also smaller, are available from specialist catalogs. Calandrinia blooms in about 15 weeks from seed, so it is best started in-

Callistephus blooms in late summer, when many other flowers have faded. It often self-sows to reappear the next spring.

doors about six weeks before the last spring frost date. It can also be propagated from cuttings.

Callirhoe involucrata
Wine cup, poppy mallow

Callirhoe is a trailer for hot, dry places, good for the edge of a bed or to cover rocks. Stems grow about 1 foot (30 cm) long, decorated all summer with cupped cherry-red mallow flowers. It resents transplanting, so seeds should be sown in late spring directly where the plants will grow. Do not water when plants go dormant after blooming. Native from Texas to Wyoming, callirhoe may overwinter where winters are not too harsh and the soil is very dry.

Callistephus chinensis
Chinese aster

The annual asters are now grouped under the genus *Callistephus*. Although not lovers of parched soil, they do well in full sun and respond quickly to an occasional evening watering. Resembling

large centaureas in their double form, they bloom in white and the bluish palette from lilac to purple, as well as pink and red. Better for the dry garden, and more beautiful in any case, I think, are the tall singles such as 'Single California Mix,' which self-seeds faithfully, producing welcome drifts of pink and purple beginning in late August, when many other flowers are finished.

Like its relatives the asters, callistephus is vulnerable to the fungal disease aster yellows, which causes plants to become yellow and die in midsummer. Pull out infected plants, and where the disease is a problem, rotate asters from one area to another each year.

Catharanthus hybrids
Vinca, periwinkle

Once labeled *Vinca rosea*, this relative of the hardy perennial trailing periwinkle has similar starry flowers but has been assigned its own genus. Under any name, this tender perennial is a recent arrival on the horticultural market. Only since

1991 have brightly colored cultivars been available, but now they are among the most popular annuals for hot, dry places and sunny hanging baskets—for places where impatiens, another long-blooming plant of similar height and flower size, does not thrive. Flowers about 1½ inches (3.8 cm) wide bloom in white and shades of pink through magenta. Many cultivars are now popularly available as transplants, but if you want to grow your own, the seeds should be sown indoors about eight weeks before the last spring frost date. *C. roseus* contains alkaloids widely used in the treatment of leukemia and other cancers.

Centaurea species
Cornflower, bachelor's button

Certain centaureas known as knapweed are pests of the midwestern plains, demonstrating the ability of the genus to endure neglect and dry soil. *C. cyanus* can also be too much of a good thing in some places. One common name, cornflower, comes from its infestation of farm fields in its native Europe. Known more affectionately as bachelor's button, centaurea is one of the few annuals I have grown, other than *Salvia horminum*, that will survive drought during germination. *C. cyanus* thrives on sandy soil, produces its bright blue flowers in summer's hot weather and drops its seeds around it to reappear the next year. The typical blue color is a perfect complement to the many white, yellow and orange daisies that grow in similar conditions. There are also white and pink cultivars and at least one brown one, 'Black Ball.' The usual height is 2 feet (60 cm) on stems that are slender but seldom need staking. There are also dwarf varieties.

C. americana is 3 feet (1 m) tall, with stiff stems and lilac-colored flowers as wide as 5 inches (13 cm). 'Jolly Joker' is a German selection.

C. cineraria (*C. maritima*, *Senecio cineraria*), known as dusty miller, is grown for its finely divided bright silver foliage. This and two other annuals called dusty miller—*Senecio viravira* and *Chrysanthemum ptarmiciflorum* (*Cineraria candicans*, *Pyrethrum ptarmiciflorum*)—are widely available as spring transplants to fill out window boxes, containers and hanging baskets in sun, although they are also good for border edges.

C. moschata (sweet sultan) has fragrant yellow flowers 2 inches (5 cm) wide on stems about 2 feet (60 cm) tall. There are several cultivars.

Cheiranthus cheiri
Wallflower

There are annual, biennial and perennial wallflowers, some grouped into the genus *Erysimum* (see page 89). Clusters of neon-orange flowers are the usual signature of *C. cheiri*, an annual or biennial that will survive on sandy hillsides once established. There are also cream, yellow, apricot, purple, pink, salmon, rose and mahogany cultivars. Sow the seeds directly in the garden around the last spring frost date. The plants may bloom the first year or grow as biennials, forming a rosette of foliage the first year and blooming the second. Most grow about 20 inches (50 cm) tall. Wallflowers often self-sow.

Cladanthus arabicus
Palm Springs daisy

All summer and into fall, cladanthus produces a crop of fragrant yellow daisies as wide as 2 inches (5 cm) on a mound of slender 2-foot-tall (60 cm) stems. The flowers are reminiscent of its close relative chamomile, and the foliage is finely divided. Sow the seeds in the garden in spring, just covering them, or give them an early start indoors.

Cleome spinosa
Spider flower

With its stately self-supporting stems, about 3 feet (1 m) tall, topped in summer by delicate, spidery flowers with threadlike stamens, cleome looks like nothing else in the garden. The foliage is deeply divided and decorative. Gardeners either love it or dislike its airy presence. The usual flower colors are pink and white, although there is also a violet cultivar. Sow seeds directly in the garden in early spring, and thin to 6 inches (15 cm) apart. It is a good specimen plant grown in a bed on its own, or it can fill the back of a sunny border. If the flowers are left to mature, cleome will self-sow.

Rows of pink, rose and white Cosmos bipinnatus *grow alongside orange, red and yellow* Cosmos sulphureus.

Coreopsis species
Tickseed, calliopsis

Perennial types of coreopsis are described on pages 85 and 86. The annuals are apt to be taller and may reappear every year too, because they often self-sow. On stems as tall as 3 feet (1 m), golden yellow flowers bloom all summer, no matter how dry or hot the weather (unlike many drought-tolerant plants, coreopsis is not averse to high temperatures). It can thus be a good companion for plants such as California poppy, whose blooming declines in hot weather. There are single and double forms of coreopsis, and some are bicolored mahogany and yellow. Sow the seeds outdoors in early spring directly where they will grow.

Cosmos species
Cosmos

Cosmos is a lover of warmth and sun that does well with frequent watering but will also survive a certain amount of dry weather, although stems will be shorter. It prefers sandy soil. Most cultivars of *C. bipinnatus*, which grows around 3 feet (1 m) tall and has flowers as wide as 5 inches (13 cm) in the pink, rose and white color range, will self-sow, while *C. sulphureus*, generally shorter and with smaller yellow, orange or red flowers, is less likely to do so. *C. atrosanguineus* has 2-to-3-foot (60-90 cm) stems bearing single dark red 1½-inch (3.8 cm) flowers with orange centers.

Sow seeds directly outdoors anytime in spring. Alternatively, seeds can be sown indoors six weeks before the last spring frost date. Transplants are also widely available in spring, but cosmos must be transplanted carefully, or it will be set back. Wait until nights are warm.

Cynoglossum amabile
Chinese forget-me-not, hound's tongue

Brilliant blue flowers very much like the biennial or perennial forget-me-not identify the biennial or annual version, a reliable self-sower when it is happy—in sandy soil, in weather that is not too hot and preferably with some shade. There are also whites and pinks. Cynoglossum grows about 18 inches (45 cm) tall, with slender mounding stems. Sow the seeds in early spring directly where they will grow. Late sowings will not bloom until next year.

Dyssodia (Thymophylla) tenuiloba
Golden fleece, Dahlberg daisy

Easy from seed and likely to self-sow where conditions suit it—in well-drained soil in sun—this native of the southern United States and Mexico forms a bushy plant up to 1 foot (30 cm) tall, covered with small daisies that may be orange, yellow or white with yellow centers. 'Shooting Star' is golden. Blooming is best when the weather cools in late summer. Sow seeds directly outdoors anytime in spring, or start them early indoors. Blooming begins about four months from germination.

Echium species
Blueweed

Viper's bugloss, or blueweed (*E. vulgare*), is a beautiful but coarse, prickly weed that blooms in early summer where I live. The bees enjoy it, and it is an attractive roadside companion for the oxeye daisies (*Chrysanthemum leucanthemum*) that bloom at the same time. The flowers open bright pink, then turn the brilliant blue of its relatives the forget-me-nots. There are a few slightly more refined cultivars for the garden, all with similar spires of blue, white, pink or purple flowers. They may form a deep taproot and flat rosette of foliage the first year and flower stems the next. They self-sow. There are also some showier annual or biennial relatives. *E. lycopsis* (*E. plantagineum*) grows as tall as 3 feet (1 m), with 10-inch (25 cm) spikes of flowers in summer. *E. russicum* (*E. rubrum*) has tubular red flowers.

Eschscholzia californica
California poppy

Considering that it is native to California, where it is perennial, this lovely poppy is surprisingly tolerant of bitter winters—or, rather, its seeds are. Not long after the snow has gone, the appearance of delicate blue-green foliage, similar to that of young dill, shows that it has self-seeded and will bloom again by midsummer. The easiest way to start a patch is simply to broadcast the seeds on the ground anytime in spring; they will await the right soil temperature and moisture level for sprouting. Although drought-tolerant once rooted, they will not sprout or begin growing without moisture. Seeding can be done until the end of June for flowers the same season. A lax stem about 1 foot (30 cm) tall grows a mass of bluish foliage. When the plants are 2 inches (5 cm) high, thin them to 4 inches (10 cm) apart. Like all poppies, *E. californica* resents transplanting.

The color of the wild species is brilliant orange, but there are now whites, yellows, pinks, purples and crimsons, in single-, semidouble- and double-flowered forms. Although the California poppy is drought-tolerant, it flowers better when the weather is not hot. If the plants receive some water during the hottest weather, they may bloom again as temperatures fall.

E. caespitosa is smaller, just 6 inches (15 cm), with scented yellow poppies, and is therefore good for a border edge.

Euphorbia marginata
Snow on the mountain

A good foliage filler between brighter flowers, *E. marginata* looks unremarkable until, in midsummer, it produces beautifully variegated bracts at the tips, green with white edges, which are topped by small white flowers. This is one of the plants that will self-sow and, at about 2 feet (60 cm) tall, looks good almost anywhere. It is most easily sown directly in the garden anytime in spring.

Everlastings
There are several similar daisies with brightly colored bracts that dry on the stem in the garden and keep their shape all winter. All are best picked in bud or when they are just beginning to bloom, as they will open a little more after picking and are less attractive when open flat. They can be wired if stiff stems are needed. All are easy from seed sown directly in the garden around the last spring frost date or planted indoors several weeks earlier, then transplanted out after the last frost.

Ammobium alatum (winged everlasting) has

winged 2-foot (60 cm) stems bearing silvery white flowers with yellow centers.

Helichrysum bracteatum, or *H. monstrosum* (strawflower), is the most common of the everlastings, available in a choice of heights up to 3 feet (1 m) and in shades of yellow, orange, pink, violet, red and white. *H. cassianum* bears sprays of small, starry white flowers. Additional species are available from specialists. Helichrysum seeds must be sown on the soil surface, as they need light to germinate.

Helipterum roseum (rose everlasting) is available in several cultivars that bloom in shades of pink, rose and white. Leaves are grayish, and stems are generally about 18 inches (45 cm) tall. Additional species are available from specialist sources.

Xeranthemum annuum, the best of the everlastings for poor, dry soil, has white, pink, rose or purple flowers, single or double, and woolly white foliage on 20-inch (50 cm) stems.

Additional annual everlastings for the dry garden include *Gomphrena globosa*, *Limonium sinuatum* and grasses.

Gomphrena globosa
Globe amaranth

Globe amaranth was a favorite of the pioneers because it was easy to grow, pretty in the garden and lasted all winter in a vase without water, but they knew it only in shades of purple, pink and white. The palette now includes orange, red and bicolors. For dried arrangements, cut the stems when the cloverlike flowers are newly opened; the bracts keep their color well, and the stiff stems need no wiring. Seeds can be sown directly in the spring garden.

Grasses
There are many annual ornamental grasses (for perennial grasses, see pages 46 to 49). These grasses form a clump; they don't spend long enough in the garden to spread by rhizome and become groundcovers. Some self-sow to return next year, and most can be sown directly in the garden, although obviously this is a dangerous practice, since all grass seedlings look much alike, and you may end up weeding out your precious ornamentals. Smaller grasses look best in drifts of several plants but should be thinned to at least 6 inches (15 cm) apart.

Annual grasses are grown primarily for their decorative seedheads, which are not only attractive in the garden but also useful in dried arrangements, especially if picked before they are fully open. The foliage of the annuals is generally quite ordinary-looking, so plant them among and behind other plants with more attractive leaves.

Following are some of the best annual grasses for dry places. Their demands are few. Ornamental-grass specialist Peter Loewer writes, "As long as the soil drains and is capable of supporting a good crop of weeds, the annual grasses do quite well."

Agrostis nebulosa (cloud grass), which grows 8 to 20 inches (20-50 cm) tall in sun or partial shade, is well named for its delicate, billowy appearance during its brief blooming period. It dies back soon after blooming in early to midsummer, so plan to mask or fill its spot with something longer-lasting.

Avena sterilis (animated oats) grows as tall as 3 feet (1 m) and is named for the twisting and turning of the 2-inch (5 cm) flowers as the humidity changes.

Briza maxima (quaking grass, puffed wheat) has seedheads that shiver in the slightest breeze. The plants grow 1 to 3 feet (30-90 cm) tall, and foliage turns from green through golden to brown during the season. A smaller, more delicate form is *B. minor* (little quaking grass), which grows about 6 to 14 inches (15-35 cm) tall and blooms just after *B. maxima*. It dies soon after flowering. If you want to add either grass to an arrangement, pick it just before the seedheads open.

Bromus lanceolatus (*B. macrostachys*) and *B. madritensis* are two types of bromegrass, plants that are especially useful for dried arrangements. They grow as tall as 2 feet (60 cm), with erect, bristly spikes that last all summer. Stay away from other bromegrasses, which may be invasive.

Hordeum jubatum (squirrel's-tail grass, foxtail barley) has 2-foot (60 cm) stalks topped in summer with lovely plumes that may be green, red or purple. Although decorative, this species is considered a noxious weed in some places.

Lagurus ovatus (hare's-tail grass) grows about 1 foot (30 cm) tall, with grayish foliage and fluffy

Hordeum jubatum *is an annual grass that can be beautiful in its place but has become a noxious weed in some areas.*

bunny-tail seedheads that suit dried arrangements. Like lamb's ears, this is a pettable plant that children love. The only grass included in a trial of 55 summer-flowering annuals at the Chicago Botanic Garden in 1994, *L. ovatus* was judged "excellent overall," with no pests or diseases. Peak flowering began in early July and continued throughout the season.

Lamarckia aurea (golden top) has shimmering golden panicles that fade by midsummer, when the plants should be removed or replaced. It grows about 2 feet (60 cm) tall.

Pennisetum setaceum (*P. ruppelii*) is an annual form of fountain grass that resembles the perennial *P. alopecuroides*. It forms an arching 3-foot-tall (1 m) clump that has been artfully grouped at the Denver Botanic Gardens with ruby grass and white nicotiana. Fountain grass has attractive foliage all season and rosy 10-inch (25 cm) flower spikes in late summer. The cultivars 'Rubrum' and 'Cuprem' are deep wine-red. *P. villosum*, or *P. longistylum* (feathertop grass), is about half as tall, with long, feathery flowerheads, pale green or white

fading to beige. It, too, has good-looking foliage all season and can be eye-catching edging a path. Both species of pennisetum are good container plants.

Rhynchelytrum repens, or *R. roseum, Tricholaena rosea* (ruby grass, Natal grass, champagne grass), a tender perennial that is weedy in the southern states, has rosy red seedheads on 2-to-3-foot (60-90 cm) stems from July to October. This is popular in fresh, not dried, arrangements; instead of cutting, pull the stems carefully from the leaf sheaths. Offsets can be planted in pots in fall and overwintered indoors in a cool window.

Setaria glauca, or *S. lutescens* (foxtail grass, Italian millet), is an important cereal crop in China and is also grown for birdseed. It grows as tall as 3 feet (1 m) and is topped in summer by orange bristles that glow in the sun. This grass will die in prolonged drought.

Zea mays japonica (japonica, striped maize) is a sweet-corn relative that grows up to 6 feet (1.8 m) tall, with leaves striped green, cream and pink. It was a favorite of Victorian gardeners.

Gypsophila elegans
Baby's-breath

Like its perennial cousin *G. paniculata* (see page 91), annual baby's-breath prefers dry, alkaline soil, where its wiry stems yield a crop of tiny, white or pink flowers that are perfect fillers for garden, container, window box or vase. If you want continuous cutting, sow the seeds every couple of weeks through spring and early summer. Plants take three months to flower from seed. Stems grow 12 to 30 inches (30-75 cm) tall, depending on the cultivar and growing conditions.

Helianthus annuus
Sunflower

Sunflowers are the crowning glories of hot, sunny gardens, although not necessarily dry ones. Like many other daisies, they do best with some moisture, especially in early summer, when they are growing rapidly. There are many varieties: short-stemmed types with huge flowers, tall-stemmed branching types with small flowers—excellent for cutting—and tall-stemmed types with large flowers, including those, such as the 10-foot (3 m) 'Russian Giant,' grown for their large, edible, protein-rich seeds. Flower colors range from white and the palest yellow through golden to dark orange, bronze and red. All are easy from seed sown directly in the garden anytime in spring and thinned to stand at least 1 foot (30 cm) apart, farther for the tall types. In a windy spot, they may need staking. Deadhead the finished flowers, and save their seeds for next year. They often self-sow, and seedlings transplant well.

Many parts of sunflowers are toxic to neighboring plants, especially the hulls on any seeds that fall. Grow them where they will neither shade nor compete with other flowers.

Kochia scoparia (Bassia scoparia)
Burning bush

This foliage annual is a noxious weed in some places, evidence of its ability to thrive in dry conditions. It forms a neat, dense 2-foot-tall (60 cm) globe of tiny leaves that opens out somewhat when the inconspicuous flowers bloom in late summer, then turns brilliant crimson in fall. It often self-sows. Kochia can be used to form a temporary windbreak on the windward edge of a vegetable or flower garden, or it can be grown as a foliage contrast between more floriferous plants. It makes an excellent container plant on its own or surrounded by portulaca or sanvitalia. Seeds can be sown *in situ* in early spring, and the seedlings should be thinned to 2 feet (60 cm) apart.

Lantana camara (L. hybrida)
Yellow sage

In Hawaii, this tender shrub has become weedy, but in the North, it is coaxed along as an annual especially prized for containers in sun. Although lantana can exceed 6 feet (1.8 m), given sufficient warmth and time, and can be trained as a show-stopping standard, it most often grows about 2 feet (60 cm) in northern containers. Rounded heads of tiny verbenalike flowers, which appear until frost, open yellow and then mature to red or white, so several colors appear on the same stem. There are other colors as well. The bluish fruits are poisonous. Lantana needs regular watering until it becomes established but, by midsummer, is drought-resistant. Seeds must be sown indoors about eight weeks before the last spring frost date.

Layia elegans (L. platyglossa)
Tidy tips

A neat perimeter of white tips encircles the 2-inch (5 cm) bright yellow petals of this unusual daisy. Reddish stems grow 12 to 18 inches (30-45 cm) tall, with flowers all season until frost. They are excellent for cutting. Seeds can be sown directly in the garden in spring.

Limonium sinuatum
Statice

Best known for spikes of blue flowers as tall as 2 to 3 feet (60-90 cm), this everlasting annual also blooms in shades of white, rose and yellow. The papery flowers dry easily right in the garden and should be cut for everlasting arrangements as soon as the flowers begin to open. Give statice sandy soil mixed with plenty of compost, and grow it in sun

New sunflowers on the market are meant as cut flowers and decorations for the garden rather than sources of edible seeds.

or a little shade. Seeds are best sown indoors about eight weeks before the last spring frost date. *L. suworowii* has slender spikes of rose-colored flowers that resemble chenille.

Lobularia maritima
Sweet alyssum

This modest but accommodating plant puts up with almost anything, from damp soil and a little shade to conditions that are quite dry and sunny, and although it is an annual, it often self-sows to decorate border edges again the next year. Buy transplants, start seeds early indoors, or sow the seeds directly on the soil anytime in spring; they will wait until the temperature is right for germination. Sweet alyssum has relaxed stems about 6 inches (15 cm) long that grow into a tangled mass only a few inches high, suitable for filling the spaces between other plants. There are white, pink, rose and purple varieties, all lightly scented. Shear it back after flowering to keep it neat and encourage more buds, but leave some to go to seed.

Malva sylvestris
Tree mallow

Often listed as perennial, *M. sylvestris* is a dependably self-sowing annual in my garden. It grows 3 to 4 feet (1-1.2 m) tall and is self-supporting, with silky flowers held against the central stem. There are several cultivars. 'Bibor Felho' has large 3-inch (7.5 cm) deep purple flowers. 'Zebrina' has dark purple stripes on a pale background. The edible flowers bloom from midsummer until fall. Collect seeds when the seedpods dry, or let some seeds fall for the next year's crop. Like many mallows, they can become leggy unless thinned to stand at least a hand's length apart. Cut the stems back in late summer after blooming to keep that area of the garden looking neat.

Matricaria species
Mayweed

There are several decorative cousins of the herb chamomile that have similar lax, slender stems and small daisy flowers, generally white or

Succulent foliage that looks frosted has given mesembryanthemum, planted here with lobelia, the moniker ice plant.

yellow. All love sun and survive in poor soil, provided it is well drained. *M. grandiflora* 'Gold Pompoms' has unusual rounded flowerheads that dry well for everlasting bouquets. All can be sown directly outdoors in early spring. Some self-sow.

Melampodium paludosum
Melampodium, African zinnia

This recent garden arrival, which is covered with small yellow daisies all summer, is an excellent cut flower and a good choice for containers or window boxes in sun. Even in poor, dry soil, it forms a shrubby mound 8 to 10 inches (20-25 cm) tall. It sometimes self-sows. Sow seeds two weeks before the last spring frost date, and transplant into the garden four weeks later.

Mesembryanthemum criniflorum (Dorotheanthus species)
Ice plant, Livingstone daisy

Succulent foliage that looks as though it is frosted with ice crystals is well adapted to deflect-ing summer's heat. Mesembryanthemum, the name for cultivated forms of dorotheanthus, is a favorite plant for dry southern roadsides and is just as adaptable to sunny northern containers that are never watered. Daisies a little wider than 1 inch (2.5 cm), in shades of pink, peach, orange and rose, bloom just above the ground on reclining stems. The flowers close at night and in cloudy weather and do not open until afternoon. Search specialist seed houses for several unusual species of dorotheanthus, all of which are suited to the driest, sunniest garden spots.

Osteospermum (Dimorphotheca) species
Cape marigold, African daisy

Many of the choice daisies for dry places hail from southern Africa. This group has stems about 2 feet (60 cm) tall and large flowers as wide as 3 inches (7.5 cm), in shades of white, cream, pink, orange, yellow, buff and purple. The undersides of the petals are often purplish or brown. New cultivars appear on the market every year, some with odd spoon-shaped petals. Flowers close at night and in cloudy weather. Buy transplants, or start seeds indoors several weeks before the last spring frost date, as they need a long season for the best show.

Petunia species
Petunia

There are petunias and petunias. In the dry garden, don't bother with the big floppy hybrids that need pinching and regular watering unless you want them for containers or window boxes and are prepared to look after them every day. Instead, look for multifloras or minifloras, such as the Fantasy series. Also better in stressful places are the Surfinias and Supertunias, types that must be vegetatively reproduced. They are tender perennials, so you can clip back the plants and bring them indoors in fall or take cuttings to overwinter for next year.

I have good luck, too, with *P. hybrida* (which, despite its name, is not a hybrid), from J.L. Hudson in California. There are pink and white varieties. They self-sow in fall, sprout in midspring, need ruthless thinning and begin blooming by mid-July. Flowering continues through fall. All petunias will survive a few light fall frosts.

Phacelia campanularia
Desert bluebell

You may have to search the specialist seed houses to find this native of the California deserts, but it is worth the trouble. The plant is tough enough to survive in the cracks in a sidewalk, a perfect partner, in color and form, to its western companion the California poppy. Relaxed stems grow 6 inches (15 cm) long, and the 1-inch (2.5 cm) flower is an intense deep blue. It is excellent massed along a border's edge, between taller plants or in a container filled with sandy soil. It flowers in about two months from seeds sown directly in the garden a couple of weeks before the last spring frost date.

Phlox drummondii
Annual phlox

If there were a contest for cutest cultivar name, Thompson & Morgan's 'Phlox of Sheep'

would have won in 1996. Like other types of annual phlox, it is an excellent garden plant, with flowers much like those of perennial phlox but on shorter stems, only about 10 inches (25 cm). Annual phlox survives in sandy or otherwise well-drained soil in sun or partial shade. Like sheep, it does look best in flocks. Seeds can be sown directly outdoors a couple of weeks before the last spring frost date—they need temperatures cooler than 75 degrees F (24°C) to sprout. Thin seedlings to 6 inches (15 cm) apart; they resent transplanting. The flowers, in shades of white, pink, lilac, red, blue, yellow and bicolored, are good for cutting and continue to bloom almost until frost.

Polygonum species
Knotweed, smartweed, fleece flower

Annual varieties of this genus, whose name means "many knees"—referring to the jointed stems—show up from time to time in seed catalogs. Some members of the genus are very weedy, and all can take a beating. Several are described on page 60.

P. capitatum is called pink punching balls by one seed catalog. A 3-to-4-inch (7.5-10 cm) groundcover, it produces ½-inch (1 cm) pink globe flowers. It requires watering only during the driest weather, loves heat and needs well-drained soil. A tender perennial that flowers the first year from seed, it is hardy in zone 9, where it may become weedy.

P. orientale (kiss-me-over-the-garden-gate) is a pioneer favorite that can grow as tall as 6 feet (1.8 m), with green leaves and bright pink flower tassels at the tips. It needs some moisture to grow to its full height and to keep the leaves from wilting, but it will survive from year to year in dry ground, although it will be much shorter. It self-sows dependably.

Portulaca grandiflora
Moss rose

Of all the annuals suited to really dry places, portulaca is the easiest to find as a bedding plant in spring, which is not a bad way to go unless you want to start the tiny seeds several weeks early indoors or sow them directly in the garden anytime in spring. One advantage of growing from seed is

In the author's garden, golden rudbeckia is contrasted with the white of dwarf Shasta daisies.

that you can buy a single color instead of the mixtures generally available as transplants. Colors available from Stokes Seeds, for instance, include cream, pink, magenta, yellow, orange and mango (see Sources). The seeds are simply scattered on the soil surface, which should be kept moist until germination. An individual plant will form a mound 4 to 6 inches (10-15 cm) high and about 1 foot (30 cm) wide, creating a short-lived groundcover for the front of a sunny bed, between herbs or in a container. Flowers close at night and on cloudy days and are late to open in the morning—one old name is eleven o'clock—although breeders are working to counteract this tendency; the Sundial series stays open longer. Portulaca sometimes self-sows. In my garden, seedlings are ½ inch (1 cm) high by the first week of June and are easy to transplant elsewhere.

A close relative is *P. oleracea*, the annual weed purslane, an edible groundcover with succulent foliage that can thicken soups or flavor salads.

Rudbeckia species
Black-eyed Susan, gloriosa daisy

There are annual, biennial and perennial rudbeckias, large-flowered daisies in the color range of yellow through orange to brown, plain or bicolored, single or double, with brown centers. Easiest in the dry garden is *R. hirta*, which may behave as an annual or a biennial. It can be sown directly in the garden anytime in spring and will self-sow thereafter. Flowers as wide as 5 inches (13 cm) begin blooming in early July and may continue until midfall, a bright presence as other flowers come and go. Stems are 2 to 3 feet (60-90 cm) long and self-supporting. *R. amplexicaulis* is smaller in every way, with 1-inch (2.5 cm) bright yellow daisies on 2-foot (60 cm) stems.

Salvia species
Salvia, sage

S. splendens, the common annual bedding salvia with its bright plume flowers, needs a fairly steady water supply, although it does well in heat and sun. There are other annuals, however, that live up to the salvia reputation as plants for dry places and most have the grayish foliage to prove it.

S. argentea (silver sage) is one of the most unusual, with huge, downy, silvery leaves that form a flat clump as wide as 3 feet (1 m), which is extended even more by lateral rosettes growing out from the mother plant. Leave plenty of room when you plant it, or the mature plants will blanket their neighbors. This is an excellent choice for the front of a sunny, dry border. The small flower stalks that appear in late summer should be allowed to set seed for self-sowing but can be cut back otherwise. Plants sometimes survive the winter.

S. coccinea is a Texan perennial grown as an annual in the North. It has spikes of brilliant red flowers on 2-foot (60 cm) stems. The heart-shaped foliage is fuzzy and aromatic.

S. farinacea (mealy cup sage) is a fairly tender perennial generally grown in the North as an annual. On stems about 2 feet (60 cm) tall, it has slender spikes of pale blue to white flowers and thin, gray-green leaves. Among the best-known cultivars are the blue 'Blue Bedder,' the deep blue

Though associated with the Virgin Mary, Silybum marianum *has big, thorny leaves that are far from meek and mild.*

or white 'Victoria,' which grows up to 18 inches (45 cm) tall, and the All-America Selection 'Strata.'

S. horminum (clary sage) is one of the best flowering annuals for dry soil. It has grayish leaves and looks modest until after a few weeks, when it develops pastel-colored petal-like bracts along the 2-foot (60 cm) stems. Colors include white, pink, rose, lilac, purple and blue. Excellent in a vase, either fresh or dried, it looks best in masses and often self-sows.

Sanvitalia procumbens
Creeping zinnia

Trailing 6-inch (15 cm) stems tipped with 1-inch (2.5 cm) yellow or orange daisies make sanvitalia a good choice for the front of a sunny border, a hanging basket or a sunny container. The usual selection is single, but there is also a double-flowered form. 'Mandarin Orange' is an All-America Selection. Once blooming starts in midsummer, it continues until fall frosts. Sanvitalia prefers light, sandy soil in sun and needs careful transplanting.

Silybum marianum
Our Lady's thistle

Legend has it that the white streaks on this remarkable plant came from the Virgin Mary's milk. Its thorniness, however, is far from meek and mild. Huge leaves that grow in a rosette as wide as 4 feet (1.2 m) have long thorns around the perimeter. Grow silybum in a place where you need not tend it or walk too close to its big, mottled leaves. In summer, purple thistle flowers bloom atop vertical stems. It is easy from seeds sown directly in the garden anytime in spring and often self-sows.

Tagetes species
Marigold

Although lovers of sun and warmth, marigolds are not the best flowers for dry places. As with most other flowers, double varieties and triploids tend to need more coddling than the wilder singles. Among the best types for dry places are the small-flowered singles such as the Gem series, *T. tenuifolia* and the signet marigolds (*T. signata*

Among the marigolds that are best suited to drought are the dwarfs and singles, such as the cultivar 'Granada.'

pumila). These produce large quantities of seed that the gardener can gather in late summer; they sometimes self-sow. If the season is extended, summer seedlings may reach blooming size before fall frosts, which rapidly kill them. Useful in vegetable gardens are the so-called French marigolds (*T. patula*), proven repellents for certain harmful varieties of tiny soil-dwelling worms called nematodes.

Tithonia rotundifolia (T. speciosa)
Mexican sunflower

In warm sun and soil that is well drained but occasionally moist, this impressive annual can form a bush of stiff stems 6 feet (1.8 m) tall, with large, velvety leaves and neon-orange sunflowers with yellow centers on the usual cultivar 'Goldfinger.' In dry ground and where nights are cool, it is only half as tall. Flowers bloom freely until fall frost. Sow the seeds indoors six to eight weeks before the last spring frost date, and set the plants out 2 feet (60 cm) apart in sun. Tithonia is good at the back of a sunny border or as a specimen.

Ursinia species
Ursinia

There are several species of this South African daisy available from mail-order seed houses. They resemble gazanias, with wide, usually bright orange or yellow flowers (which close at night and in cloudy weather) that bloom all summer on stems about 1 foot (30 cm) tall. The hairy, feathery foliage of *U. anethoides* is strongly scented. Sow the seeds indoors six weeks before the last spring frost date, and thin seedlings to 6 inches (15 cm) apart.

Venidium fastuosum
Monarch of the veldt

Flowers 4 inches (10 cm) wide resemble target shooters' bull's-eyes, with brown centers circled by concentric rings of yellow or white and brown, but even more fascinating are the white woolly leaves and stems of this drought beater. Stems grow about 30 inches (75 cm) tall. Like many African daisies, the flowers close at night and on cloudy days. Sow seeds indoors about four weeks before the last spring frost date, and transplant into well-drained soil in a sunny place after danger of frost has passed. Deadhead frequently.

Verbena species
Verbena

The usual annual verbena is *V.* x *hybrida*, a somewhat drought-resistant constant bloomer popular for hanging baskets and window boxes in sun. It is widely available as a spring bedding plant, although seeds can be sown directly in the garden a couple of weeks before the last spring frost date or a few weeks earlier indoors. Even tougher, although grown from cuttings instead of seed, is Tapien™ verbena, a compact hybrid developed in Japan. It is mildew-resistant and spreads quickly but does not overpower other plants. This is a good temporary groundcover for a hot, sunny spot. As of 1998, it is available in five colors— deep violet, pink, light blue, rose bicolor and lavender—and will tolerate frosts to 23 degrees F (–5°C). Take cuttings indoors to overwinter in a cool, bright spot. Very different and not suited to containers is *V. bonariensis,* which grows as tall as 5 feet (1.5 m) and has dark purple flowers that attract butterflies. It often self-sows.

Zinnia species
Zinnia

Like marigolds, zinnias have been selected and hybridized into hundreds of forms, some so mop-headed that they have to be tended like lapdogs. They are not good candidates for dry or windy places. On the other hand, the less celebrated singles, some of which are lovely, have retained their inborn ability to withstand stressful weather. *Z. angustifolia* (*Z. linearis*) 'Crystal White' was a 1997 All-America Selection (AAS) winner with white single daisies on mounding 10-inch (25 cm) plants. Also good is the Star series, which includes orange, yellow and white selections. Grown in masses planted 6 inches (15 cm) apart, *Z. angustifolia* makes a good temporary groundcover in sun. The taller *Z. haageana* (Mexican zinnia), about 15 inches (38 cm), has single or double, often bicolored flowers in shades of orange, maroon, red,

Double zinnias such as 'Border Beauty Scarlet' need more watering than the small-flowered species.

brown, cream, pink and purple. Its best-known cultivars are the AAS winners 'Persian Carpet' and 'Old Mexico.' Their flowers resemble small dahlias.

Single zinnias are easiest to grow by sowing the large seeds directly in the garden after the last spring frost date. They do best in full sun with some moisture, especially until they germinate and for a couple of weeks afterward. When watering, try to water the soil rather than the plants— zinnias are susceptible to mildew. Spray weekly with a mixture of 1 teaspoon (5 mL) baking soda to 1 quart (1 L) water. Pick the flowers when newly opened for indoor arrangements, or deadhead them when faded if you want extended color in the garden.

Herbs

◆ 7

"I GREW SWEET BASIL, SAGE, SUMMER SAVORY, BORAGE, HOREHOUND, DILL.
MY GRANDFATHER'S HOUSE HAD A HUGE GARDEN AT THE BACK IN WHICH
I WORKED AS LITTLE AS POSSIBLE, BUT THE HERBS WERE DIFFERENT."

—Margaret Laurence, *Dance on the Earth: A Memoir*, 1989

In her autobiography, Margaret Laurence describes her passion for growing herbs at her childhood home on the prairies in Neepawa, Manitoba. Like many gardeners, she found that herbs, for all their exotic reputation in the kitchen, were quite easy in the garden, even a dry prairie plot tended by a novice. If vegetables need regular watering in dry places, herbs are more self-sufficient. Many of the most popular hardy perennial herbs belong to two plant families that have strong survival instincts: the mint family (Labiatae) and the dill family (Umbelliferae). The former group includes many natives of dry, sunny places, while the latter has taproots that descend quickly to moister depths.

Agastache foeniculum
Anise-hyssop, licorice mint

This mint relative has foliage with the distinct scent of licorice. Although sometimes described as perennial, it is an annual in my zone-4 garden, where it self-sows so plentifully that its constant survival is assured. It grows 2 to 3 feet (60-90 cm) tall, looking much like its relative catnip, with 4- to-6-inch (10-15 cm) spires of lilac-colored flowers for four to five weeks in summer. Like catnip, it will wilt during a long dry spell but revives quickly after a brief watering and can even be grown in sand. It is easy from seeds sown directly in the garden anytime in spring. Anise-hyssop makes a delicious tea served hot or cold, either on its own or blended with other herbs.

Allium species
Chives, garlic

Chives (*A. schoenoprasum*) thrive in moist, fertile soil but will also survive in dry ground, although the leaves will be smaller and more slender. Whether the soil is dry or moist, give the herb a spot with some sun. It is decorative in a flower garden, with its tubular deep green foliage and lilac umbels, which keep their color through most of June and lure bees and monarch butterflies. Grow it from seed or bulbs. Once it takes hold, this plant can be divided easily anytime during the year. Chives will self-sow if some flowers are left to go to seed, but seedlings are easily pulled out where they are not wanted. Self-sown chives grow all through one of my flowerbeds.

A. sativum (garlic) is not ornamental and requires richer well-watered soil, so it should be confined to the vegetable garden. Garlic needs a long season to fill out fully, and if planted in late fall, it can take advantage of the cool, moist soil of winter and early spring to get a head start. Plant locally grown cloves if possible. Mulch plants after they sprout in spring. In trials in Saskatoon, Saskatchewan, the best cultivars for overwintering were 'California Late,' 'Mexican' and 'Polish.'

A. tuberosum (garlic chives), which have a distinctive garlic flavor, are a little less vigorous than regular chives but are ornamental enough for a flowerbed. They have flatter leaves and taller stems bearing white flowers.

Anethum graveolens
Dill

Dill thrives in rich, moist soil, where it may reach 3 feet (1 m) in height, yet it will grow, although not as tall, in very dry soil, provided the seeds have enough moisture to germinate and the seedlings can get their roots down before the soil dries. Even in a dry garden, dill often self-sows to reappear the next year. The ferny foliage is used in salads, the seeds in pickles and vinegars. If you need dill in quantity for pickling, broadcast the seeds anytime in spring and thin the seedlings to 4 inches (10 cm) apart. Dill is also pretty enough to grow as an ornamental in flowerbeds; the dwarf variety 'Fernleaf' was bred for that purpose.

Armoracia rusticana
Horseradish

The thick, fleshy taproots that are grated to make a pungent sauce carry horseradish through all kinds of inclement weather, from floods to deep freezes to summer-long droughts. In other words, horseradish can be very hard to get rid of once you have it in the garden, and if you till the roots, you will have it everywhere. For the strongest flavor, harvest the roots when the ground is cold, either just before it freezes in fall or just after it thaws in spring. Horseradish can be immediately grated and made into sauce—beware its eye-stinging powers—or it can be stored whole for several weeks in a cool, moist environment, such as a plastic bag in the coolest part of the refrigerator.

Artemisia species
French tarragon, wormwood

Artemisias are dependable inhabitants of the dry garden (see page 31), and *A. dracunculus sativa* (French tarragon) is no exception, despite a delicate anise flavor that suggests *haute cuisine*. It is unimpressive-looking, with slender green leaves on a bushy, lax plant 12 to 18 inches (30-45 cm) tall. It can be grown only from plant divisions or cuttings. If your tarragon has been grown from seed or has no flavor, it is probably Russian tarragon, a plant not worth including in the herb garden.

A. absinthium (wormwood) has an ancient reputation as a medicine for both internal and external use, but its power gained notoriety in Europe a century ago when absinthe, a liqueur that contains it, proved addictive and physically and mentally destructive. There are a few ornamental forms, all around knee height, with bright silver leaves that are eye-catching from summer until early winter. 'Lambrook Silver' is widely available. 'Powis Castle' has performed especially well at the Xeriscape Demonstration Garden in Plainview, New York. Wormwood has woody stems that do not die back to the ground in winter. In some areas, it is invasive.

Calendula officinalis
Pot marigold, English marigold

This is the plant called marigold in England. *C. officinalis* has a long history of medicinal and "pot" (cooking) use in Britain and Europe. Like the marigolds of North American gardens, which are members of the genus *Tagetes*, the usual flower colors of calendula are orange and yellow, although the single or double flowers can also appear in shades of cream and apricot. There are many cultivars, from tiny to 30 inches (75 cm) tall. All are edible; the fresh petals can be used as a saffron substitute. Calendula is easily grown from seeds sown ¼ inch (6 mm) deep directly in the garden in early spring. It can tolerate poor, dry soil but does best in partial shade and appreciates cool weather. Deadhead spent flowers.

Calendula flowers brighten the garden as well as salads and cooked dishes, where they can be used as a saffron substitute.

Chrysanthemum species

Costmary, feverfew

    C. balsamita (costmary, alecost or bibleleaf) grows alongside my dusty driveway, utterly neglected and gradually invading the surrounding grass. Its foliage has a sweet fragrance not quite like anything else. It grows about 3 feet (1 m) tall in any soil and produces insignificant yellow daisies in summer. The leaves are used, fresh or dried, to make tea, dried to mix into potpourri or, as in the past, used to make bookmarks; hence, bibleleaf.

    C. parthenium (*Matricaria eximia, M. parthenium*), known as feverfew, is another plant that survives in the most inhospitable places and has a proven reputation as a medicine for migraine headaches. The foliage is yellow-green with a bitter scent; the flowers are decorative small white daisies. It is a hardy perennial but often self-sows, and some seedlings should be allowed to grow and replace older plants, because they become un-productive and woody in a few years. Grown in masses, feverfew can create a groundcover 1 foot (30 cm) high that is green all winter. There is a double-flowered form and another with golden foliage, sometimes called golden feather.

Echinacea species

Coneflower

    See pages 87 and 88. Because echinaceas are highly regarded as stimulants to the immune system, they are as suitable for the herb garden as for the perennial border. To make a medicinal tincture, dig up the entire plant in summer or fall, clean, chop and steep the roots just covered in vodka for a couple of weeks, then strain and bottle the liquid. A few drops taken daily with garlic are said to enhance overall health.

Galium verum

Lady's bedstraw

    The common name is descriptive enough—this airy, fragrant herb was once harvested to stuff mattresses. No wonder it can be found in present-day pioneer villages, where it still grows with no tending whatsoever. The leaves grow in whorls around the stems, like those of its relative sweet woodruff. Left unclipped, it forms a leafy clump about 14 inches (35 cm) tall.

Hyssopus officinalis
Hyssop

Still accepted in the herb garden, hyssop is one of many ancient herbs no longer used much in either medicine or the kitchen. Hyssop has several aesthetic virtues. It forms a neat shrub about 1 foot (30 cm) tall, covered with tiny dark green leaves that persist for most of the winter. In late summer, spikes as tall as 2 feet (60 cm) are decorated with whorls of small flowers, usually blue but sometimes white or pink. Hyssop is an ideal plant for edging a herb bed. It will put up with shearing or clipping and is easy to propagate from spring cuttings (see page 28), so you can make a row from a single plant in a season. An easier but slower way to obtain new plants is to sow seeds indoors in early spring. Hyssop prefers well-drained, slightly alkaline soil in sun. It is hardy to zone 2 but is short-lived, so cuttings should be taken every two or three years to renew it.

Lavandula species
Lavender

Lavender's gray-blue foliage denotes a plant that likes to dry thoroughly between waterings. It needs well-drained soil. In areas that are wet in winter, lavender should be grown in a raised bed, on a slope or in a container of sandy soil. Give it full sun or a bit of shade and little or no fertilizer. In places where it is not hardy, it can be confined to a pot and wintered indoors. In marginal areas, pots can be buried to their rim in the soil for winter, then mulched. A couple of species and cultivars are hardier than most. 'Lady,' an All-America Selection that can be grown from seed, survives some winters in my zone-4 garden, although I bury its pot to the rim and mulch it with straw in fall. It grows about 1 foot (30 cm) tall and almost as wide, with spikes of fragrant lilac flowers in summer. Lavender is easy to propagate from cuttings (see page 28).

L. angustifolia (English lavender) is hardy to about zone 4. 'Hidcote' and 'Munstead' are common cultivars.

L. dentata (French lavender) is a tender perennial that can survive only light frosts.

The hybrid *L.* x *intermedia* (*L. angustifolia* x *L. latifolia*), sometimes called lavendin, is slightly less hardy than *L. angustifolia.* Cultivars include 'Grosso' and 'Provence.'

In trials involving six varieties of lavender at Ohio State University in Columbus, Ohio, where winter temperatures fell to minus 24 degrees F (−31°C), the best survivor was 'Hidcote,' followed by 'Munstead.' More than half of the *L.* x *intermedia* plants survived, but all the *L. dentata* plants died.

Levisticum officinale
Lovage

Looking like an overgrown celery plant, this related plant is as much a lover of rich, moist soil as its better-known cousin. But perhaps because lovage is a perennial, it will survive far worse conditions. I have seen a plant put up a few leaves year after year in a parched, weedy spot in a few inches of soil. Another plant in a corner of my vegetable garden grows 6 feet (1.8 m) tall and ferny, with no watering or other care. In late summer, the dry flower stalks should be broken off at the base and discarded.

Leaves and young stems can be used as a substitute for parsley or celery; the leafy stems are especially good as stir sticks in tomato drinks. Known in Europe as the magi plant, lovage is a good seasoning for vegetable and meat soups. Leaves can be frozen or dried for winter.

Marrubium species
Horehound

Not popular as a kitchen herb, horehound is best known for horehound "candies," bitter-tasting confections once prescribed for colds and probably consigned to the same spot in the medicine cabinet as castor oil. But horehound earns its place in the herb garden today by reputation and appearance, because its grayish foliage is handsome all season. *M. vulgare* is the usual herb-garden occupant. The cultivar 'Green Pompom' has small white flowers followed by decorative round green seedheads at intervals up stems 1 foot (30 cm) tall or more. *M. incanum* (woolly horehound) is more ornamental and drought-resistant, with woolly white foliage. Plants grow about 1 foot (30 cm) tall and are hardy to zone 5. Mulch with straw after the soil freezes to help ensure survival. Propagate by division or from cuttings.

Matricaria species
Chamomile

The annual type of chamomile (*M. recutita*, *Chamomilla recutita*), called German, Hungarian or wild chamomile, self-seeds profusely, producing a tangle of willowy stems about 1 foot (30 cm) tall, topped by small white-petaled daisies in early summer. The chamomile-tea fragrance is noticeable after every rain or if you brush by the plants. Annual chamomile will survive with practically no care once the seeds have germinated, but it does need weeding and an open area where it can colonize. Seeds can be sown in fall or spring.

Chamaemelum nobile (*Anthemis nobilis*) is the hardy perennial chamomile, also known as Roman chamomile, which is sown, harvested and used the same way as the annual. It is hardy to zone 4. In the herb garden, it makes a good 9-inch (23 cm) groundcover that can even be mowed or stepped on. There are several ornamental biennial or hardy perennial *Anthemis* species with white, yellow or orange flowers.

Chamomile, primarily the flower, has well-documented uses as an antiseptic or healing herb. The ancient Egyptians considered the plant sacred, a gift from the sun god to heal the effects of sunstroke and hypothermia. Handpick the flowers in summer, and use them fresh or dry them to store. They can be used on their own or combined with other herbs to make tea.

Mentha species
Mint

The hardy perennial mints have a reputation for being not only tolerant of soggy ground but water guzzlers as well—these plants will thrive un-

Annual chamomile self-seeds profusely, forming a fragrant tangle of stems and flowers every summer.

der a drippy eavestrough or in a bog garden, where they are apt to take over. Yet neglected mint growing in the sunny, dry ground by my kitchen door has survived for years without regular watering. After a long dry spell, it looks a bit threadbare but quickly responds to rain or watering, when it resumes the invasive habits for which mints are well known.

Because of their wandering rhizomes, mints should be kept away from smaller plants and are good candidates for a big pot, but the pot must be protected in winter beyond zone 6 by being buried up to its rim in fall. If you grow mint in a pot, water it regularly and prune it back to keep it looking lush and neat. Divide the plant when it is crowded, to encourage new growth. For best flavor, pick leaves and stem tips before flowering. Leaves dry easily and retain their flavor well for winter teas and condiments. The best-flavored mints are grown from cuttings or plant divisions, not from seed. Most commonly available are *M.* x *piperita* (peppermint), whose leaves have smooth edges,

Like the common form, golden oregano needs winter mulching and is not reliably perennial beyond about zone 5.

and *M. spicata* (spearmint), whose leaves are jagged. Other species and varieties have subtly different flavors and foliage that may be silver or variegated.

Myrrhis odorata
Sweet cicely, anise fern, great chervil

This ferny perennial is seldom used in cooking nowadays—the common name sweet cicely suggests the former use of the leaves as a natural sweetener—but it is a beautiful plant for the back of a border in partial shade and good soil. Grow it for its beauty, and you may discover that the anise-flavored leaves are delicious in salads or herbal teas. The soil should be deep and well drained. Umbels of white flowers are borne on strong 3-foot-tall (1 m) stalks in early summer. The seedpods drop hard, black seeds that can be used as a seasoning or left to sprout.

Grow it from seed, or purchase plants. Sweet cicely gradually expands where it is content, but it is not overly invasive. Division should be done in early spring as soon as the shoots appear.

Nepeta cataria
Catnip

Catnip grows wild and weedy at my place, where its early-spring sprouting is heralded by snuffling cats. As it grows, the cats chew it and later roll in it. Eventually, plants reach as tall as 3 feet (1 m) and are topped with spires of pink flowers. Catnip grows despite season-long neglect, although it can look threadbare and seedy by late summer. It resembles anise-hyssop and has a similar tendency to self-sow profusely. Harvest shoot tips while they are still lush and green in spring and early summer, let them dry on trays in the sun or in a barely warm oven, then stuff them into small cloth bags for cat toys. Or use fresh or dried catnip to make a soothing herbal tea for humans.

Origanum vulgare
Oregano

Perennial oregano spreads into an attractive 1-foot (30 cm) mound of small, grayish leaves that makes a good groundcover around taller plants or at the front of a sunny herb garden. Not only is the regular variety decorative, but selections are available that are specially meant for edging flowerbeds. 'Hopleys' has rose-colored flowers. 'Aureum' is golden, although not strongly flavored. 'Compacta' and *O. pulchellum* grow just 6 inches (15 cm) tall. The latter has pale pink flowers and dark pink bracts.

Oregano needs well-drained soil to survive the winter and is dependably hardy only to about zone 5, so where winters are colder, it should be mulched heavily or brought indoors.

Portulaca oleracea sativa
French purslane

The cultivated form of this weedy annual grows into a spreading mat of small, succulent leaves in hot, dry weather and in the driest sandy ground. The young foliage, rich in vitamin C and antioxidants, is very nutritious and can be cooked in soups or added to salads. Purslane grows easily from seed and self-sows.

Rosmarinus officinalis
Rosemary

Despite its grayish foliage, rosemary needs frequent watering, but if it is grown in a pot—the usual situation in northern gardens—this is an easy job. Give it a spot in partial shade, with the container partly buried to help insulate the roots and cut down on watering needs.

To start a new plant, strip the foliage from a bottom branch and bend the stem gently where it will contact the ground. Make sure this layer is held firmly in place, and stake the branch tip to hold it upright. It should root by the end of the growing season and can then be cut from the parent plant. Rosemary is also easy from cuttings (see page 28). Bring the pot indoors to overwinter in a cool, bright location.

Ruta graveolens
Rue, herb of grace

Rue means regret. This herb has a strong, bitter fragrance once associated with sadness or unpleasantness and certainly with evil, which rue was thought to counteract by its very presence. But rue doesn't take sides. If it protects the gardener, it also endangers the gardener. It is poisonous in large amounts, and merely handling the plant gives some people an itchy rash and blisters that are intensified by exposure to sunlight. Wear gardening gloves unless you know that you are not sensitive to it. It is not the herb for every garden. However, deeply indented bluish foliage and yellow summer flowers make this a beautiful 1-foot-tall (30 cm) shrubby perennial that can be used as a herb-garden hedge. It needs sun and good soil but tends to be short-lived.

Salvia officinalis
Sage

Many sages there are, but only this one carries the species name *officinalis*, designating it as an official plant of the herbalists and apothecaries—a medicinal staple. The genus name *Salvia* means a plant that saves, and our own word "sage" suggests wisdom and goodness. An old saying asks, "Why should a man die while sage grows in his garden?" Now sage is primarily a cooking herb. It is also beautiful, with grayish leaves on woody stems that generally grow upright. Sage does better in well-drained, dryish, sunny soil than in dampness or shade, but its perennial habits may fail after just a couple of years. Renew it frequently. Fortunately, it is quite easy from seed or tip cuttings (see page 28).

Satureja species
Savory

Sow the seeds of summer savory (*S. hortensis*) in early spring directly in a sunny spot in the garden or in a large pot. After the seeds germinate, the wiry stems grow quickly to 1 foot (30 cm) or taller, with tiny, dark green leaves that can be stripped off and added to salads, sausages and cooked vegetable dishes. Harvesting is best done before the small pink or white flowers open in summer. This is an easy annual, and its flavor is generally more esteemed than that of its hardy perennial cousin winter savory (*S. montana*). Winter savory also tolerates dry ground and prefers alkaline soil. The creeping form (*S. repandra*) is a good ground-

Unusual colors of thyme, such as the lemon-scented Doone Valley, are generally less hardy than other thymes.

cover for a sunny herb garden. *S. biflora* is a lemon-scented tender perennial. All perennial types can be grown from seed or propagated from cuttings.

Symphytum grandiflorum
Comfrey

A herb of ancient reputation, comfrey excels as a garden plant, although it is no longer recommended for internal use because of its content of possibly carcinogenic alkaloids. It forms a rounded mound of big green leaves 3 feet (1 m) or more high and even wider, reminiscent of those of its cousin borage. A crop of tubular, bell-shaped flowers, usually pink or white, appears in summer. If it has become badly wilted after your summer vacation away from the garden, it can be cut back and will regrow. Comfrey is a strong plant that will grow in either sun or shade. Situate the plant carefully at the outset, because it is difficult to eradicate once it is settled. It can be divided easily in spring before flowering.

Tanacetum vulgare
Tansy

Not to be confused with *Senecio jacobaea,* another plant that is called tansy or ragwort, true tansy has fragrant, ferny foliage once used as a seasoning and occasionally used now to repel rodents in gardens and houses. The yellow flowers, which bloom in clusters, can be cut and dried as everlastings. Stems grow about 2 feet (60 cm) tall. Like many drought-tolerant plants, tansy has wandering rhizomes that can quickly spread beyond bounds. Rather than living to regret planting tansy, confine it to a large pot. The attractive cultivar 'Fernleaf,' which cannot be grown from seed, is less invasive but, nevertheless, should not be trusted among delicate plants.

Teucrium chamaedrys
Germander

Along with lavender and santolina, germander is a common edging plant for the sinuous beds of English knot gardens. It is seldom used today as a medicinal herb, yet it remains decoratively useful because it is compact and evergreen, has small, glossy green leaves and woody stems and is hardy to about zone 4. It seldom exceeds 1 foot (30 cm) in height. There is also a creeping cultivar. Purplish pink flowers bloom in summer.

Where the climate is too cold for it to overwinter in the garden, a few cuttings should be kept in a cold frame or a cool place indoors until spring. Germander is easy from seed, best given an early start indoors. *T. scorodonia* (wood germander) has yellow flowers and self-sows. It has naturalized throughout Ontario and parts of the Midwest.

Thymus species
Thyme

Easy, hardy and possessed of a wide spectrum of flavors—from citrus to caraway to unmistakably thyme—the thymes are low-growing herbs that will put up with neglect in terms of watering but not weeding. Most are easily outpaced by grasses and other weeds. Ground-covering species are described on page 64. Among culinary varieties, the standard is *T. vulgaris* (common thyme), which forms a low mat that can fill in between other plants in a herb garden or anywhere else that has sun and well-drained soil. There are two strains: English (German or winter) thyme, which has broad, dark green leaves, and French (summer) thyme, which has narrow grayish leaves and a sweeter flavor. Just as hardy, to about zone 4, are caraway thyme (*T. herba-barona*) and lemon thyme (*T.* x *citriodorus*). There are additional flavors and leaf colors in perennial thymes, but not all are hardy, although well-drained soil in sun will increase your chances of overwintering them. If in doubt, take entire plants or root cuttings indoors in winter and keep them in a cool, bright place.

Valeriana officinalis
Valerian, garden heliotrope

This somewhat carrotlike plant, whose roots are still used to make a sedative, produces a clump of ferny foliage above which 3-foot-tall (1 m) self-supporting stems hold umbels of white flowers in June, a time when no other lacy white flowers are available to fill out vases and perennial beds. The flowers are sweetly fragrant and attract bees, butterflies and the small wasps that feed on insect pests. Cut the flower stems back to the ground after the blooms fade. Altogether a lovely and totally dependable plant, hardy to zone 2 and needing no fertilizing or watering, valerian is equally suited to a flowerbed or a herb garden, although it will need regular dividing, preferably in spring.

According to British plantswoman Kay Sanecki, a compost accelerator can be made from approximately equal portions of fresh valerian, dandelion, chamomile, nettle, yarrow and oak bark. Spread a thin layer of leaves, bark or whole plants, fresh or dry, between other compost ingredients, then add water.

PLOTS AND POTS
The classic perennial herb garden is a geometrically designed plot in which gray foliage predominates. It must be located in a place that is mostly sunny but sheltered from strong winds. Often, the herb garden is walled or hedged. Paths, paved or not, divide it into sections, and at the center, there is often an eye-catching feature such as a sundial. Plants not used in cooking but traditionally labeled as herbs, such as wormwood and rue, may be included for visual and historical interest. Horehound and germander, for example, make a good hardy low hedge for the perimeter, amenable to clipping. Where it is hardy, sanvitalia acts similarly. Annual herbs are generally grown elsewhere, amongst vegetables or annual flowers.

Many herbs grow well in pots. For instance, tender perennial herbs such as

To ensure the survival of prized herbs such as these thymes, overwinter indoors.

rosemary, lemon verbena and bay, which must be wintered indoors beyond zone 7, can live in a pot year-round. Give them a sandy soil mixture, and when they are indoors, allow the soil to dry between waterings. They need plenty of light in a place that is preferably cooler than 70 degrees F (21°C) by day and even cooler but above freezing by night. Hardy potted herbs left outdoors should be buried up to their rims in fall, then mulched.

Roses and Shrubs

◆ 8 ◆

"Do not scatter shrubs indiscriminately as individual specimen plants. These shrubs must not detract from the desired garden picture, which may be the home itself, some structural element of it or the landscape planting."

—L.C. Sherk and A.R. Buckley, *Ornamental Shrubs for Canada*, 1968

Many shrubs and trees are suited to dry gardens. Some may seem surprising. Willows, for instance, which are tolerant of wet ground, will survive in dry conditions after they have rooted for a couple of years. Because most trees can survive the short droughts described in this book, this chapter concentrates, instead, on shrubs.

What's the difference between a shrub and a tree? Shrubs are often smaller, but not always. More important is that although both shrubs and trees have permanent stems or trunks—if they died back to the ground in winter, they would be better called perennials or, to be more precise, herbaceous perennials—trees have just one stem, while shrubs have more. But it's not quite that clear, either. You can confuse the issue by pruning a shrub to one stem or grafting what would otherwise be a shrub onto a single trunk, like weeping caragana. So some species that don't grow too big or too fast can be either shrub or tree, depending on how they are pruned and trained. And shrubs living at the edge of their limit of hardiness may go the other way and act like herbaceous perennials, dying back to the ground in winter and resprouting in spring. Many roses do that.

Amelanchier species
Shadbush, Juneberry, saskatoon

Also known as snowy mespilus, serviceberry and shadblow, these spring-flowering members of the rose family boast admirable drought tolerance and hardiness—many to zone 1. They grow as tall as 15 feet (4.5 m) and may be equally wide. None is especially interesting after blooming time, but most have the advantage of offering edible berries that, if not picked by people, will be relished by birds. *A. alnifolia* (saskatoon) is grown for its delicious fruit. Look for improved cultivars such as 'Smoky.' There are many cultivars of the less hardy (to zone 4) but more profusely flowering *A.* x *grandiflora* and *A. laevis*. All tolerate wet soil as well as dry.

Aralia species
Aralia

These big, spiny shrubs are too domineering for a small garden. They are armed with spines and spread by suckers. But they are undemanding and eye-catching where there is room for them. They grow around 15 feet (4.5 m) tall and almost as wide.

A. elata (Japanese angelica tree), the hardiest (zone 4), is a large shrub or small tree from Asia. The compound leaves may be as long as 3 feet (1 m). Spikes of flowers bloom in summer, followed by black fruit that is enjoyed by birds. Some variegated forms are even showier. The foliage of 'Variegata' is edged and blotched with creamy white.

A. spinosa (Hercules club, devil's walking stick) is a fairly tender shrub (zone 6) that is too big for a small city garden. It can reach 25 feet (7.5 m) where it is content.

Aronia species
Chokeberry

Chokeberries are native North American shrubs with showy white or rose-colored spring blossoms, followed by decorative fruit that lasts well into winter. The fall color is good. All are excellent for massing or for including in shrub or perennial borders.

A. arbutifolia (red chokeberry) is hardy to at least zone 4. The cultivar 'Brilliantissima' has white blossoms, a big crop of glossy red fruits (technically pomes) that resemble tiny pears and bright scarlet fall foliage. It grows 8 feet (2.4 m) or taller in full sun and almost any soil.

A. melanocarpa (black chokeberry) grows roughly half as tall. The cultivar 'Autumn Magic' has wine-red foliage in fall and shiny purple-black fruits that are edible but bitter. It is hardy to zone 3 or 4.

Caragana species
Siberian pea shrub, pea tree

Many drought-tolerant shrubs are members of the pea family (Leguminosae). These plants are capable of synthesizing their own soil-nitrogen supply, enriching the soil for neighboring plants, and can be relatively self-sufficient otherwise. This legume has the small, gray-green opposite leaves and summer flowers typical of the family. Caragana flowers are usually bright yellow. Extremely drought-tolerant, hardy (zone 2) and easy to grow, caragana is a good plant to include in any dry gar-

den. Prune it immediately after it flowers. Following 11 years of trials to determine the most self-reliant plants for the Midwest, the University of Minnesota recommended caragana for hedges and screens in difficult places.

C. arborescens (common caragana) grows at the foot of my driveway. Purchased as an unwatered half-price bargain in a discount-store cardboard box, it quickly revived in the garden only to be driven over during a winter storm. Righted the following spring, it again recovered. This is a plant for abusive situations, where it can grow as tall as a leggy 18 feet (5.5 m) but should be pruned to stay shorter and denser. In rich soil, it is invasive. More discreet is the justifiably popular weeping form, 'Pendula,' which looks unpleasantly like an umbrella for the first couple of years but becomes increasingly graceful as its branches multiply and lengthen. It is so top-heavy that it should be staked for at least the first year, longer in a windy spot. 'Walker' is another weeping form. The variety 'Sutherland' has a vertical shape as tall as 20 feet (6 m), ideal for windbreaks. 'Fernleaf,' named for its distinctive foliage, is about the same height.

C. pygmaea (*C. aurantiaca*), known as pygmy caragana, forms a compact fine-textured mound of arched, spreading branches only 2 to 4 feet (60-120 cm) tall, suitable for the perennial border. The Devonian Botanic Garden near Edmonton, Alberta, uses this species as a low hedge around its herb garden. More difficult to find, although more ornamental, are the equally hardy *C. jubata*, *C. frutex* and *C. sinica*. Caragana is easy from seed, which is the best way to obtain unusual species.

Caryopteris x clandonensis
Blue mist shrub, bluebeard, blue spirea

As its common names indicate, *C. x clandonensis* is known for a beautiful show of blue flowers, although there is also a white version. If it is pruned every year, the shrub grows less than 2 to 3 feet (60-90 cm) tall, with gray foliage and fuzzy flowers for several weeks in late summer.

Although this was one of the star performers during the 1995 drought at the Xeriscape Demonstration Garden in Plainview, New York, it was not

Cotinus, also called smoke tree or smoke bush, has long, hairlike flower stalks that appear for weeks in great abundance.

sufficiently winter-hardy to survive at the trial garden at the University of Maine at Orono (zone 4). It is hardy in protected places in zone 5, although it will suffer tip dieback in winter; it is safer in zone 6. Farther north, it can be grown in a cool greenhouse. The flowers of 'Dark Knight' are violet-blue, 'Blue Mist' are pale blue and 'Heavenly Blue' are medium blue. Give caryopteris sun and preferably a light-textured limy soil. Prune it back to the ground in early spring, as it flowers on new growth.

Cotinus coggygria
Smoke bush, smoke tree

This farmyard favorite, hardy to about zone 5 depending on the cultivar, is named for the unusual foggy appearance of the shrub in bloom. The misty look comes from thousands of hairs that extend from clusters of tiny flowers. After the flowers fade, the hairs continue to grow, so the effect can last for weeks. Cotinus grows as tall as 10 to 15 feet (3-4.5 m) and almost as wide. The lower branches can be removed to create a small multi-stemmed tree, or the entire plant can be cut back to 2 feet (60 cm) or so every winter to keep it growing as a small, dense, profusely flowering shrub, since cotinus blooms on new wood. Leaf color is remarkably intense on new growth, another incentive to prune heavily. In zone 3 and sometimes 4, this annual dieback happens naturally, and the shrub may act much like a herbaceous perennial. Such is the case with the cultivars 'Nordine,' 'Royal Purple' (dark purple foliage) and 'Velvet Cloak' (red foliage), all grown in the trial garden of the University of Maine at Orono (zone 4). The hardier 'Pink Champagne' suffered little or no damage. There are many additional cultivars, most with green leaves. 'Daydream,' from the Arnold Arboretum in Boston, stays a neat 10 feet (3 m).

Give smoke bush sun for most of the day. It can put up with almost any soil and has no major pest or disease problems. A relative of sumac (*Rhus* species), smoke bush is sometimes incorrectly labeled *Rhus cotinus*.

Cotoneaster species

Cotoneaster

Cotoneasters are members of the rose family, mostly from China, that may be evergreen or deciduous. They have small white or pink flowers, followed by red or black fruits (correctly called pomes) like tiny apples. These fruits persist into winter, contributing to the year-round attractiveness of the shrubs. If you look far enough, you can find at least 13 species of cotoneaster on the market. All prefer sun and well-drained soil, preferably alkaline. Several grow laterally and so create good groundcovers (see pages 53 and 54). Others form neat shrubs. For maximum fruit production, prune cotoneaster only as needed.

The hardiest cotoneasters proved self-reliant after 11 years of field trials at the University of Minnesota, maintaining a good appearance whether or not they were irrigated. In trials at the garden of the University of Maine at Orono (zone 4), two species thrived: *C. lucidus* (hedge cotoneaster), which is deciduous and grows about 10 feet (3 m) tall, with black fruit; and *C. racemiflorus aureus*, deciduous, to 8 feet (2.4 m) tall, with bright red fruit. Not included in the Maine trial but hardy to zone 2 are *C. acutifolius* (Peking cotoneaster), which is deciduous, to 10 feet (3 m) tall, with black fruit; and *C. integerrimus* (European cotoneaster), also deciduous, 4 to 7 feet (1.2-2 m) tall, with red fruit.

Cytisus species

Broom

Difficult to grow north of zone 5 but a weedy pest where it is most comfortable—in places like the Pacific Northwest and Cape Cod—*C. scoparius* (Scotch broom), which has a cloud of brilliant yellow pea flowers in early spring, exemplifies the ability of the genus to survive in poor soil. It can put up with sand or gravel, even on slopes and in strong winds, provided it is in sun and the ground is well drained. For zone 5 and sheltered places in zone 4, the hardiest species are *C. purpureus* (*Genista purpurea*), or purple broom, 2 feet (60 cm) tall, with white, pink or purple flowers; and *C.* x *praecox* (*Genista praecox*), known as War-

'Emerald Gaiety' is a hardy euonymus cultivar that is suitable for a protected place in zone 5.

minster broom, to 10 feet (3 m), with hairy leaves and pale yellow flowers. There are bright yellow and white cultivars as well. Prune broom back after flowering to keep it from becoming straggly. Broom should be transplanted when small or purchased as a container plant, because large plants do not move well. See also *Genista* (page 143).

Elaeagnus commutata

Silverberry

Two members of this genus, *E. angustifolia* (Russian olive) and *E. umbellata* (autumn olive), are Asian imports that have become invasive in parts of midwestern and eastern North America. But silverberry, the only North American cousin, is not on the hit list, although it, too, is suited to poor ground and dry, windy hillsides. It is a shrubby version of the Russian olive tree and is hardy to zone 2, with beautiful silvery leaves. It grows as tall as 12 feet (3.7 m) and has fragrant flowers, followed by silvery fruit. Although it is a native plant—to eastern Canada and the north-eastern United States—and thus cannot be condemned as an alien invader, it does spread by suckers, so it should be grown where you can mow around it or where it is contained by paving.

Euonymus species
Spindle tree

E. fortunei (wintercreeper) attracts a lot of attention at plant nurseries in spring, with its waxy leaves in variegated shades of gold, cream and green. Despite its showy looks and evergreen foliage, it is an easy shrub where it is hardy, prized for foundation or specimen plantings and for sunny or lightly shaded perennial borders, anywhere the soil is not wet. It can be kept at just 3 to 4 feet (90-120 cm). *E. fortunei* is most safely grown in zone-6 or warmer gardens, but among the hardiest cultivars, suitable for protected places in zone 5, are 'Emerald Cushion,' 'Emerald Gaiety,' 'Silver Edge,' 'Vegetus' and 'Waterdown.'

E. alatus (winged euonymus, burning bush), which is taller and hardier than *E. fortunei* (to zone 4), is considered invasive in midwestern and eastern North America and thus should be kept out of gardens in these areas. It has corky protrusions on the bark—the wings described by its common name—which add to its interest. The cultivar 'Compacta' reaches only about 4 feet (1.2 m), while most others grow twice as tall.

Forsythia species
Forsythia

Like lilac, forsythia is nothing more than a modest green shrub after the flowers are gone, but that matters little to northern gardeners who eagerly await its early show of bright yellow flowers. It is the first spring shrub to bloom—if it does. Until the 1970s, forsythia was a disappointment most springs in zone-5 or cooler gardens, because only buds protected by spring snow bloomed, unless the winter and spring had been exceptionally mild. During the past couple of decades, however, a number of hardier cultivars have been developed, mostly hybrids of *F. ovata* and *F. europaea*. One of the first was 'Northern Gold,' but even more

reliable is 'Happy Centennial,' a 1986 Canadian introduction.

At the Minnesota Landscape Arboretum, 'New Hampshire Gold,' 'Northern Gold' and 'Northern Sun' were found best able to withstand average Minnesota winters, including temperatures as low as minus 33 degrees F (–36°C), although all suffered flower-bud death when temperatures fluctuated. ('Happy Centennial' was not included in the Minnesota trial.) 'Vermont Sun,' a selection of *F. mandschurica*, came out of dormancy earliest of the plants in the Minnesota trials and ended up less hardy than the others by mid-March. For warmer climatic zones, there are more profusely flowering species and cultivars, such as *F.* x *intermedia* 'Beatrix Farrand,' developed at the Arnold Arboretum in Boston.

Allow forsythia plenty of room to grow, roughly 3 feet (1 m) all around, so that it can be allowed to grow as it looks best, to its full height of 7 to 9 feet (2-2.7 m). After blooming, prune to shape, trimming the oldest stems close to the ground to create replacements. An overgrown plant can be cut back almost to the ground immediately after blooming, but there will be little flowering the following year.

Genista species
Dyer's greenwood, Spanish gorse

Very similar to their relatives in the genus *Cytisus* (see page 142), these shrubs are also tolerant of poor, dry soil in sun, and most have a mass of golden pealike flowers in spring, although some bloom white. They grow 1 to 3 feet (30-90 cm) tall, depending on the species and cultivar. While the most common in zone 7 is *G. hispanica* (Spanish gorse, broom), which is a prickly pest on Vancouver Island, the best known in places with colder winters is *G. tinctoria* (dyer's greenwood) and its dwarf forms 'Golden Dwarf' and the double-flowered 'Plena.' They are hardy to zone 4. Almost as hardy is the summer-blooming *G. lydia*, about 2 feet (60 cm) tall. Like cytisus, genista resents transplanting. It should be obtained as a container-grown plant and moved when small. Some can be used as groundcovers (see page 55).

Genista tinctoria *resents transplanting and needs sun and perfectly drained soil, but it can be reliable and long-lived.*

Heptacodium miconioides
Seven son flower

This native of China is still little known in North America but is already acclaimed. It was introduced to the United States in 1980 by the Arnold Arboretum in Boston and was awarded a Gold Medal in 1994 by the Pennsylvania Horticultural Society for its beauty, uniqueness and pest and disease resistance. It can be kept smallish as a shrub or allowed to grow into a tree about 20 feet (6 m) tall. There are small, fragrant, creamy white flowers in late summer or fall, followed by fruit that is purple when ripe. The dark green leaves hang on well into fall, when they turn yellow. The tan bark exfoliates and is therefore attractive in winter. Seven son flower does best in sun but will tolerate shade and almost any soil. It is hardy to zone 4.

Hibiscus syriacus
Rose of Sharon

The only hardy shrub in the genus *Hibiscus*, safest in zone-6 or warmer gardens, rose of Sharon is surprisingly drought-tolerant once established. 'Diana,' a white-flowered cultivar, was one of the star performers during the 1995 drought at the Xeriscape Demonstration Garden in Plainview, New York. Rose of Sharon grows as tall as 15 feet (4.5 m) and almost as wide, although it is usually only half that height in the northern part of its range. Its chief value is late-summer blooming when most other shrubs are finished, but otherwise, it is unremarkable. There are many cultivars with single or double flowers in shades of white through pink to rose, magenta and violet-blue, some bicolored.

Although the usual route is to buy plants, it is not difficult to grow from seed. Young plants are susceptible to winterkill in the northern part of their hardiness range, so they should be mulched for at least the first two winters. Water deeply during prolonged droughts. Prune in early spring to encourage flowering, which occurs on new wood. The name rose of Sharon, incidentally, is also used for the unrelated zone-7 yellow-flowered ground-cover *Hypericum calycinum*.

Hippophaë rhamnoides
Sea buckthorn

There are several dry-garden plants whose common name includes the word "sea"—such as sea lavender, sea holly and this shrub—indicating a plant that can grow in salty, sandy seaside gardens. Sea buckthorn can even be used to create a windbreak on a beach. These large, spiny shrubs or small trees have attractive, narrow silver leaves resembling willow, and the females will bear bright orange fruit, provided you grow at least one male for as many as six females. The berries, which are edible but too acidic to be eaten by birds, will last all winter, making this a choice shrub for winter color. The species generally grows about 12 feet (3.7 m) tall and equally wide, although there are taller cultivars, and it is hardy to zone 2. As is the case with many tough plants, sea buckthorn can be aggressive and hard to get rid of. It suckers freely, so keep it out of perennial borders. It looks best when given its own corner. Sea buckthorn is quite easy from ripe seeds sown outdoors in fall.

Hypericum species
St.-John's-wort

There are herbaceous and woody forms of this genus. The common name attests either to its use by St. John the healer or to its blooming time around the date commemorating the saint's beheading, June 24. The plant's yellow flowers turn red when crushed, suggesting blood. "Wort" is simply an old name for any healing plant. The hardy perennial *H. perforatum*, which has proven antibiotic and healing qualities, is the species most often used in medicine.

Hypericum is also gratifyingly easy to grow, provided you choose a species hardy and drought-resistant enough for your garden. Most thrive in full sun and dry, sandy soil, although a little shade will prolong flowering. One deciduous shrub recommended for the Midwest by the Ohio Nursery and Landscape Association in 1994 was *H. patulum* 'Sunburst,' which has blue-green leaves and large yellow flowers in summer. It grows about 5 feet (1.5 m) tall and wide. It did exceptionally well during the 1995 drought at the Xeriscape Demonstration Garden in Plainview, New York.

The evergreen North American species *H. kalmianum*, about 3 feet (1 m) tall, and the cultivar *H. patulum* 'Sungold' fared best in the trial garden at the University of Maine at Orono, where all other *Hypericum* species and cultivars that were tested succumbed to the zone-4 winter.

Recommended for warmer gardens is *H. prolificum* (bush broom, shrubby St.-John's-wort), an evergreen North American native that grows 3 to 5 feet (1-1.5 m) tall or more, with clusters of small flowers throughout much of the summer.

Ilex glabra
Inkberry

Hollies are generally not very winter-hardy and are happiest in wet, organic soils, but inkberry is an exception. Although it prefers moist conditions and can be found in swamps, it will thrive in dry places and even puts up with salty soil once established. In common with all broad-leaved evergreens, it isn't suitable for exposed places or windbreaks but can be included in a perennial border or a sheltered corner. The small flowers attract bees. There are interesting white-fruited cultivars of inkberry, but the more usual black-fruited types are known not for showy fruit, which is mostly hidden, but for their lovely, dark green, leathery foliage. This is the only evergreen species of *Ilex* that is native to Canada—its range extends south to Florida—with some cultivars hardy to zone 4. A list of common names, which include winterberry and Appalachian tea, attests to its versatility. It grows around 5 to 8 feet (1.5-2.4 m) tall and equally wide. Inkberry puts out stolons, so it is easy to transplant or divide, but it is not badly invasive.

Juniperus species
Juniper

One of the evergreen shrubs most likely to succeed in dry, sunny gardens—and unhappy in shade and damp—juniper is available in so many shapes, sizes and foliage colors that an attractive minimal-care garden could be created using little else. In downtown office gardens, scrunched between concrete sidewalks and walls, junipers create a reliable and refreshing spread of green, whether bright, dull, bluish or gold. An all-juniper design is too static for a home garden, but junipers planted among other shrubs and perennials can provide a dependable background that looks good all year. In winter, junipers add color to perennial beds that may otherwise be empty, providing foliage and sometimes berries as well. The females are distinguished among coniferous evergreens by their blue, black or reddish berries. Common juniper (*J. communis*) berries are used to flavor gin, which takes its name from the plant. About 2 pounds (1 kg) of berries flavor 100 gallons (380 L) of gin. The berries have also been used medicinally, especially as a diuretic and urinary antiseptic. Common juniper is hardy to zone 2, but there are dozens of cultivars, some much tenderer.

Because some junipers grow very large and do so quite quickly, make sure that the diminutive plant you buy will not overwhelm your garden, or be prepared to move neighboring plants outward every couple of years. There are two species of mat-forming junipers described as groundcovers on pages 57 to 59, and there are also upright spreading and columnar types.

J. chinensis (Chinese juniper). The best-known Chinese junipers are called pfitzers, selections with ascending branches. The first of these, 'Pfitzeriana,' bred in Germany in 1899 and still recommended as an easy hedge for full sun, has been hybridized into green, blue and gold-tipped cultivars, usually 3 to 4 feet (90-120 cm) tall but sometimes dwarf and sometimes much taller; 'Hetzii' may reach 15 feet (4.5 m). The green pfitzers are less hardy than the golden types. 'Gold Star,' hardy to zone 2, forms a dense low-growing mound up to 2 feet (60 cm) tall. Its juvenile foliage, produced at the branch tips, is bright gold throughout the life of the plant. 'Mint Julep,' also known as 'Seagreen,' is one of the best of the greens. In zone-4 or colder gardens, it should be protected from the wind.

J. scopulorum (Western red cedar, Colorado red cedar, Rocky Mountain juniper) is hardy to zone 2. It forms a pyramidal shape. Popular cultivars include 'Blue Heaven' and 'Wichita Blue.' These grow quickly to a height of 10 to 20 feet (3-6 m), too

tall for foundation plantings and small gardens but good as specimens in a lawn or along a driveway. 'Skyrocket' may be the narrowest of vertical junipers.

J. virginiana (Eastern red cedar) is also very hardy, to zone 3, but should not be planted near hawthorn, which is an alternate host for cedar apple rust, a fungus that produces ugly growths on junipers. It should also be kept out of commercial apple-growing areas, as it contributes to a rust disease of apples. Most cultivars, such as the dark green 'Emerald Sentinel,' are pyramidal, although some, such as the silver-blue 'Gray Owl,' are wide-spreading.

Upright junipers should be spiraled round with twine in late fall to prevent snow and ice damage. If grown in a windy place, they may need staking for the first year or two. Wearing gloves, shear them every spring if you want to retain a tight, formal shape. Also in spring, trim away any dead needles and cut broken branches back to the closest joint.

Kerria japonica
Japanese rose

This Chinese member of the rose family forms a rounded shrub about 4 to 6 feet (1.2-1.8 m) tall and wide. It is deciduous, but the stems remain green and decorative all winter. The buttercuplike flowers are pretty in spring but short-lived, unless you grow the double-flowered form 'Pleniflora.' 'Pleniflora' did not survive the winter in the trial garden at the University of Maine at Orono (zone 4). 'Picta' ('Variegata'), which offers variegated green-and-white foliage, thrived during the 1995 drought at the Xeriscape Demonstration Garden in Plainview, New York.

Kerria needs well-drained soil and should be grown out of the wind in partial shade. In the coldest part of its range, in exposed spots in zone 5, branch tips may be lost to winterkill and should be pruned off, but the shrub generally recovers quickly in spring.

Kolkwitzia amabilis
Beauty bush

An old-fashioned favorite, this honeysuckle cousin is valued for its fountain shape and spectac-

One of the brightest green Juniperus chinensis *cultivars, 'Mint Julep' may need winter protection in zone-4 gardens.*

ular crop of fragrant pink bell-shaped flowers in late spring. Beauty bush is easy to grow but can be overly eager. It is hardy to zone 4 and will put up with virtually any soil if given full sun, but it needs regular pruning as soon as the flowers fade to keep it from becoming leggy. It grows 6 to 10 feet (1.8-3 m) tall and about the same width, with heavily textured leaves. It is too large for most small gardens and not especially interesting when blooming is over. The cultivars may be less winter-hardy.

Lespedeza species
Bush clover

A little-known member of the pea family, lespedeza can be considered a shrub or a perennial, because after a cold winter, it may die back to the ground. In any case, it should be cut back hard in spring to keep the growth dense and to ensure a good crop of flowers, which bloom on new growth. The plant has blue-green foliage and white, pink or purple flowers in summer or fall, when few other shrubs are in bloom. Lespedeza

is very easy from seeds, which are large and can be sown in spring just like sweet peas. Give lespedeza well-drained soil in full sun.

L. bicolor, the hardiest species, to about zone 4, can exceed 8 feet (2.4 m) in height, with arching branches and purple flowers in summer and fall.

L. japonica, hardy to zone 6, has white flowers in fall.

L. thunbergii has rosy purple flowers in fall. The cultivar 'Gibraltar' has improved flowering. Both can be propagated from softwood cuttings (see page 28).

Lonicera species
Honeysuckle

Some honeysuckles need considerable moisture to thrive, and honeysuckles vary from hardy to tender, depending on the species and cultivar, but winter and drought damage are only two of the hazards awaiting this otherwise choice shrub, a favorite of bees, birds and butterflies.

Certain honeysuckles are susceptible to

damage by the honeysuckle aphid, which entered North America on imported plants during the 1970s. Infected plants develop the clumps and deformities known as witches'-broom. Deformed twigs and sometimes entire plants may die. Horticulturists at North Dakota State University evaluated honeysuckles' aphid resistance. Among the plants that fared best were a few that also have considerable drought resistance: *L. maackii* (Amur honeysuckle) and its cultivars 'Cling Red' and 'Rem Red'; and *L. tatarica* (Tatarian honeysuckle) 'Arnold Red.'

L. maackii can reach 10 to 15 feet (3-4.5 m) tall and wide, with a fabulous show of fragrant fall flowers, followed by red berries. It can be invasive and is hardy to zone 2.

L. tatarica grows 8 to 10 feet (2.4-3 m) tall and bears white, pink or red flowers in spring, followed by red berries that are decorative in summer. The species is hardy to zone 2 but invasive. 'Arnold Red,' which has dark red flowers, is a bit less hardy and not invasive. The Devonian Botanic Garden of the University of Alberta reports that 'Arnold Red' is resistant to aphids but produces no root suckers, so it is difficult to propagate and therefore can be hard to find.

A honeysuckle that will likely become better known in the next decade is *L. caerulea* (blue honeysuckle), a favorite plant in Siberia because of its extreme winter hardiness and early, dependable production of berries high in vitamin C. It grows as tall and wide as 6 feet (1.8 m). For fruit production, you have to grow at least two different varieties. It must be planted in fall, because spring growth is early and rapid.

Honeysuckle looks and does best if severely pruned every year immediately after flowering. Remove the oldest branches to the base.

Myrica pensylvanica
Bayberry, wax myrtle

A shrub of the seashore of eastern North America, bayberry thrives in sandy, acidic soil, spreads by suckers to form colonies and can be used to stabilize dry hillsides in full sun to light shade. It grows about 8 feet (2.4 m) tall and wide,

The flowers of a well-established Lonicera tatarica *hedge attract colorful monarch butterflies in June.*

with dull green foliage. The sexes are on separate plants, so if you want berries, you must grow at least one female and one male. The tiny berries, which are waxy and grayish and have a distinctive fragrance, are used to make bayberry candles. They persist into winter unless eaten by birds. Bayberry is hardy to zone 3.

Philadelphus species
Mock orange

Mock orange is one of many flowering shrubs that is interesting only when in bloom, unless you choose a variety with unusual foliage. The flowers, however, are lovely: white, spring-blooming and, best of all, strongly and sweetly perfumed. Double flowers last longer in bloom than singles. Species and cultivars range from hardy to tender, so if you live where winters are harsh, choose carefully. Among the hardiest types are *P. schrenkii* (Manchurian mock orange), zone 2, and *P. coronarius,* zone 3. *P. coronarius* 'Aureus' is a choice selection with golden leaves. 'Variegatus' has leaves bordered with white.

The eventual height of philadelphus depends on the species and cultivar, from 3-foot (1 m) *P.* 'Silver Rain,' or 'Silver Showers,' to 9-foot (2.7 m) *P.* x *virginalis* (virginal mock orange), an old-fashioned hybrid that has been surpassed by neater cultivars which bloom more profusely and for a longer period.

Mock orange will grow well in any decent soil, provided it is well drained. Prune the branches back immediately after blooming in spring, in the manner of forsythia, so that new wood can produce flowers next spring. Overgrown leggy plants can be cut back entirely to just above the ground and will regrow, although blooming may be delayed a year.

Physocarpus opulifolius
Ninebark

Although it looks somewhat like spirea and is sometimes called *Spiraea opulifolia*, *P. opulifolius* has more interesting features. The unfurling leaves are bright yellow in early spring. Next, in spring or early summer, comes a good show of light pink flowers. Although small, they are produced in large clusters. The red seedpods that follow are attractive in floral arrangements, and all year, there is interesting peeling bark which reveals beautiful brown inner bark. Ninebark does fine in ordinary soil and full sun, where it can quickly grow taller than 5 to 8 feet (1.5-2.4 m), and is hardy to zone 2. The cultivars 'Luteus,' 'Pygmy Gold' and 'Dart's Gold' have yellow foliage and are smaller than the species. 'Nanus,' or 'Nana,' is a dwarf form about 4 feet (1.2 m) tall, sometimes used for a hedge.

Pinus species
Pine

Tree-sized pines are better known, but there are several small species and cultivars as well. They are among the best evergreens for dry, sandy places. Most popular and always hardy, although extremely variable in eventual size, is the mugho pine (*P. mugo*). Some cultivars stay small, while others may eventually grow up to 30 feet (9 m) tall

and wide, overwhelming foundation plantings and shrub borders. For mughos that stay small, search for 'Big Tuna,' to 10 feet (3 m) tall and 6 feet (1.8 m) wide; 'Mops,' about half as tall; and the even smaller 'Allen's Dwarf,' 'Gnome,' 'Valley Cushion,' 'Oregon Jade' and 'Green Candle.'

Additional small pines are choice finds for rock gardens, although they can also be pretty along paths and in perennial borders, providing long-lasting color after their bedmates fade in winter. Look for blue-green *P. strobus* 'Nana,' *P. densiflora* 'Umbraculifera' and the dwarf forms of *P. sylvestris* (Scots pine), such as 'Watereri,' which eventually reaches almost 9 feet (2.7 m) tall. The groundcover types are described on page 60.

To keep pines small and dense, pinch off all or a portion of the new candles of growth each spring.

Potentilla fruticosa
Cinquefoil

This shrubby form of potentilla is hardy to about zone 2 and thrives in hot sun, although it needs occasional watering and appreciates soil with some humus. The small, narrow leaflets grow in groups of five, origin of the common name cinquefoil (five leaves). Flowering begins in late spring and may continue for most of the summer. The usual flower color is sunny yellow, but there are also light and dark oranges, reds and pinks, all with yellow undertones. The pinks and reds fade as they mature, one reason the white-flowered cultivars, such as 'Abbotswood,' 'McKay's White' and 'Snowflake,' are among the most decorative. The best of the yellows may be 'Gold Star,' with its unusually large flowers, or 'Goldfinger,' with bright flowers and dark green foliage until fall. From the University of Manitoba comes the double pink 'Pink Beauty.' 'Floppy Disc' has bright pink flowers, while 'Primrose Beauty' has silvery foliage and creamy yellow flowers.

The more upright varieties may reach almost 5 feet (1.5 m), although they can be kept smaller. 'Sutter's Gold' is one of the smallest, about 1 foot (30 cm) tall.

Clip back potentilla branches after flowering to keep the shrub dense and floriferous. It can be cut back to the ground every three to five years. Otherwise, remove one-third of the canes every year in late winter. Potentilla is susceptible to infestation by spider mites, which can be killed with insecticidal soap spray.

Prunus species

Cherry, plum

Sweet cherries, edible plums and other large-fruited flag bearers of the genus *Prunus* need plenty of water in hot weather, but there are smaller-fruited types that are remarkably hardy. All produce edible fruit that, if not sweet enough for humans to eat straight off the branch, is always cherished by birds and other wildlife. Usually, the fruit makes delicious preserves. The plants use the moisture in the spring soil to produce flowers and berries, and once established, the plants survive dry summers and cold winters, but the soil must be well drained. In a trial of *Prunus* at the Agriculture Canada station in Morden, Manitoba, the first to flower, starting April 20, were *P. armeniaca* and *P. salicina,* followed shortly by *P. tomentosa* (Nanking, Hansen's bush cherry), *P. americana, P. nigra, P.* x *nigrella, P. triloba simplex, P. pensylvanica* and *P. spinosa.* The station tested 11 other species, all hardy and productive on the prairies. The following are three of the best shrubs for dry places:

P. besseyi (Western sand cherry, bush cherry) is a North American prairie native with sweet fruit. Hybrids of sand cherry and plum have produced so-called cherry plums, small trees that bear edible fruits which look like cherry-sized plums. Cultivars include 'Opata' and 'Sapa.'

P. x *cistena* (purple sand cherry) is valued as one of the few hardy shrubs with purple foliage. Small white or pink spring flowers are followed by dark purple fruit. It is hardy to zone 3. Prune it back in spring to keep the growth dense. It can reach 10 feet (3 m) in protected places.

P. maritima (beach plum) is native to the east coast of North America and hardy to zone 4. It has masses of white spring flowers that bloom before the leaves appear. The purple or yellow fruit makes excellent jelly. It grows 3 to 6 feet (1-1.8 m) tall and may be twice as wide.

Rhus species

Sumac

Sumac can be considered either a shrub or a small tree and comes in species and varieties from 3 to 30 feet (1-9 m) tall or more. One of the most prized woody ornamentals in Europe—because of its toughness coupled with, paradoxically, its tropical-looking foliage and beautiful purple flowers—sumac is less popular in North America. It is native to this continent, and *R. typhina* (*R. hirta*), known as staghorn sumac, is a rampant spreader that most gardeners would fear welcoming into their manicured beds. It spreads by aggressive suckers that may sprout some distance from the mother plant.

Although there are no entirely sucker-free sumacs yet, the cultivars are more refined than their wild forebears. *R. typhina* 'Dissecta' and 'Laciniata,' for instance, are beautiful cut-leaved forms that are less invasive, although even these are best grown as specimens surrounded by a lawn or patio. Mowing or pavement will keep them confined. On the positive side, this aggressiveness suits most sumacs to colonizing dry hills and occupying gravelly beds where little else will look as comely. As well as the deciduous types, such as *R. typhina* and the three species below, there are evergreens that are not listed here because they need warm winters.

R. aromatica (*R. canadensis*), or fragrant sumac, has cultivars that grow just 3 feet (1 m) tall, making it an excellent choice for dry, rocky slopes or in front of taller shrubs. The leaves are aromatic, and it is hardy to zone 3. Just 2 feet (60 cm) tall, the cultivar 'Gro-low' is one of the shrubs recommended for sustainable landscapes by the University of Massachusetts.

R. copallina (shining sumac, flame leaf sumac) can reach 30 feet (9 m) and is hardy to zone 5. It has glossy, dark green leaves that turn scarlet in fall.

R. glabra (smooth sumac) is recommended as one of the best hardy drought-tolerant shrubs by North Dakota State University in Fargo. It is hardy to zone 3 and grows 6 to 10 feet (1.8-3 m) tall. 'Flavescens' has yellow fruit and yellow fall color.

In most species, there are separate male and female plants, but many cultivars have flowers of both sexes on the same plant.

Many cousins of cherries and plums, such as Prunus tomentosa, *are suited to harsh climates and have edible fruit.*

Ribes alpinum
Mountain currant, alpine currant

Scarlet berries on the female plants mark this hardy shrub as a relative of the gooseberry and the red and black currant. Although mountain currant can be susceptible to powdery mildew, it is, nevertheless, an excellent plant for massing or for hedges. It is hardy to zone 3 and is considered one of the best drought-tolerant shrubs by North Dakota State University in Fargo. The foliage is dense and dark green on the species, and the plant is strongly upright, to 7 feet (2 m) tall, although it can be sheared regularly to keep it smaller. It will grow in full sun or shade.

Because some *Ribes* species, including females of *R. alpinum*, can be hosts of white pine blister rust fungus, a potentially devastating disease of white pines, some states prohibit importation of all *Ribes* species. As of 1996, these states were Michigan, New Hampshire, North Carolina, Pennsylvania, Rhode Island, South Carolina and Vermont. Several additional states prohibit importation of some but not all species. Contact your provincial department of agriculture or extension department agent for more information.

Rosa species
Rose

To disagree with Gertrude Stein ("a rose is a rose is a rose"), there are roses, roses and roses. Gardeners dealing with drought and wind have to look past the obvious. The biggest-flowered, most luxuriant roses—the ones most gardeners want to grow—are plants for deep, fertile soils, gentle rains and mild winters. Even so, they can be touchy and susceptible to diseases. On the other hand, a rose is the provincial flower of Alberta; *R. acicularis* grows wild and untended where summers are dry and winters are cold. It is just one among many species and selections that are very hardy and self-reliant. The trade-off in added toughness is generally smaller flowers that sometimes, although not always, bloom for a brief season. The wild species have single flowers, the type with just

Foliage that is beautiful all year but especially so in fall is a gift of Rhus typhina, *which is a rampant spreader.*

five petals, but many of the cultivars are fully double.

Among species roses for dry gardens are the following:

R. blanda (Hudson's Bay rose) grows up to 5 feet (1.5 m) tall and blooms just once but has a long-lasting display of red fruits called hips. It can bloom at its branch tips even after winter temperatures as low as minus 45 degrees F (−43°C).

R. carolina (Carolina rose, pasture rose) grows about 3 feet (1 m) tall and spreads by underground stems to form dense thickets. Small pink flowers in June are followed by red hips.

R. virginiana (Virginia rose) has single, pale pink to magenta flowers followed by red hips. It spreads by underground stems to create dense thickets almost 5 feet (1.5 m) high. It can be cut back to the ground and will revive.

Species roses can be hard to find on the market, but some can be transplanted from nearby roadsides and fields, provided you leave part of the plant in place. They can also be grown from seed,

if you have patience. The seeds do require a period of cold to germinate, so the easiest method is to sow them just under the soil surface in pots left outdoors in a sheltered place. Sprouts may appear the first spring or a year later. Blooming should occur the second or third year after sprouting.

Among cultivated varieties, most of the hardiest types are grouped as shrub roses, which have woody permanent stems. They can be short or tall, and the flowers may be single or double and any color. Some shrub roses are heirlooms, also known as Old Garden roses, varieties introduced at least a century ago. Several nurseries specialize in these. Hardy heirlooms include cultivars of *R.* x *alba* and *R. gallica*, both hardy to minus 30 degrees F (−34°C), *R. spinosissima* (Scotch rose) and *R. foetida* (yellow rose), from southwestern Asia. Yellow roses recommended for cold, dry gardens include 'Persian Yellow,' 'Harison's Yellow' and 'Hazeldean,' the hardiest of all. Unfortunately, 'Hazeldean' is difficult to propagate and hard to find.

Some of the best hybrids for tough places include in their background *R. rugosa* (rugosa rose), a native of northern Japan. *R. rugosa* roses are hardy to zone 2 unless otherwise specified. They may bloom just once in early summer, but their wrinkled (rugose) foliage is also decorative. Many yield especially large and colorful hips that remain on the plant until winter and are not only ornamental but tasty and rich in ascorbic acid. The hips can be made into jellies, syrups and herbal teas. There are scores of cultivars with *R. rugosa* in their parentage. Best of all the cultivars tested at several botanical gardens in Wisconsin, Minnesota, Illinois and Ohio was 'Frau Dagmar Hastrup' ('Frau Dagmar Hartopp'), about 3 feet (1 m) tall, with fragrant, light pink single flowers and large red hips that are showy into winter. The following cultivars were also recommended after the same trials:

'Blanc Double de Coubert' grows as tall as 6 feet (1.8 m), with fragrant, white semidouble flowers and no hips.

'Belle Poitevine' is about 4 feet (1.2 m) tall, with large, pink semidouble flowers.

'Hansa' has clusters of fragrant, reddish violet flowers on strong, self-supporting stems 3 to 4 feet

(90-120 cm) tall. 'Hansa' is widely available on the prairies but tends to become leggy and needs severe pruning back after flowering.

'Therese Bugnet' is a large, extremely hardy shrub rose to 6 feet (1.8 m) tall, with medium-pink double flowers and a few hips. It is slightly susceptible to black spot and more so to rose stem girdler.

Among climbers for difficult places are several *R. kordesii* hybrids in the Canadian rose series named for explorers, including 9-to-10-foot (2.7-3 m) dark pink 'John Cabot,' 6-foot (1.8 m) pink 'John Davis' and 9-foot (2.7 m) 'William Baffin.' All will survive temperatures of at least minus 35 degrees F (–37°C). Perhaps best of all is 'Henry Kelsey,' whose rose-red semidouble flowers have golden stamens.

Roses need full sun or just a little shade, protection from strong winds and, in their first year, weekly watering. Give them a spot with deep, rich, weed-free and preferably slightly acidic soil without competition from other plants. Dig a large hole so that the roots will not be cramped, and plant them in spring. On grafted plants in cold-winter areas, make sure the bud union, where the plant is grafted onto the roots, is 2 to 3 inches (5-7.5 cm) below the soil surface. Mulch around the stem in summer with about 4 inches (10 cm) of grass clippings or straw for moisture retention, and in winter, mulch all but the toughest roses with soil and fallen leaves or pile evergreen branches around the plants.

Pruning depends on the rose type, but in general, the hardy types can put up with heavy shearing if they become overly large. In early spring, always remove any dead or damaged shoots and give the plant the shape you want. Suckers that sprout up from the base can be pruned off. This is optional in wild roses but recommended for grafted roses, as the suckers will not be the preferred variety.

Roses are susceptible to a number of diseases, especially the fungal disease black spot. Choose resistant varieties, or spray the plants weekly with a solution of 1 teaspoon (5 mL) baking soda (sodium bicarbonate) dissolved in 1 quart (1 L) water. A further refinement of this recipe, developed at Cornell University, is effective against other fungi as well. It calls for 1 tablespoon (15 mL) horticultural oil, such as Sunspray, and 1 tablespoon (15 mL) baking soda in 1 gallon (4 L) water. Spray once a week, preferably during cool, overcast weather.

Shepherdia species
Buffaloberry

These native North American shrubs will grow in windy places where the soil is rocky and dry, preferably alkaline. *S. argentea* (silver buffaloberry) grows stiffly upright, with attractive, coarsely textured silvery leaves and sour red or yellow fruit that can be used in jellies and jams. It grows 10 feet (3 m) or taller and about as wide. *S. canadensis* (russet buffaloberry, soapberry) has leaves that are green on top and silvery underneath and is somewhat smaller, about 6 to 8 feet (1.8-2.4 m), with insipid, soapy-tasting fruit. The sexes are separate, so you must grow both a female and a male for fruit. Either species of buffaloberry can be grown as a backdrop for a perennial border or used for a shelterbelt or hedge, trimmed or untrimmed, in areas as cold as zone 3.

Spiraea species
Spirea

Spirea is one of the best-selling deciduous shrubs, mostly because a host of new cultivars offers bright spring foliage, summer flowers, winter hardiness and summer adaptability. Some have spectacular fall color as well, and they are adaptable, useful as hedges or specimens or within a shrub or perennial border. They fare best in sun and will put up with almost any soil, although leaves grow larger with occasional watering.

The old-fashioned *S. x vanhouttei* (bridal-wreath)—at 6 feet (1.8 m), one of the tallest hardy types—was common in farmyard gardens a century ago. It is distinguished by gracefully weeping branches and trusses of white flowers. Branches cut in late spring can be forced indoors.

Within the perennial border, try some of the dwarf species, such as cultivars of *S. japonica*. The 12-inch (30 cm) 'Alpina' has rose-colored flowers from early summer until fall. 'Goldmound,' a

Canadian introduction, grows 18 inches (45 cm) tall and has pink late-spring flowers and golden foliage. It does best in sandy loam in sun and is hardy to zone 3. 'Little Princess,' 2 feet (60 cm) tall, has pink flowers and bright green foliage that turns red in fall.

S. bumalda is also fairly small, about 2 to 3 feet (60-90 cm). One of the hardiest cultivars is 'Goldflame' (zone 4), whose red spring foliage lightens to pink, yellow or green. There are pink flowers in summer, and the foliage turns red in fall.

Plants with variegated foliage are generally less hardy than their plain-leaved counterparts, and spireas are no exception. Where they will survive, the variegated forms—better known for the beauty of their foliage than their flowers—can be arresting within a border of other shrubs, including evergreens.

Spirea can be pruned back almost to the ground when it looks leggy and needs renewing. Light annual pruning will increase flowering. White-flowered types of spirea should be pruned immediately after blooming, both to remove old canes and to shear back overgrown tops. The others bloom on new growth produced in spring and therefore can be either left unpruned or pruned in early spring before growth begins.

Symphoricarpos species
Snowberry, coralberry, waxberry

Grown chiefly for its white berries that stay on the branches into winter, *S. albus* (snowberry, waxberry) is otherwise unremarkable. Deciduous cousins of honeysuckles, symphoricarpos are North American native shrubs that thrive in sun or shade and almost any soil. They are tolerant of city air pollution, and all are easy to grow from seed or cuttings or by simply removing a sucker. *S. albus* grows about 3 feet (1 m) tall; the variety *laevigatus*, which is more commonly available, is twice as tall and is hardy to zone 2.

S. x *chenaultii* (Chenault coralberry) grows about 3 feet (1 m) tall, has reddish berries and is hardy to zone 5. See page 64 for the prostrate cultivar 'Hancock.'

S. doorenbosii 'Mother of Pearl' is 4 feet (1.2 m) tall, with clusters of pearl-pink berries at its branch tips. It is hardy to zone 5.

S. orbiculatus (*S. vulgaris*), known as coralberry or Indian currant, grows about 5 to 7 feet (1.5-2 m) tall. It has persistent coral-colored fruit and grayish foliage that turns crimson in fall. It suckers freely and should be kept out of perennial beds, but it can be used on a dry hillside or allowed to form a clump in an out-of-the-way corner.

Syringa species
Lilac

Spring where I live wouldn't be the same without the couple of weeks in late May when every breeze carries the sweet perfume of lilacs. Introduced by the pioneers, lilacs have spread far beyond gardens and now grow wild along country roadsides. Common lilacs (*S. vulgaris*) will, if allowed, gradually colonize acres with their invasive suckers. In gardens, they can be domineering too, but fortunately, there are garden lilacs with more modest spreading habits—or none at all. There are literally hundreds of varieties from which to choose; the collection at the Royal Botanical Gardens in Burlington, Ontario, numbers almost 700 varieties. All lilacs except *S. potaninii* are hardy to at least zone 4.

S. vulgaris species and cultivars tend to grow tall, up to 25 feet (7.5 m), but they can be kept shorter with annual pruning. The standard by which lilacs are measured is the group of French hybrids, cultivars of *S. vulgaris* developed around the turn of the century. Several are still popular, including 'Madame Lemoine,' whose yellow buds open pure white. Another good *S. vulgaris* cultivar is the pink double 'Edward J. Gardner,' introduced in Minnesota in 1950. 'Krasavitsa Moskvy' is a Russian introduction with pink buds opening into white double flowers. 'Sensation' has dark purple petals edged with white.

Among the most self-reliant lilacs, according to 11 years of field trials at the University of Minnesota, are *S.* x *persica* (Persian lilac), 4 to 8 feet (1.2-2.4 m) tall, and *S.* x *chinensis* (Chinese or Rouen lilac), roughly twice as tall. Both types have dark green leaves and fragrant May flowers. The

This hardy Rosa spinosissima *cultivar yields a big crop of fruits, called hips, in Beaverlodge, in northern Alberta.*

Chinese lilac has pink flowers with a light perfume.

S. meyeri 'Palibin' (*S. palibiniana*, *S. velutina*), known as dwarf Korean lilac or Meyer's lilac, is one of the most restrained, staying less than 5 to 6 feet (1.5-1.8 m) tall. The pale lavender flowers, which bloom around the same time as *S. vulgaris*, are fragrant, and the foliage is attractive in all seasons, turning pinkish as it fades in fall. This is a good hedge plant, with the added bonus that it resists powdery mildew.

Around the same size is *S. patula* (Korean lilac). 'Miss Kim,' released from New Hampshire in 1960, bears a huge crop of fragrant, lilac-colored flowers in June. It is slow-growing, easy to restrain with pruning and resistant to powdery mildew, but it needs well-drained soil.

S. reticulata (Japanese tree lilac) blooms later, into July. The flowers are creamy yellow but not especially fragrant. The cultivar 'Ivory Silk' was awarded a Gold Medal in 1996 by the Pennsylvania Horticultural Society. In 20 years, it reaches about 20 feet (6 m) high and roughly half as wide.

S. x *hyacinthiflora* 'Excel,' developed in Manitoba, is another excellent garden variety that is disease-resistant and produces an abundant crop of fragrant flowers. One release by F.L. Skinner of Dropmore, Manitoba, is 'Assessippi.' Along with 'Excel,' it blooms heavily a few days before the wild lilac, on a shrub that forms a neat globe shape.

Newly planted lilacs may not bloom for several years. Provided they are in sun and not heavily pruned or fertilized, the gardener will eventually be rewarded. Lilacs should be pruned immediately after blooming. Any later, and you risk cutting away next year's buds. Prune out the oldest stems at the base. Also cut away all suckers or basal sprouts except those growing near your pruning cuts. The chief detriment of lilacs, aside from the invasiveness of some varieties, is that after their period of gorgeous, fragrant bloom, they are unremarkable—a common shortcoming of spring-flowering shrubs. Plant the self-contained types of lilac behind and among other things, rather than as specimens on their own, so that they do not

Like many spring-flowering shrubs, the otherwise modest lilac can be the focal point of the garden when it is in bloom.

command too much attention beyond their brief spell in the limelight. Suckering lilacs should be kept away from other perennials and shrubs. Mowing or paving will contain them.

Tamarix species
Tamarisk

These unusual shrubs or small trees look evergreen but are deciduous. Like broad-leaved deciduous trees, they change color in autumn, often turning bright gold before the leaves fall. Their soft, scalelike leaves resemble heather or yew. Tiny, feathery flowers grow in dense clusers. Tamarisks can withstand salty air and wind, so they are frequently planted on sandy seaside slopes. In fact, some have become weedy pests on streambanks in the western United States. Tamarisks do best in full sun in perfectly drained alkaline soil. They should be pruned every year to keep them from looking leggy. Except as noted, prune them in early spring before growth begins, as they flower on the current year's wood.

T. odessana (Odessa tamarisk) grows 4 to 6 feet (1.2-1.8 m) tall, is hardy to zone 3 and has pink flowers in late summer.

T. parviflora (small-flowered tamarisk) grows about 15 feet (4.5 m) tall. It has reddish bark and pink flowers in late spring on the previous year's growth, so it should be pruned after flowering. It is hardy to zone 4.

T. pentandra (*T. ramosissima*), known as Amur tamarisk and five-stamen tamarisk, grows about half as tall as *T. parviflora*. Masses of pink flowers bloom on new growth in summer. The species is considered hardy to zone 3 or 4 and, indeed, is rated one of the best trees for both drought tolerance and hardiness by a researcher at the North Dakota State University in Fargo. It may winterkill to the ground in exposed places but will generally regrow in spring. Cultivars vary in hardiness. The species suffered some tip dieback at the Central Experimental Farm in Ottawa, Ontario (zone 4), as did the cultivar 'Summer Glow' (also called 'Summerglow' or 'Rubra') at the trial gardens at the University of Maine at Orono (also zone 4), but 'Pink Cascade' did not survive there.

Amur tamarisk is useful for a hardy hedge, but it should not be trimmed closely for shape, as this may remove the flower buds.

Taxus species
Yew

There are two faces of yews: They suit lush English landscapes, where they are favorites for pruning into perfect hedging and topiary bunnies and chess pieces, and they are also among the evergreens most tolerant of dry ground, even in shade. Some, especially *T. canadensis* (Canada yew)—a straggly creeper not often available for sale—are very hardy, to zone 3, while *T. baccata* (English yew) is quite tender, to zone 7. What they have in common are waxy evergreen needles, soft to the touch, and an ability to regrow from buds all along the stems, not just at the tips, so they can be repeatedly pruned, even quite far down the stems. None are hardy on the Canadian prairies or in open areas of the American Midwest.

T. cuspidata (Japanese yew), hardy to zone 4, can grow as tall as 25 feet (7.5 m). A number of its cultivars are compact and slow-growing.

Favorites of northern nursery people are cultivars of *T.* x *media*, such as 'Tauntonii,' which has a low-spreading habit, good green color all year, heat tolerance and resistance to winter windburn. The cultivar 'Hicksii' (Hicks' yew) grows narrow and upright to about 15 feet (4.5 m). There are many other excellent cultivars hardy to zone 4, although they may suffer from occasional tip dieback. They take full sun to part shade but should be kept out of the windiest, most exposed places.

Viburnum species
Viburnum

Known for globes of showy, fragrant flowers, viburnums are considered shrubs for kind climates, yet some can survive in trying conditions, although they are admittedly less spectacular. In a spot sheltered from strong winds and with a bit of shade, some of the deciduous viburnums are hardy, self-reliant and drought-resistant, especially if the soil

Hardy and independent, the common lilac (Syringa vulgaris) can colonize acres with its invasive suckers.

is acidic and rich in humus. They will produce flowers, berries for birds and season-long foliage. Both of the following species are hardy to zone 2:

V. lantana (wayfaring tree) forms a shrub or small tree about 15 feet (4.5 m) high, with wrinkled, gray-green leaves that turn red in fall. Flat clusters of spring flowers become clusters of red berries that are a favorite of birds. The cultivar 'Mohican' is smaller, with orange-red fruit.

V. lentago (sheepberry, nannyberry) was a star performer during the 1995 drought at the Xeriscape Demonstration Garden in Plainview, New York. It can reach 20 to 30 feet (6-9 m) tall. The leaves are green and lustrous. Creamy white flowers are followed by juicy blue-black berries enjoyed by birds.

Sources

◆

Publications

Cactus and Succulent Journal
Cactus and Succulent Society of America, Inc.
Box 3010
Santa Barbara, CA 93130

Environmental Landscape News
California Xeriscape Foundation
16176 Mesa Robles Drive
Hacienda Heights, CA 91745

Ornamental Grasses for Cold Climates
Publication BU-6411-YG
MES Distribution Center
20 Coffey Hall, 1420 Eckles Avenue
University of Minnesota
St. Paul, MN 55108-6069
fax: 612-625-6281

Restoring Canada's Native Prairies
The Manitoba Naturalists Society
401-63 Albert Street
Winnipeg, MB R3B 1G4

Trickle Irrigation in the Eastern United States
Northeast Regional Agricultural
   Engineering Service
152 Riley Robb Hall
Cornell University
Ithaca, NY 14853

Equipment

Aquapore Moisture Systems, Inc.
610 South 80th Avenue
Phoenix, AZ 85043
800-635-8379; fax: 602-936-9040
Soaker and sprinkler hoses.

Dramm Quality Watering Products
P.O. Box 1960
Manitowoc, WI 54221-1960
800-258-0848 or 414-684-0227;
fax: 414-684-4499
Watering equipment.

Dripworks
380 Maple Street
Willits, CA 95490
800-522-3747; fax: 707-459-9645
Watering equipment and information.

Forest City Models & Patterns
352 Sovereign Road
London, ON N6M 1A8
519-451-6211
Plastic water barrels.

Gardener's Supply Company
128 Intervale Road
Burlington, VT 05401-2850
800-853-1700
Rain barrels, composters and other gardening
equipment. Catalog free.

The Great American Rain Barrel Co. Inc.
1715 Hyde Park Avenue
Hyde Park, MA 02136
Phone/fax: 800-251-2352 or 508-668-8465
Plastic rain barrels and associated equipment.

International Irrigation Systems
L.P.O. Box 360, 1555 Third Street
Niagara Falls, NY 14304
or:
P.O. Box 1133
St. Catharines, ON L2R 7A3
905-688-4090; fax: 905-688-4093
Irrigro drip-irrigation systems.

Kourik Drip Irrigation Systems
217 San Anselmo Avenue
San Anselmo, CA 94960
707-766-9303

Lee Valley Tools Ltd.
1080 Morrison Drive
Ottawa, ON K2H 8K7
800-267-8767 or 613-596-0350;
fax: 800-668-1807
Compost bins, rain barrels, watering
equipment, tools. Catalog free.

The Natural Gardening Company
217 San Anselmo Avenue
San Anselmo, CA 94960
707-766-9303; fax: 707-766-9747
Compost bins, drip irrigation, organic gardening
supplies.

Rain Control
P.O. Box 662
Adrian, MI 49221
800-536-RAIN or 517-263-5226;
fax: 517-263-6153
Suppliers of Irri-Gator drip systems.

Season Extenders
Dept. 2701
971 Nichols Avenue
Stratford, CT 06497
Garden equipment, including composters,
irrigation supplies. Catalog free.

The Urban Farmer Store
2833 Vicente Street
San Francisco, CA 94116
415-661-2204; fax: 415-661-7826
Garden supplies. Drip-irrigation manual free.

Seeds and Plants

CANADA
Alberta Nurseries & Seeds Ltd.
Box 20
Bowden, AB T0M 0K0
403-224-3545; fax: 403-224-2455
Shrubs, seeds for vegetables, flowers.
Catalog free.

Alyssa's Garden
Box 6250
Fort St. John, BC V1J 4H7
250-785-2220; fax: 250-785-2213
Lilies, peonies, daylilies, perennials.
Catalog $2.

Bluestem Ornamental Grasses
1949 Fife Road
Christina Lake, BC V0H 1E3
Phone/fax: 250-447-6363
Ornamental grasses. Catalog $2.

Boughen Nurseries Valley River Ltd.
Box 12
Valley River, MB R0L 2B0
204-638-7618; fax: 204-638-7172
Shrubs, trees, hardy roses. Catalog free.

Chuck Chapman Iris
11 Harts Lane
Guelph, ON N1L 1B1
509-823-8744
Irises. Catalog $2.

The Conservancy
51563 Range Road, 212A
Sherwood Park, AB T8G 1B1
Seeds for flowers, grasses, shrubs.
Catalog $2.

Corn Hill Nursery Ltd.
RR 5, Route 890
Petitcodiac, NB E0A 2H0
506-756-3635; fax: 506-756-1087
Shrubs, hardy roses. Catalog $2.

Cruikshank's Inc.
780 Birchmount Road, Unit 16
Scarborough, ON M1K 5H4
416-750-9249; fax: 416-750-8522
Hardy and tender bulbs, irises, perennials,
clematises. Catalog $3.

Dominion Seed House
Box 2500
Georgetown, ON L7G 5L6
905-873-3037 or 800-784-3037;
fax: 800-567-4594
Perennials, seeds for flowers, vegetables.

Erikson's Daylily Gardens
24642 51st Avenue
Langley, BC V2Z 1H9
604-856-5758
Daylilies. Catalog $2.

Fraser's Thimble Farms
175 Arbutus Road
Salt Spring Island, BC V8K 1A3
Phone/fax: 250-537-5788
Perennials, including many geraniums
(cranesbills). Catalog $2.

Gardens North
5984 Third Line Road North, RR 3
North Gower, ON K0A 2T0
Phone/fax: 613-489-0065
Seeds for hardy perennials, common and rare.
Catalog $4.

Hardy Roses for the North
Box 2048
Grand Forks, BC V0H 1H0
250-442-8442; fax: 250-442-2766
Hardy roses, some perennials, vines.
Catalog $4.

The Heather Farm
Box 2206
Sardis, BC V2R 1A6
604-823-4884
Heaths, heathers. Send SASE for list.

Holes Greenhouses & Gardens Ltd.
101 Bellerose Drive
St. Albert, AB T8N 8N8
403-459-6498
Hardy perennials, grasses, shrubs, trees.
Catalog free.

Honeywood Lilies
Box 68
Parkside, SK S0J 2A0
306-747-3296
Lilies, peonies. Catalog $2.

Iris & Plus
1269 Rte. 139, Box 903
Sutton, PQ J0E 2K0
514-538-2048; fax: 514-538-7353
Irises, daylilies, peonies, perennials. Catalog $2.

The Lily Nook
Box 846
Neepawa, MB R0J 1H0
204-476-3225
Lilies. Catalog $2.

Living Prairie Museum
2795 Ness Avenue
Winnipeg, MB R3J 3S4
204-832-0167
Seeds for prairie native plants. List $1.

Mason Hogue Gardens
3520 Durham Road 1, RR 4
Uxbridge, ON L9P 1R4
Drought-tolerant perennials, grasses, shrubs,
clematises. Catalog $2.

McConnell Nurseries Inc.
Box 269
Port Burwell, ON N0J 1T0
519-660-6200
Perennials, roses, shrubs. Catalog free.

McMillen's Iris Garden
RR 1
Norwich, ON N0J 1P0
519-468-6508
Irises, daylilies. Catalog $2.

Meadowsweet Farms
24640 Sixteenth Avenue
South Langley, BC V2Z 1J4
604-530-2611; fax: 604-530-9996
Perennials, grasses. Catalog $2.

Parkland Perennials
Box 3683
Spruce Grove, AB T7X 3A9
Phone/fax: 403-963-7307
Lilies, irises, daylilies, peonies. Catalog free.

Peek's Perennials
Box 6443
Edson, AB T7E 1T8
403-723-5701
Grasses, perennials, hardy to zone 2. Catalog $2.

W.H. Perron & Co. Ltd.
CP 408
Ville de Laval, PQ H7S 2A6
514-682-9071; fax: 514-682-4959
Bulbs, perennials, seeds for flowers, vegetables.
Catalog free.

Prairie Habitats
Box 1
Argyle, MB R0C 0B0
204-467-9371
Seeds for prairie native plants. List $2.

Prism Perennials
C-45, S-25, RR 1
Castlegar, BC V1N 3H7
604-365-3753; fax: 604-365-3735
Perennials, irises, daylilies, grasses. List $2.

Richters
357 Highway 47
Goodwood, ON L0C 1A0
905-640-6677; fax: 905-640-6641
Herb seeds and plants. Catalog free.

Stokes Seeds
Box 10
St. Catharines, ON L2R 6R6
Seeds for vegetables, annuals, herbs, perennials.
Catalog free.

T&T Seeds
Box 1710
Winnipeg, MB R3C 3P6
204-956-2777; fax: 204-956-1994
Hardy shrubs and perennials, seeds for flowers,
vegetables. Catalog $2.

UNITED STATES

Alpine Gardens
12446 County Highway F
Stitzer, WI 43825
608-822-6382
Hardy sedums, sempervivums, cacti.
Catalog $2.

Ambergate Gardens
8015 Krey Avenue
Waconia, MN 55387-9616
Phone/fax: 612-443-2248
Perennials, including many grasses and
selections for sun. Catalog $2.

American Daylilies & Perennials
Box 210
Grain Valley, MO 64029
800-770-2777
Daylilies, peonies, lantanas. Catalog $5.

Appalachian Gardens
Box 82
Waynesboro, PA 17268-0082
717-762-4312; fax: 717-762-7532
Shrubs, trees. Catalog free.

B&D Lilies
330 P Street
Port Townsend, WA 98368
Daylilies, irises, lilies. Fall catalog $3.

Borbeleta Gardens
15980 Canby Avenue
Faribault, MN 55021-7652
507-334-2807; fax: 507-334-0365
Lilies, irises, daylilies, peonies. Catalog $3.

Busse Gardens
5873 Oliver Avenue SW
Cokato, MN 55321
800-544-3192
Hardy perennials. Catalog $2.

Companion Plants
7247 North Coolville Ridge
Athens, OH 45701
614-592-4643
Organically grown herb plants, seeds. Catalog $3

Cooper's Garden
2345 Decatur Avenue N
Golden Valley, MN 55427
Phone/fax: 612-542-9447
Irises, perennials. Catalog $1.

The Daffodil Mart
7463 Heath Trail
Gloucester, VA 23061
800-255-2852
Bulbs. Catalog free.

Dooley Gardens
210 North High Drive NE
Hutchinson, MN 55350
612-587-3050
Garden chrysanthemums. Catalog free.

Dutch Gardens
P.O. Box 200
Adelphia, NJ 07710-0200
800-818-3861
Flower bulbs, perennials. Catalog free.

Goodwin Creek Gardens
P.O. Box 83
Williams, OR 97544
Rare lavenders and oreganos, other herbs.
Catalog $1.

Heard Gardens Ltd.
5355 Merle Hay Road
Johnston, IA 50131
515-276-4533
Lilacs. Catalog $2.

Heaths & Heathers
E. 502 Haskell Hill Road
Shelton, WA 98584
Hardy heaths and heathers. Catalog $1.

Dry-Land Gardening

Heronswood Nursery
7530 288th Street NE
Kingston, WA 98346
Perennials, shrubs, grasses, trees. Catalog $4.

High Country Gardens
2902 Rufina Street
Santa Fe, NM 87505-2929
800-925-9387
Xeriscaping plants and plans. Catalog free.

J.L. Hudson, Seedsman
Star Route 2, Box 337
La Honda, CA 94020
Seeds for unusual annuals, perennials, vegetables.
Catalog $1.

Intermountain Cactus
1478 North 750 East
Kaysville, UT 84037
801-546-2006
Hardy cacti. Catalog $1.

Kurt Bluemel Inc.
2740 Green Lane
Baldwin, MD 21013
301-557-7229
Ornamental grasses. Catalog $2.

Limerock Ornamental Grasses, Inc.
70 Sawmill Road
Port Matilda, PA 16870
814-692-2272; fax: 814-692-9848
Ornamental grasses. Catalog $3.

Lowe's Own Root Roses
6 Sheffield Road
Nashua, NH 03062
603-888-2214
All types of roses on their own roots. Catalog $2.

Midwest Cactus
P.O. Box 163
New Melle, MO 63365
314-828-5389
Hardy cacti, yuccas and sedums. Catalog $2.

Musser Forests
P.O. Box 340
Indiana, PA 15701
412-465-5685
Shrubs, groundcovers, tree seedlings. Catalog free.

Netherland Bulb Co.
13 McFadden Road
Easton, PA 18045-7819
800-755-2852
Flower bulbs, perennials. Catalog free.

Park Seed Company
Cokesbury Road
Greenwood, SC 29647-0001
800-845-3369
Seeds for flowers, vegetables. Catalog free.

Prairie Moon Nursery, Alan Wade
Route 3, Box 163
Winona, MN 55987
507-452-1362; fax: 507-454-5238
Native prairie plants. Catalog $2.

Prairie Nursery
Box 306
Westfield, WI 53964
608-296-3679
Native prairie perennials. Catalog $3.

Prairie Ridge Nursery
9738 Overland Road
Mt. Horeb, WI 53572-2832
608-437-5245; fax: 608-437-8982
Native prairie plants. Catalog $3.

Schreiner's Iris Gardens
3625 Quinaby Road NE
Salem, OR 97303
Irises. Catalog $2.

Siskiyou Rare Plant Nursery
2825 Cummings Road
Medford, OR 97501
503-772-6846
Dwarf plants for alpine conditions. Catalog $2.

Stock Seed Farms
28008 Mill Road
Murdock, NE 68407
800-759-1520
Grasses, including buffalo grass. List free.

Stokes Seeds
Box 548
Buffalo, NY 14240-0548
800-263-7233; fax: 905-684-8411
Vegetables, annuals, perennials. Catalog free.

Thompson & Morgan Inc.
P.O. Box 1308
Jackson, NJ 08527-0308
800-263-7233; fax: 888-466-4769
Seeds for annuals, perennials, vegetables.
Catalog free.

Tripple Brook Farm
37 Middle Road
Southampton, MA 01073
413-527-4626

Shrubs, grasses, cacti and other perennials.
Catalog 50¢.

Twombly Nursery
163 Barn Hill Road
Monroe, CT 06468
203-261-2133; fax: 203-261-9230
Shrubs, trees, perennials, grasses, bamboos.
Catalog $3.

Wayside Gardens
1 Garden Lane
Hodges, SC 29695-0001
Perennials, shrubs, trees, vines, bulbs, roses.
Catalog free.

INTERNATIONAL
Chiltern Seeds
Bortree Stile
Ulverston, Cambria
England LA12 7PB
Seeds for unusual annuals, perennials, shrubs.
Catalog £2 or $2 (U.S.).

Index

Photo Credits

◆

Jennifer Bennett:
24, 26, 28, 32, 34, 42, 49, 53, 61, 62, 64, 68, 75,
76, 77, 83, 88, 97, 100, 103, 111, 113, 116, 119,
121, 122, 125, 126, 131, 133, 134, 136, 138,
142, 147, 148, 151, 155

Stephen Errington:
112

Turid Forsyth:
6 (tree peony), 21, 29, 57, 66, 69, 71, 74, 80,
87, 110, 127, 128, 137, 141, 159 (Asiatic hybrid
lilies), 160 (ornamental grasses), 162 ('Sweet
Million' tomatoes), 165 (fritillaria)

John Ruskay:
8, 9, 10, 11, 12, 14, 16, 19, 20, 22, 23, 31, 35,
37, 38, 41, 44, 45, 47, 48, 50, 54, 55, 58, 60, 65,
70, 73, 78, 84, 90, 93, 94, 98, 105, 106, 107,
108, 114, 124, 144, 152, 156, 157

National Garden Bureau:
36